# STUDYING
# S·M·A·R·T

**THINKING AND STUDY SKILLS
FOR SCHOOL AND THE WORKPLACE**

# STUDYING
# S·M·A·R·T

**THINKING AND STUDY SKILLS
FOR SCHOOL AND THE WORKPLACE**

**NEILD B. OLDHAM**

**PARADIGM**

**Developmental Editors**  Sonja Brown and Russ Blixt
**Copy Editor**  Roberta Mantus
**Text Design/Production**  The Oldham Publishing Service
**Cover Design**  Ruth Laird Fen
**Illustrations**  Jorel Williams

**ACKNOWLEDGEMENTS**

The author thanks the following instructors and technical experts who contributed to this workbook:

John Neimeyer
Patricia Stevens College
St. Louis, Missouri

Jay Hollowell
Commonwealth College
Virginia Beach, Virginia

**Library of Congress Cataloging-in-Publication Data**

Oldham, Neild B.
    Studying smart: thinking and study skills for school and the workplace / Neild B. Oldham.
    p. cm.
    ISBN 1-56118-528-0
    1. Study, Method of. I. Title.
LB2395.O44 1993
371.3'028'12—dc20                                                        92-31850
                                                                                       CIP

© 1993 by Paradigm Publishing Inc.
280 East Case Ave., St. Paul, MN 55101

All rights reserved. No part of this publication may be reproduced, stored in a retrieval system, or transmitted, in any form or by any means, electronic, mechanical, photocopying, recording, or otherwise, without the written permission of Paradigm Publishing Inc.

Printed in the United States of America.

10 9 8 7 6 5 4 3 2 1

# Table of Contents

Preface . . . . . . . . . . . . . . . . . . . . . . . . . . . . vii

UNIT I: THINKING . . . . . . . . . . . . . . . . . . . . 1
   Chapter 1: Thinking Creatively and Critically . . . . 5
   Chapter 2: Thinking for Yourself . . . . . . . . . . . 29

UNIT II: PLANNING . . . . . . . . . . . . . . . . . . . 45
   Chapter 3: Finding a Vision; Setting Goals . . . . . 49
   Chapter 4: Managing Time . . . . . . . . . . . . . . 75
   Chapter 5: Managing Stress . . . . . . . . . . . . . 97

UNIT III: LEARNING . . . . . . . . . . . . . . . . . . 117
   Chapter 6: Reading Strategies . . . . . . . . . . . . 123
   Chapter 7: Taking Reading Notes . . . . . . . . . . 149
   Chapter 8: Listening Effectively . . . . . . . . . . . 169
   Chapter 9: Taking Listening Notes . . . . . . . . . . 187

UNIT IV: USING YOUR KNOWLEDGE . . . . . . . . . . 203
   Chapter 10: Taking Objective Tests . . . . . . . . . 207
   Chapter 11: Taking Essay Tests . . . . . . . . . . . 223
   Chapter 12: Succeeding in the Workplace . . . . . 239

PERFORMANCE MASTERY: Using Your Skills . . . . . . . . . 253

Index . . . . . . . . . . . . . . . . . . . . . . . . . . . 257

# Preface

This is a course on thinking and study skills, but it is also more than that. The skills you need to study effectively are the same skills you need to perform well on the job. Furthermore, these skills will contribute to the quality and satisfaction of your life. How well you apply your thinking and study skills now will affect the quality and satisfaction of your future life.

## EVALUATE YOUR LEARNING STYLE

No two people are identical. No two people learn in the same way. This book is a guide—a way to help you become an effective learner. Some of the ideas and activities will be extremely helpful to you. You may find others less helpful, but they may be just what a classmate needs.

Your own abilities and individual learning style will influence what you learn as you study this book. If you have problems concentrating during lectures or reading, you will find suggestions for improving your concentration. If you are an excellent student, you may discover new techniques for studying and test-taking. Knowing your unique learning style will help you learn. A visual person may learn best by reading. A poor reader may find it easier to learn from lectures or audiotape. A hands-on learner may prefer to learn by doing.

## THINK OF YOURSELF AS A GOOD STUDENT

Think of yourself as a good student, and let it become a self-fulfilling prophecy. As a good student, learning will be your goal.

### Make Learning Central to Your Daily Life

Establish a learning routine. Attend every class and seminar, do your assignments promptly, review your class notes, and prepare for tomorrow's class. Leave plenty of time in your daily schedule for study.

### Clarify Reasons For Learning

To be an effective learner, you need to clarify your reasons for learning. Then, you can concentrate on achieving your purpose—your reason for being in class, reading an assignment, attending a seminar. Knowing why you want to learn will help you to learn.

# UNIT 1
# THINKING

**When you have completed this unit, you will be able to apply creative and critical thinking skills to new situations.**

Thinking is a skill. You can learn the rules and principles for thinking as you can for any skill. As with all skills, the extent to which you develop your ability to perform the skill depends on the extent to which you practice it. This course will teach you the rules and principles for the skill of thinking and will give you suggestions for applying them. The rest is up to you.

Thinking skills and study skills go together. They are skills that you will use all your life. Developing thinking skills is a base for learning and studying. The goal of formal education is to teach you how to think and to learn. If you were to finish your formal education without any specific skills except thinking and study skills, you would succeed in whatever career you choose. That is how important these skills are.

There are two basic types of thinking:

>Creative thinking.

>Critical thinking.

You use **creative thinking** to produce ideas, to think of possible courses of action, and to solve problems. You use **critical thinking** to evaluate ideas—your own as well as those of others. Creative and critical thinking skills are important if you want to *think for yourself* rather than *be told what to think*.

In this unit, you will learn about these types of thinking and some techniques to develop and use.

## WHAT DO YOU DO WHEN YOU THINK?

You are thinking all the time. That is, mental images or symbols or words float through your mind constantly. You could not read this book, watch a videocassette, or perform any activity without some mental action occurring. Thinking includes:

- Imagining.
- Remembering.
- Problem-solving.

You have done all these things, of course. You have thought creatively and critically at different times. When you wanted to buy a new car, the latest video, or a compact disc, you used creative thinking to trigger ideas on where you could get the necessary money. You then thought critically about these different ideas so that you could act on the best one.

## WHY STUDY THINKING?

You may wonder at this point why you need to learn how to do something that you have been doing all your life. The answer is that random mental activity—images and ideas just floating around in your head—rarely, if ever, serves any purpose. Unless you order these ideas and direct your thinking toward a specific purpose, you mostly waste your mental activity. You are not really thinking—certainly not creatively or critically.

Some people, facing the need to make a decision, become trapped in pointless mental activity to the point of agony. They mentally repeat the same meaningless arguments over and over.

> *Maybe I should do this.*
> *No, I should do that.*
> *No, no, I really should do this.*
> *Yes . . . no . . . perhaps . . . I wonder.*

This is not creative or critical thinking. It is mental activity that achieves no purpose.

Thinking to achieve a purpose—thinking creatively and critically—is a skill that you can learn, develop, and improve.

As a student, your two main activities will be reading and listening. You may consider reading and listening to be passive activities. You need only sit and let your eyes pick up the information from the printed page or let your ears pick up the words the lecturer is sending your way. Not so—reading and listening are actions that require effort and participation on your part. They require good creative and critical thinking skills.

If you read without creative and critical thinking, your mind wanders, you do not absorb the information, you will not likely remember it, and, if you do remember it, you will almost certainly not understand it. The same is true of listening. You must think, creatively and critically, about what you are hearing. Otherwise, you will be daydreaming and the words will be meaningless sounds droning against your ears.

To repeat, thinking skills and study skills go together. Study skills include reading and listening as well as developing good habits, such as setting aside a time to study each day, managing your time to finish assignments on time, and avoiding distractions. You use your study skills to acquire information. You use your thinking skills to process, evaluate, comprehend, and store what you read and hear. In this unit, you will learn about creative and critical thinking as well as how to think as an individual.

# 1 Thinking Creatively and Critically

**When you have completed this chapter, you will be able to apply creative and critical thinking skills to study effectively, to solve problems, and to check ideas, facts, and opinions.**

You will read about creative and critical thinking in separate sections of this chapter even though in life the two types of thinking are inseparable. This learning arrangement reflects the different emphases of creative and critical thinking.

When thinking creatively, you want to be creative, to produce. You do not want to block your imagination or stop ideas occurring to you by raising questions and challenges, which is the prime purpose of critical thinking.

When thinking critically, you question and challenge. You raise questions and judge ideas before accepting and acting on them. First, you must think creatively to develop the ideas.

Remember, however, that to achieve some worthwhile result with your mental efforts, you must do both. Creative and critical thinking work hand in hand. Together they constitute the successful thinking process.

# CREATIVE THINKING

Everyone can and does think creatively. Creative thinking is not a skill that only a few talented writers, artists, scientists, or performers have. Even very young children think creatively. Perhaps we should say that children—preschool age, for example—think creatively more often and more naturally than older people.

A reason for this is that at an early age, people have not yet "learned" that creative thinking is supposed to be something only a few can do. Nor have they "learned" all the reasons why this, that, or the other thing is not possible or should not be done.

Perhaps you can recall when you were young. You looked at a brand new world and your mind was wide open to all possibilities. Nothing restricted or limited your thinking as to what was possible. Your natural ability to think creatively, to be ready to try anything, was probably the greatest single learning tool you had when you were young and first exploring life.

> *Why is grass green?*
> *Why is the sky blue?*

Many adults consider these childish, *silly* questions. Actually, they are creative questions, and it was by asking such creative questions that we learned and grew.

Although no longer a child, you still have that ability to think creatively, and thinking creatively—being open to all the possibilities—is always a great learning tool.

Unfortunately, many people, as they grow older, stop using their ability to think creatively. This is not surprising. They have heard, probably a thousand times, as they grew older, "Oh, you can't do that." or "That's a silly idea." or "That's not practical."

Certainly, not everything is possible. We must all learn this important lesson. In learning that lesson, unfortunately, we sometimes jump to wrong conclusions: Stop asking "silly" questions. Ban those unique thoughts. We stop exercising our natural ability to think creatively and, through lack of use, this ability gradually fades. We decide that letting our minds explore all the options is kid stuff and has no place in the life of a serious adult. We are wrong.

Those adults who continue to exercise their power to think creatively continue to ask "silly" questions, often with startling results. An adult wondering why grass is green discovers chlorophyll, describes the process of photosynthesis, and, ultimately, contributes to the collective knowledge of the world by unlocking one of nature's secrets.

You may not unlock one of nature's secrets with your creative thinking, but you can certainly use it to improve your ability to learn as well as to solve problems.

> The tracks of Amtrak railroad between New Haven, Connecticut, and Boston, Massachusetts, run along the coast of Connecticut. The tracks were put there early in this century. Electric locomotives now pull the trains between New York City and New Haven. At New Haven, diesel engines are put on for the run to Boston. In 1991, Amtrak announced it would electrify the tracks between New Haven and Boston. This would eliminate the delay caused by switching engines in New Haven. Also, the electric locomotives would be faster, quieter, and less polluting.
>
> Some residents of Connecticut did not like the idea of towers and wires carrying electricity strung along their shore. The tracks themselves were bad enough visually, and they cut off access to the shore in many places as well as blocking tidal flow. Over a period of approximately 90 years, Connecticut residents had learned to accept the tracks, but many did not want the added visual pollution of electric wires and poles. Even more were also concerned about safety not only because of the electric wires, but because of the faster trains.
>
> During the public discussion, one Connecticut resident proposed a breathtaking idea: move the tracks away from the shore and put them next to the interstate highway! Sure, it would cost billions, but the country was in a severe recession and the project would provide jobs. Moving the tracks would open up a lot of valuable shore front property, the sale of which could help cover the cost. He also gave other reasons to support the idea.
>
> The response was immediate and mostly predictable.
> *Ridiculous! Impossible! Too costly! Insane!*
> Only one or two people thought it was an idea worth exploring.
>
> Whatever finally happens, the man with the idea and those few who supported him were thinking creatively. The rest were exhibiting an all-too familiar mindset by responding negatively.
>
> For the most part, the naysayers were not even thinking critically. As you will learn, critical thinking is more than finding fault.

The quick rejection of what is new or unusual is the opposite of creative thinking. It effectively suffocates creative thinking. To think creatively, you must avoid having this reaction yourself, not only to your own ideas but to the ideas of others. Furthermore, to persevere with your own creative thinking, you must be ready to deal with this kind of suffocating reaction from others.

## Creative Thinking and Learning

How is creative thinking linked to learning? Memorizing one or two facts is not creative thinking. You might be able to parrot the facts back on a test, but that does not mean you understand them. Coming to understand the facts so as to be able to restate them in your own words is creative thinking. Consider this simple example:

> *Early in school, we memorized the equation 2 plus 2 equals 4. We also memorized the equation that 4 minus 2 equals 2. When we realize that these equations are two ways of representing the same relationship of the numbers, we have understood them. We have thought creatively about them.*

How does this simple example illustrate creative thinking? What actually has taken place? What is the connection with learning? The answer is that the individual has connected two previously separate ideas to create a new idea or a new way of seeing something and is able to state that idea in other words. The individual has learned something. The essence of creative thinking is:

> *Making connections between bits and pieces of existing or old information to create a wholly new idea.*

The idea might be new to the world or might be new only to the individual. Whichever it is, when this happens, it means that the individual has exercised his or her creative thinking skills.

## Steps in Creative Thinking

To stimulate your ability to think creatively, think of the word IDEA. Each letter in *idea* suggests steps in creative thinking:

> I—Illuminate your problem or purpose.
> D—Develop possible solutions.
> E—Ease off for a while.
> A—Arrive at a solution (outcome).

What you are trying to achieve will determine whether you take the step of easing off. You should always take the first two steps. The more important and complex your situation, the more important steps one and two are.

### Illuminate Your Problem

In this first step, you illuminate what you want to achieve or the problem you want to solve. Be as specific as you possibly can. Gather as much information as you can about the situation.

If you do not illuminate your problem clearly before you look for a solution, you will not find a solution or will find the wrong one, which could be worse.

> Journalism always interested Betsy, although she expects to get a job as a paralegal. She reads the paper regularly and loves to argue about politics. One day she reads in the paper about a summer course in journalism. She says to herself, "I would love to take that course. How can I find a way to do it?"

**Develop Possible Solutions**

You need to think of possible solutions or things you can do to solve a problem or reach your goal. Make lists of these possibilities.

It is difficult to think of alternatives when the first obvious one that occurs to you satisfies you. Always take the time to think of others. Avoid deciding before listing as many choices as possible. You may later find that the first solution you thought of was not the best.

> Betsy knows there are plenty of reasons why she should not take the journalism course: She should not spend the money. She should take a course more related to the paralegal field, and so on. However, she says to herself, "There's no harm in a little daydreaming. What good reasons can I think of for taking the course?" She makes a list of everything that comes into her head, laughing to herself over a couple of them.
> ✓ The course starts at 7:30 in the morning so she'll have to get up early—something she's been trying to make a habit.
> ✓ She wants to know more about what it would be like to work with newspaper reporters.
> ✓ She'll find out about what goes into putting together a newspaper and why some news receives a lot of attention and other news very little.
> ✓ The course would provide a nice break from her regular classes.
> ✓ She wants to break up with her boyfriend, so keeping very busy all summer would help.
> ✓ She wants to write a letter to the editor of the paper about the lack of money to keep open the local swimming pool, but doesn't quite have the nerve. Maybe she will after taking the course.
> ✓ The course is offered near where she will be working, so it won't mean any more time or money spent on traveling.

Sometimes a problem may seem to have only one solution. Rarely is this true. Some problems just require greater effort to think of alternative solutions. That effort will almost always be worthwhile.

### Ease Off for a While

Depending on your goal, you may or may not take this step. You may move right to the outcome step after thinking of all possible solutions and testing the pros and cons.

If, however, you have been trying to create a work of art, gain insight and knowledge from studying, or have a difficult problem to solve, you will often find it necessary to take this step. You could call this the *incubation* or *hatching* step.

In this step, you take a rest. You no longer consciously think about the problem. You have identified the problem and gathered and reviewed all the facts you can think of. But you have not gained any insight, reached any conclusion, or created anything new. Despite all your research and review, no outcome occurs to you.

So you put it out of your thoughts. You let your subconscious work on it. After a while, when you have not consciously thought about it, the solution you have been searching for often suddenly occurs to you. You have moved to the outcome stage.

Experts do not know exactly how or why this process works, but it does. In his book, *The Origin of Consciousness in the Breakdown of the Bicameral Mind*, (Pelican Books, NY, 1976, p. 44) Julian Jaynes quotes the British physicist Wolfgang Kohler.

> *We often talk about the three B's, the Bus, the Bath, and the Bed. That is where the great discoveries are made in our science.*

Kohler's point is that many people have had their greatest insights or discoveries when they were not actively thinking about the problem at all. A part of creative thinking is letting your subconscious help you out.

You must realize, however, that this will happen *only* after you have spent considerable time consciously gathering and reviewing all available data. No worthwhile outcome occurs without effort.

▶ The deadline for signing up for the journalism course is several weeks away. Betsy decides to put it out of her mind for a while. Several days later while going to class, she finds herself daydreaming about being in the journalism class.

  She envisions herself learning about how to interview famous people. That evening while reading the paper, she finds herself trying to rewrite a headline that does not seem to go with the article.

**Arrive at a Solution**

If nothing occurs to you after not actively thinking of the problem for a while, you must begin thinking actively again, starting with the first step. Restating the problem and thinking of new possible results, after a period of rest, will often move you along to the outcome step.

You are at this step when you have gained the insight, acquired the knowledge. You analyze all possible solutions to make sure you select the best possible one. Doing this may result in your rejecting all the solutions you have thought of so far.

▶ Betsy talks to her brother about a murder trial that has been reported in the paper for several weeks. She has read that the jury has been sequestered (kept out of contact with other people) so they cannot discuss the trial with anyone or read about it in the newspaper. The paper quotes one of the attorneys extensively.

Betsy sees a connection between the legal profession and journalism and finds her reason to take the journalism course. Not only is she interested in it, but it might also teach her things worth knowing about working with the press when she goes to work for a law firm. Perhaps she will look for a firm that specializes in criminal law.

Betsy has thought creatively about the course. She did not reject the idea immediately when several reasons for not taking it were obvious. She brainstormed for possible reasons to take it, some of which were pretty ridiculous, she admitted. However, she had opened up her mind and stimulated her thinking. When a really good reason for taking the course came to her, she was able to recognize it.

## Techniques for Thinking Creatively

To think creatively you must open up your mind. Push aside familiar thoughts and knowledge. Think about the impossible as possible, of up as down. To think creatively, avoid conforming to the standard. Do not let negative reactions of others stop you. Keep an open mind to all possibilities or alternatives. Be alert to a good idea, which could appear at an unexpected moment. Here are some ways to stimulate your creative thinking.

### Brainstorm

Brainstorming is a technique in which you just let your mind go. You use this in step two of creative thinking when you are thinking of all possibilities along with their pluses and minuses. Initially, you avoid judging any ideas, you just write them all down as they occur.

### Use All Sources of Help

When defining your problem and particularly when considering all possible solutions, do not rely solely on yourself. Ask others—friends, relatives, teachers—to help you. Conduct research. Depending on your problem or the desired outcome, you can find help in magazines and books. You have to take the final step yourself, but you can and should get as much help as possible in the first two steps.

### Ask Yourself Questions

Stimulate your creative thinking by asking yourself questions. Ask them mentally. Ask them out loud. Ask them in writing.

Suppose you performed poorly on your last test. You have a problem. You need to decide what you should do to improve your grades. Before making such a decision, you need to know why you did poorly. You must answer such questions as:

>*What exactly is the problem?*
>*What could have happened?*
>*What are the possible reasons?*

Some answers might be:

>*You did not understand the material.*
>*You failed to study.*
>*You did not study effectively enough.*
>*You did not study the right material.*
>*You were not feeling well.*
>*You stayed up too late the night before.*
>*You missed a class and did not know a test was scheduled.*

As you can see, there are many different reasons for failing a test. Before you can decide what action to take, you must consider all these possible reasons to identify the problem you must solve.

### Write It Down

Writing is an invaluable aid to thinking. You will read more than once in this text to *write it down*. Writing something down not only helps you remember it, but it makes you see it in another light. Writing your ideas down gives them a substance and weight that moves them out of the realm of daydreaming and into the practical world of action.

At step one in creative thinking, when you illuminate your purpose, write it down. When you look at the written purpose, it may not seem complete or right. In which case, redefine your purpose and write it down again. Keep doing this until the results satisfy you.

At step two, write down all the possibilities you can think of. Writing down the possibilities helps you think of more as well as gives you a written, concrete list to examine.

## CRITICAL THINKING

When you think of someone being critical, you may think of him or her as finding fault and being negative.

> *Oh, you're always criticizing me! Why are you so critical?*

This usage is confirmed by dictionaries. *The Oxford Universal Dictionary* gives the first definition of critical as

> *Given to judging; especially fault-finding, censorious.*

There is, however, more to critical thinking than finding fault. Critical thinking requires judging all aspects of what is under review—both the good and the bad. Critics, for example, apply critical thinking to review movies, television shows, art, records, and books.

A competent critic tells us what is *right* about the object of the review as well as what is wrong. The second definition of *critical* in *The Oxford Universal Dictionary* reflects this aspect of critical thinking:

> *Involving or exercising careful judgment.*

So, critical thinking does not mean rejecting everything or simply finding fault. It means that you must examine things closely before you reach a conclusion.

Movie, television, or book critics are not the only ones who use critical thinking. Critical thinking is an important part of everyone's daily life. You read, see, and hear facts, opinions, and ideas constantly. In any given day, you receive a huge amount of information. Some of it you ignore; a lot of it you take in. You must think critically to judge all this material.

You think critically to recognize propaganda for what it is, to separate fact from fiction, opinion from fact, and the worthwhile from the worthless. If you never think critically and simply accept every idea that comes your way, you are not a free, independent person. You can neither truly learn nor grow.

You must also think critically to evaluate your own thoughts. This is important and difficult. If you do not think critically about your own ideas and decisions, however, you will make mistakes. Thinking critically about your own ideas is difficult because you are so familiar with your own ideas that you tend to be uncritical of them.

### Critical Thinking as a Study Skill

Being able to evaluate what you read, see, and hear is a basic study skill. To study is to read and listen. As you read in the introduction to this unit, reading and listening are not passive activities. Thinking critically is an important active part of them.

The ability to tell the difference between facts and opinions is a necessity if you want to learn and make the best decisions for yourself. Information from television, radio, books, newspapers, and other sources bombards you daily. You must be able to sort through all that information and decide what information is accurate and what is not. Determining what is fact and what is opinion is not always easy, and the ability to think critically is necessary for doing this. If you cannot separate fact from opinion, you will often come to wrong conclusions and take wrong actions.

What are facts and opinions and why is knowing which you are dealing with important?

A fact is a statement that you can prove true. For example, the Sears Tower in Chicago is 1,454 feet tall. That is a fact. You can prove it by measuring the height of the building. You can prove a person's age by counting the number of years that have passed since the date on the person's birth certificate. George Washington was the first president of the United States. That is a fact. You can prove it by reading newspapers and other materials written or printed in George Washington's time.

An opinion is a statement that has not yet been proved right or wrong. Some opinions can never be proved right or wrong. For example, an opinion often describes what a person thinks or feels is true. The statement, "The Mercedes-Benz is the best automobile ever built," is this type of opinion. It is impossible to prove that the Mercedes-Benz is the best automobile ever built. Everyone would first have to agree on what makes a car "the best." If one of the criteria was speed, for instance, there are several cars, past and present, faster than a Mercedes.

Another type of opinion that cannot be proved right or wrong is one that describes what a person likes or does not like. "That lady over in the far corner is beautiful" is an example. The person making the statement is saying that he or she thinks the lady in the far corner is beautiful. It does not matter if no one else in the world agrees. The person has stated an opinion.

Similarly, these statements are all opinions:

*Disneyland is too crowded.*
*Heavy metal rock music is nerve-jangling.*
*Chinese food is wonderful.*

They tell us what the speakers like or do not like. You may disagree with any of these opinions, but it would be difficult to prove any of them right or wrong. That is because these opinions indicate how people feel or think about something. When an opinion is proved to be true, it becomes a fact.

Being able to sort information into facts and opinions is important in reading, doing research, or writing a report. The words used in a statement can give you important clues. A statement of fact is often simple and straightforward. Here are some examples:

*Carl Sagan is an astronomer and author.*
*Carl Lewis, the United States track and field star,*
  *has won 7 Olympic gold medals.*
*Oliver! won the Academy Award for best picture of 1968.*

When reading or doing research, think critically about what you are reading. Watch carefully for words that express feelings or values that show approval or disapproval of something. These types of words in a statement usually mean that the statement is an opinion. Here are some examples of feeling words to watch for:

*hope, fear, wish, believe, feel, think, guess, should, must*

Some examples of value words that show approval are:

*good, better, best, interesting, pretty, wise, smart, handsome, witty, lovely, elegant*

Some examples of value words that show disapproval are:

*bad, dull, worst, terrible, ugly, boring, dumb*

Here are some opinion statements that have some clue words. See if you can pick out the word in each statement that makes it an opinion.

*Everyone should give to a charity of some kind.*

*Oliver! is the best movie musical ever made.*

*He was really upset and made an ugly scene at the party.*

The first statement was, "Everyone should give to a charity of some kind." The clue that this statement is an opinion is the feeling word, *should*.

In the statement, "*Oliver!* is the best movie musical ever made," the clue word is *best*.

In the final statement, "He was really upset and made an ugly scene at the party," the clue word is *ugly*.

Understanding the differences between facts and opinions can help you weigh and evaluate the information you collect.

## The Steps of Critical Thinking

As with creative thinking, you move through specific steps when thinking critically. In both cases, you may at times take some of these steps at a subconscious level.

Because you are reacting to a specific situation and must decide what to do, use the word SOLVE as a device to help remember the steps in critical thinking:

> S—State or summarize the problem.
> O—Organize your thoughts.
> L—Learn about your options.
> V—Validate implications of options.
> E—Evaluate and choose a solution.

You will note that the SOLVE steps of critical thinking closely parallel the IDEA steps of creative thinking. That is because you will be doing both kinds of thinking in any purposeful mental activity. The emphasis between the two types of thinking, however, is different. To train yourself to think both creatively and critically and to understand their different emphases, you need to study them separately. Now examine the steps in critical thinking.

### State or Summarize the Problem

You must state or summarize your problem as clearly and accurately as possible. Consider these two versions of the same situation. In the first, Anita clearly states her problem. In the second Sylvia does not.

> ▶ Anita's typewriter is getting old. She must type many school reports and papers. She is not the most accurate or the fastest typist. She thinks that she could use a computer to do this and probably for some personal work. A friend has a computer and thinks it's wonderful.
>
> But she hesitates because computers are expensive and she does not have much money. She identifies her problem as needing to prepare many reports and papers quickly and neatly for which she needs a computer or a new typewriter. She further identifies the problem as determining exactly what computer system and what software she would need and what she can afford.
>
> Knowing her basic problem or need—write reports, term

papers, book reviews, personal letters, and keep research notes—helps her determine the kind of computer system and software she needs.

She goes to a dealer and explains her needs. The dealer recommends that she get a simple basic model with a monochrome monitor, a good word processing program, and a dot matrix printer. The equipment is within her budget, and she requires a computer.

▶ Sylvia's typewriter is getting old. She thinks that her problem is whether or not to buy a computer. A friend tells her that she simply must get a color monitor because they are great for playing Nintendo games. Another well-meaning friend tells her she will have to get special software that can manage her files, one that has a graphic user interface. Still another says that she really must get integrated software that can do several things at once. Acting on this advice, Sylvia goes to dealers for prices. When she describes the things her friends tell her she needs, the dealer gives her a price that is beyond her budget. She decides she cannot afford a computer.

Sylvia makes a bad decision because she did not fully define and state her problem. Rather than identifying her needs, she reduces her problem to whether to buy a computer or not. She needed a simple computer with word processing software; she did not need a color monitor or special software. She could have, in fact, afforded a computer with the necessary software that would have helped her do her work and improve her study habits.

**Organize Your Thoughts**

Organizing your thoughts is important. You may have countless ideas and thoughts. As long as they are a jumble in your mind, they remain useless. A good way to organize your thoughts is to write them down. Writing things down, as you have already read, is an extremely useful tool when you are thinking.

Another good way to organize your thoughts when you are thinking critically is to weigh their pros and cons. Divide a paper into three columns. In the first column, write down all your thoughts or possibilities relating to a subject. In the second column write down all the reasons why each possibility is a good one. In the third column, write all the reasons why each one is not a good idea.

Anita took this approach when deciding what she should do regarding her old typewriter. Her list looked like the first one shown below. She lists her possibilities, no matter how silly, and the pros and cons of each, writing them down. She may have more than one pro or con per possibility. Then she can see which possibility has the best or most pro qualities and which the most con and begin eliminating the least attractive possibilities until she has the best one left.

| POSSIBILITIES | PROS | CONS |
| --- | --- | --- |
| Buy new computer | most reliable | too expensive |
| Buy used computer | less expensive | less reliable |
| Rent computer | expensive | short-term solution |
| Borrow computer | no cost | short-term solution |
| Use friend's computer | no cost | short-term solution |
| Use computer in school | least expensive | not convenient |
| Buy new typewriter | less expensive | limited in what it can do |
| Buy good used typewriter | least expensive | less reliable |
| Repair typewriter | least expensive | least reliable |
| Borrow typewriter | no cost | short-term solution |
| Make a computer | less expensive | take too long |
| Steal a computer | none | it's a crime |

## Learn About Your Options

When you are making a decision, you often are tempted to follow your instincts and choose what feels right, the first thing you think of. Resist this impulse. Learn about your options. Anita really would like to have a new computer, and it seems the perfect solution to her. She considers all the possibilities on her list and only after careful thought crosses out those that she decides are not worth pursuing further as shown below.

| POSSIBILITIES | PROS | CONS |
| --- | --- | --- |
| Buy new computer | most reliable | too expensive |
| Buy used computer | less expensive | less reliable |
| ~~Rent computer~~ | ~~expensive~~ | ~~short-term solution~~ |
| ~~Borrow computer~~ | ~~no cost~~ | ~~short-term solution~~ |
| ~~Use friend's computer~~ | ~~no cost~~ | ~~short-term solution~~ |
| ~~Use computer in school~~ | ~~least expensive~~ | ~~not convenient~~ |
| Buy new typewriter | less expensive | limited in what it can do |
| Buy good used typewriter | least expensive | less reliable |
| ~~Repair typewriter~~ | ~~least expensive~~ | ~~least reliable~~ |
| ~~Borrow typewriter~~ | ~~no cost~~ | ~~short-term solution~~ |
| ~~Make a computer~~ | ~~less expensive~~ | ~~take too long~~ |
| ~~Steal a computer~~ | ~~none~~ | ~~it's a crime~~ |

When solving a problem, write down every possibility, as Anita has done, no matter how ridiculous. Stealing a computer is out of the question of course, but it made her remember that the local police department often sells unclaimed equipment at auction. This could be a place to buy an inexpensive computer. She also decides to find out more about the cost and capabilities of a new typewriter. In learning about her options, Anita crossed out the impossible solutions and now concentrates on the possible.

**Validate Implications of Options**

When you are validating possible solutions, there is more than one way of looking at them. The type of problem you are trying to solve determines how you should validate the possible solutions.

To validate possible solutions think of the consequences and write them down. It is easier to compare and review something written than when it is only a thought floating in your mind. To help yourself think of all possible consequences, attempt to find at least one in each of these three categories for each possible solution:
1. Immediate consequences.
2. Short-term consequences. (This week, month, or year.)
3. Long-term consequences. (5 or 10 years, rest of your life.)

Sometimes, you might write "none." Most of the time, if you think about it, you will probably realize that for all but routine problems, there is, at least, an immediate and a short-term consequence.

---

▶ It is Thursday. Sylvia has a term paper due Friday morning. She has worked hard on it, doing a lot of research and creating a lot of notes. Now she is struggling with her old typewriter. One of the keys keeps sticking and as the night wears on, her typing becomes slower and more filled with errors.
   She is often erasing or striking over. It is early morning before she finishes, and the paper is filled with typos and covered with erasure smudges. She forgot to add some important information in the middle section. She does not have time to retype it and must submit it as it is. She receives a poor grade.

---

Sylvia does not define her problem to begin with and then fails to consider the consequences of not replacing her old typewriter. No one can predict the future. However, it is possible to consider potential consequences.

If Sylvia had taken time to list on a piece of scrap paper the possibilities and possible consequences of replacing her old typewriter, she might have made a different decision. Possible consequences were a poor-looking, less well-prepared paper and, ultimately, a lower grade.

If Sylvia had thought critically about her decision not to buy a computer, she may have made more of an effort to identify her problem and find a computer she could afford.

Although Sylvia's decision will be of little consequence to her life five or ten years away, it has a direct effect on the next week and perhaps months if she fails the course.

**Evaluate and Choose a Solution**

You have stated the problem, organized your thoughts, learned about your options, and validated the implications of those options. What remains are several realistic, doable courses of action. One of them will represent the solution.

You want to keep clearly and accurately in mind exactly what the problem is. You want to weigh once more the pros and cons of the choices you are about to make. You also may want to review your written lists.

Sometimes the right choice is clear to you at this point and you realize how going through the earlier steps helped to clarify your thinking. Quite often, however, the right choice is still not crystal clear to you, in which case, you need to repeat the process.

Even if your problem is to decide on a simple course of action, such as whether to join the Outdoor Club or not, you benefit from following the steps of critical thinking. Your immediate thought might be that you simply decide yes or no about joining the club. Following the steps may cause you to realize that other alternatives exist. For example, you can decide yes, but not until next year.

If following the steps helps you see variations on simple yes or no matters, the value of taking the steps becomes even more apparent when your problem is complex, such as deciding whether to pursue a degree in video production technology or in automotive technology. Whichever one you choose, you will benefit from the process of going through all the steps. You will be more comfortable in your decision after having carefully evaluated the choices.

## SUMMING UP

Everyone can and does think creatively. Sometimes people stop using their ability to think creatively as they get older and become inhibited.

A quick rejection of a new or unusual idea is the opposite of creative thinking.

Creative thinking is linked to learning. Memorizing facts is not creative thinking, but when you connect two separate ideas to create a new idea or a new way of seeing something, then you are thinking creatively.

Creative thinking refers to the mental ability to generate different and unique ideas. With creative thinking you broaden your viewpoint and see beyond the obvious, immediate, and personal.

The word *idea* suggests the steps in creative thinking:

> I—Illuminate your problem or purpose.
> D—Develop possible solutions.
> E—Ease off for a while.
> A—Arrive at a solution (outcome).

To stimulate your creative thinking, try the following techniques:

- Brainstorm
- Use all sources of help
- Ask yourself questions
- Write it down.

Critical thinking is used to evaluate and judge facts, ideas, and opinions of your own and of others. It requires judging all aspects of what is under consideration—both the good and the bad; in other words it is more than simply finding fault.

Critical thinking is a basic study skill. It includes the ability to tell the difference between facts and opinions. A fact is a statement that can be proven true. An opinion is a statement that has not been proven right or wrong. An opinion also may describe what a person likes or dislikes; it does not matter that no one else agrees.

Students need to be able to separate facts from opinions when reading, doing research, and writing reports.

Certain words usually indicate that a statement is an opinion, not a fact; for example, *hope, fear, wish, believe, feel.*

Other words, which also indicate an opinion, are value words that show approval or disapproval; for example, *good, better, smart, bad, worse, dumb.*

You can use the word *solve* as a device to help remember the steps in critical thinking:

> S—State or summarize the problem.
> O—Organize your thoughts.
> L—Learn about your options.
> V—Validate implications of options.
> E—Evaluate and choose a solution.

If you fail to do the first step, you may make a bad decision on how to solve your problem.

One way to organize your thoughts (step two) is to list the pros and cons of each one.

In step three you learn which options are possible and which ones you should not consider further.

In step four you think about the immediate, short-term and long-term consequences of possible solutions.

## ▼ DEVELOPING YOUR SKILLS

Exercise 1

### Practice Brainstorming

Refer to the story about relocating the Amtrak railroad tracks. Think of all the reasons you can why moving the tracks to run along the interstate highway away from the coast is a good idea. Think of all the reasons that moving the tracks is a bad idea. Assume that the tracks will be electrified. List your reasons on two separate sheets of paper. Head one MOVING TRACKS IS A GOOD IDEA and the other MOVING TRACKS IS A BAD IDEA.

Exercise 2

### Practice Steps of Creative Thinking

You are trying to decide whether to take some courses this coming summer. It would be nice to finish school and get your degree as soon as possible. By going to summer school, you could graduate a semester sooner. The summer school runs from June 4 to July 30. You need to be able to earn some money this coming summer as well. Last year, you had a job from June 1 to August 31. This summer, you want to visit relatives when your cousin gets married in mid-July.

- Illuminate your problem.

_____
_____
_____
_____
_____

- Develop your possible solutions.

_____
_____
_____

- Ease off for a while, if necessary.

Chapter 1                                Thinking Creatively and Critically—23

- Arrive at a solution.

_____
_____
_____
_____
_____

Exercise 3

**Practice Creative Thinking**

- Identify a problem of your own that you would like to solve and write it down.

_____
_____
_____
_____

- Develop possible solutions. (List some sources you can go to for help.)

_____
_____
_____
_____

- Write down some questions to ask yourself regarding your problem.

_____
_____
_____
_____
_____
_____
_____
_____

- List possible solutions.

_____
_____
_____
_____
_____
_____
_____
_____

Exercise 4

### Practice Using the Steps of Critical Thinking

Imagine that you work for a large company. You have just received the following memo.

> TO: All employees of XX Department
> FROM: Personnel Department
>
> A training course on the new data processing procedures will be offered this winter. Everyone in XX Department should at least be familiar with these procedures. The purpose of the course is to help you learn them faster and give you the opportunity to get help with specific difficulties you may have. No one is required to take the course.
>
> The course will be given on Saturday mornings from 9:30 to noon, beginning January 4 and ending February 3. If you would like to take this course, please contact the personnel department.

Apply the critical thinking steps to decide whether or not to take the course.

- State your problem.
- Organize your thoughts.

List all the reasons to take the course and all the reasons NOT to take the course.

| REASONS TO TAKE COURSE | REASONS **NOT** TO TAKE COURSE |
|---|---|
| | |
| | |
| | |
| | |
| | |
| | |

- Learn about your options.

Refer to your lists and cross out anything that is not worth considering further. Write the remaining reasons below.

| REASONS TO TAKE COURSE | REASONS **NOT** TO TAKE COURSE |
|---|---|
| | |
| | |
| | |

- Validate the implications of options.

Write down all the possible consequences you can think of.

## Taking the course

Immediate consequences:

_____

_____

_____

_____

Short-term consequences:

_____

_____

_____

_____

Long-term consequences:

_____

_____

_____

_____

_____

### Not taking the course

Immediate consequences:

_____

_____

_____

Short-term consequences:

_____

_____

_____

Long-term consequences:

_____

_____

_____

- Evaluate and choose a solution.

_____

_____

_____

_____

# 2 Thinking for Yourself

*After completing this chapter, you will be able to use self-awareness and self-evaluation to think for yourself.*

The goal of thinking as an individual is to make yourself a free and independent person. This requires discipline and applying the skills of creative and critical thinking. These skills will be useful throughout your life. They will give you the freedom that comes from being able to evaluate and judge what you read in the newspapers, see on television, or hear from the politician's platform. A person who only memorizes facts or accepts everything is not thinking as an individual.

## KNOW YOURSELF

Knowing yourself is essential to your success in many ways. In Chapter 3, you will learn why knowing yourself is important in developing a vision of your future. In this chapter, you learn that the first step toward being an independent individual is knowing who you are. This means more than knowing your name, address, who your parents and friends are, and what foods, clothes, and activities you enjoy. You might say that these things are *knowing where you are at*.

Before you can think as an individual, you need also to know *where you are from*. You need to make yourself aware of what people and experiences helped mold your thinking.

Many factors influence you: your parents, other family members, friends, your neighborhood, your socioeconomic background. As a result of the influence of these factors, you develop your own values and attitudes. When you think—make decisions, draw conclusions, evaluate—your values and attitudes will slant your thinking. If you remain unaware of your values and attitudes and how you developed them, you will never fully think as an individual.

You should not only make an effort to be aware of what influences shaped you and what your values and attitudes are, but you should be ready to evaluate them. That is, you should apply creative and critical thinking skills to develop new values—to refine, reject, and change old ones in response to new experiences and knowledge.

Life is not static and, as the American poet James Russell Lowell wrote, *new occasions teach new duties, time makes ancient good uncouth.* If you are unaware of your values and attitudes and how they developed, you cannot take advantage of new experiences and knowledge to grow and develop.

## KNOW YOUR VALUES

Values are your standards for judging what is important to you. You can have many values, and sometimes they conflict. You are motivated to achieve things you value. Knowing what your values are helps you focus your talents and make plans, rather than simply react.

Knowing what you value will make it easier for you to make decisions when faced with conflicting choices. For example, your answers to the following questions will indicate the kind of job you will enjoy and do well.

- Do you value working with people or things?
- Do you value independence or security?
- Do you value certainty or challenge?

### Acquiring Values

You develop and acquire values from two sources: experience and other people.

*Experience* begins molding your values from the moment of your birth. Experience is a powerful shaper of values, and can be more powerful than other people, even parents. That is because what actually happens to you has a stronger effect on you than what people tell you or demonstrate by example.

However, it is almost impossible for you to shape your values entirely without the influence of other people. Parents exert the first and strongest influence on your values. When you leave home, other people exert an influence. At first it will be mostly people in authority, such as teachers and religious leaders. When you are between the ages of 12 and 18, your peers influence you most.

## Clarifying Your Values

Acquiring and clarifying values is a lifelong process. Because we live in a time of constant change and in a society made up of many different parts, it is difficult to establish a consistent set of values. Often you will find it necessary to compromise some of your values. The problem is deciding when to compromise without becoming a hypocrite or when to hold to your values without becoming a fanatic.

Upholding the value of total individual freedom, for example, is not always practical and can be self-defeating. For example, you may value good grades and want to spend an evening studying. You find yourself, however, in a social situation in which you feel it necessary to go out for a pizza because you also value being accepted socially.

If you habitually compromise, you are in danger of failing to reach your goals. If you always give in to pressure and go get a pizza instead of studying, your grades will suffer. Acting against your values can create negative feelings, unhappiness, and guilt.

Because compromise often is necessary, it helps to know which of the values you hold are most important. Not all values are equal. Some values you will defend with your life. Others are less important. Successful people are those who can maintain their important values and be willing to compromise less important ones.

Examine and reevaluate your values every so often. Ask yourself such questions as:

- Are my values appropriate for what I am doing now?
- Do my values fit in with the changes that have occurred in my life?
- Are my values meaningful in my current situation?

If the answer to any of these questions is "no," then you must consider changing your values. You will not always change them, of course. You might decide to keep your values and change your circumstances, insofar as that is possible.

The point is to be open to change. In an entry-level job, respect for authority is a functional value because you have little experience to rely on. Lacking experience, you should value the experience of mentors or supervisors. As you gain experience, you should begin to value independence and the ability to make your own decisions. Otherwise, you will not continue to grow and succeed on the job.

Some values, such as integrity and responsibility, should always be important. Others, such as adventure and fame, may never be important to you or are important only for a short period in your life.

## THINK FOR YOURSELF

If you do not think for yourself, you are likely to reach conclusions or make decisions that are not really in your own best interests or reflect what you really feel. Thinking for yourself, however, does not mean ignoring the opinions and advice of others. It does mean being able to evaluate what you hear or read as well as your own thoughts and then acting as you think best.

Here are two situations of people thinking for themselves but with different results. Johnny is influenced by others who are important to him but also uses his own critical thinking skills. Elissa fails to use her critical thinking skills and makes a poor decision.

> Johnny is trying to decide what courses to take. A career in electronics interests him, and he wonders if taking the computer programming course might be a good idea. His older brother Frank tells him that the course is no good, the text is terrible, and the instructor awful.
> 
> He says, "Don't take the course. It's a waste of time!"
> 
> He may or may not be right. If Johnny listens to his brother and makes no effort to think critically, he will not take the course regardless of how much it might help him.
> 
> Johnny does not simply accept what his brother tells him. He thinks about it critically. He thinks that his brother's views might be slanted. He decides to talk to Elton, a classmate of Frank's.
> 
> Elton liked the computer programming course. He laughs and says to Johnny, "Your brother never liked computers. It's a good thing he switched majors. It's a good course. I learned a lot. But if I were you, Johnny, I'd find out what text they're using now. Ours was pretty bad, and the instructor knew it."
> 
> Johnny now has more information for making a decision. He realizes that a dislike of computers influenced Frank's view. He can find out what textbook is being used. He can ask Frank or

Elton if it is different from the one they used. If he is still undecided, he might talk to someone else who has taken the course or to the instructor.

Johnny thought critically about what his brother told him. He did not reject the information out-of-hand, nor did he simply accept it. He checked with another source and planned to check with still others. Compare Johnny's use of critical thinking with that of Elissa.

▶ After working as a part-time administrative assistant for several weeks, Elissa decided that she did not need to back up her work on the computer. Her school instructors always taught her to save her work on a floppy disk at the end of each session. The company she worked for even has a policy that people should do this.

None of the work she kept on a computer's hard disk, however, had ever been lost. She had never experienced a computer failure in school and none had occurred after several weeks at work. Elissa decided that computers are reliable. She began asking herself, "Why waste time at the end of the day, when I'm in a hurry to leave, making backups that are never needed?"

Based on what she believed she had learned from experience, Elissa decided to stop wasting time to make backups at the end of each day.

It was not long before the inevitable happened. Elissa came to work one day to find her computer's hard disk had accidentally been wiped clean. All of the work she had done on several previous days, including an important company report, was lost.

Elissa did not think critically about the conclusion that she arrived at before acting. If she had, she might have realized that others (instructors and supervisors), whose combined experience far exceeded hers, were in a better position to know how reliable computers were. Elissa thought that her experience with computers was sufficient to make a decision. That was not so.

Elissa's situation was different from Johnny's in that she had to think critically about her own ideas, not someone else's. As noted, that is always difficult to do. The consequences of not doing so, however, can often be serious.

### Identify Thinking Barriers

There are several barriers to creative and critical thinking that you, like everyone else, carry around with you. Unless you work to overcome them, these barriers limit the extent to which you think clearly. These barriers can prevent you from thinking as an individual. This happens when you are unaware of the barriers and let them, rather than your conscious self, control your thinking.

The most common barriers to thinking for yourself can be put into two broad groups. Each group contains patterns that block creative and critical thinking. When these thought patterns take control, you do not think as an individual.

- The first group of barriers—*fear of differences*—comes into play when you are in a new situation, are faced with a new idea, or meet some new people. You must react to each of these.

- The second group of barriers—*defensive reaction*—comes into play when you blindly defend a position, action, or belief.

## Fear of Differences

You feel most comfortable with people and things you know. That is normal. There is nothing wrong with it. Everyone feels that way. The danger to your ability to think as an individual arises when you automatically reject anything that disturbs your sense of comfort. Here are some thought patterns people automatically use when they feel threatened by what is different. These thought patterns replace active thinking.

**Glorifying Your Group.** We all belong to social groups. We are born into them, and we join them. We all want to believe that our group is best. For us to believe that, we must assume other groups are inferior. This can be harmless, as in the athletic rivalry between two schools. In some ways, it can even be helpful by stimulating constructive competition. Two classes might compete for highest academic honors. Two work teams might compete to be the most productive.

Glorifying the group, however, can quickly block independent thought. If you automatically assume that a particular group you belong to is superior or a group different from yours is inferior, you have stopped thinking. To think independently, you must make yourself look at your own group and other groups objectively. That means being able to see and talk about the flaws in your particular group as well as the positive aspects of the other group.

**Stereotyping.** This barrier to independent thinking grows out of a useful thinking tool—generalizing. You are generalizing, for example, when you say such things as "All dogs have a sharp sense of smell." "Smaller cars have better gas mileage than larger cars." "People with college degrees earn more money than those without." These are useful generalizations in that they allow you to make a point easily. They are even mostly true. That is the catch. Someone once said that:

*All generalizations are false, including this one.*

Although the statement contradicts itself, it provides a useful warning about generalizations. Stereotypes are extreme forms of generalizations. They are huge barriers to independent thinking. According to *Webster's Dictionary*, a stereotype is

*a standard mental picture . . . representing an oversimplified opinion, affective attitude, or uncritical judgment.*

A stereotype is an attitude or belief held by members of one group about members of another group. If you use stereotypes to decide about other people or things, you are not thinking independently.

**Conforming.** Conforming means to do, say, or think only what the group requires. Being different is difficult, especially when it threatens our sense of comfort in belonging to a group. People feel the urge to conform or to belong even with temporary, informal groups. Try booing when everyone else is applauding at a concert or theater and you will instantly experience discomfort.

A degree of conformity is valuable, even necessary for the maintenance of society. An extreme willingness to conform, however, represents a person's abandonment of his or her own individual critical judgment. Always try to be willing to challenge your own actions and thoughts when you find you are feeling the need to conform.

**Resisting Change.** When faced with the need to adapt to a new way of doing things or seeing things, we tend to resist. This applies to new ideas as well. People at one time resisted the idea that the earth is round. It made them uncomfortable. Rather than think about it, they preferred to hold to their old belief that the earth is flat. Otherwise, one would fall off.

The comfort of an old belief can be so great that some people will struggle to keep it rather than to accept a new one. Refusing to change is the sign of someone who has sacrificed creative and critical thinking for the sake of comfort. Work to be flexible and open to new ideas so you can examine them as an individual.

## Defensive Reaction

As mentioned, you react defensively when you blindly defend an action, a position, or a belief you hold. Rather than thinking about what is happening, you react with one of the following thought patterns.

**Don't Look at Me.** We instinctively adopt this thought pattern when something threatens our self-image or ego.

*It's not my fault!*
*I didn't do it!*

It is a familiar response of young children when warned. It is a thought pattern, unfortunately, that we tend to exhibit all our lives. When, as students, we fail to complete the homework assignment, we have many excuses—not only for the teacher but for ourselves. When late for work, we readily come up with explanations for the boss. None of it is our fault. We refuse to take responsibility.

Sometimes, of course, it really is not our fault. Often, however, it is. When it is our fault, we must see what the problem is and think about it so we can correct it. Failing this, we continue to make the same error. We do not learn, change, or grow. We are passive subjects to our thought patterns and not thinking as individuals.

**You're as Bad.** We use this automatic thought pattern when we experience criticism. It is similar to the "don't look at me" reaction and its goal is to protect our ego. We react by finding fault with the person criticizing us. If some one is finding fault for the sake of finding fault, reacting with this thought pattern might be the thing to do.

Frequently, however, criticism directed at us comes from parents, teachers, or friends trying to help us learn, grow, or develop. In such cases, the independent-minded person thinks about and evaluates the criticism before reacting or deciding what to do. Here is a simple example of the *you're as bad* response.

> "Melvin, you'd probably make fewer errors keyboarding if you didn't try to go so fast," Barbara says, trying to help her friend.
> "Yeah? Well, I notice you never cover your keyboard when you leave at night," Melvin replies.

Barbara could have been right. If he had listened, Melvin may have improved his skills and made himself a more valuable employee. Instead, he was more interested in protecting his ego. He was not being an independent thinker.

**Self-Serving Bias.** All defensive reactions are self-serving. Exaggerating our ability or conveniently forgetting an ego-threatening or personally unpleasant fact are particular examples of self-serving bias.

You may have read newspaper accounts of disputes over lottery winnings. One or more people sue the holder of the winning ticket for a share of the money. They maintain an agreement existed in which they all purchased the ticket as a joint investment. The person holding the ticket denies that any such agreement existed. Each side really believes it is right. If the people suing are right, the ticket holder is forgetting an unwanted fact. If the ticket holder is right, the challengers' memory exaggerates their right to share the ticket. Depending on the actual circumstances, one or the other side is exhibiting a self-serving bias.

Although it might soothe your ego, exaggerating your ability prevents you from learning.

> New on the job as a computer programmer, Bob wanted to impress his coworkers and supervisor with how much he knew. He brushed aside all attempts by his supervisor and coworkers to give him helpful information about the job. Also, he never asked questions. As a result, he did not learn the company's methods of doing things. He was slow and constantly making errors. When his probation period ended, so did his job.

Bob exhibited a self-serving bias by protecting his ego from having to admit he did not know everything. He was not exercising his powers to think as an individual. And, of course, he paid a high price for the sake of his ego.

It is difficult to recall facts that are not to your liking. It is equally difficult to admit you do not know everything you need to. If you recognize when you are doing this and apply creative and critical thinking skills, you can often improve your situation.

## OVERCOME THINKING BARRIERS

You are well on the way to overcoming your thinking barriers when you have admitted they exist. After that, it is a question of developing the habit of evaluating your responses and thoughts before speaking, acting, or making any decision. That does not mean you must agonize over every act or decision. In many day-to-day situations little is at stake. You can express your preference for coffee without sugar or for the beach instead of the mountains without wondering whether you are thinking for yourself.

### Consider Your Reaction

At those times, however, when you take actions that will affect your future or affect other people, practice your creative and critical thinking skills. Try to think as an individual by overcoming your personal thinking barriers. Whenever you feel your self-image or ego is under attack, take the time to consider your reaction.

### Look Beyond the Obvious

You use creative thinking to see beyond the obvious, immediate, and personal. It is probably because nothing is obvious to young children that they are natural creative thinkers. When you have become experienced, ironically, you must make an extra effort to see beyond the obvious.

### Avoid Making Quick Decisions

You constantly face problems you must solve. They range from the simple—what movie shall I go see; to the complex—what is the best career for me. In either one of these situations, you could, of course, forego creative thinking and make a snap decision. Making a snap decision about what movie to see could result in nothing more serious than the loss of a little time and some money. Making a snap decision when resolving a more complex problem, such as deciding on a career for yourself, could result in an unhappy life.

The ability to think creatively and critically can help you solve many, seemingly routine, problems. The problem of scheduling your time is one example. As a student, you often face conflicting demands on your time. You must schedule time to study, do household chores, run errands, and enjoy leisure activities. If you hold a job while attending school, you have an even greater problem in scheduling your time.

In a later lesson, you will learn techniques for setting goals and preparing schedules. You can use these techniques most effectively when you have good thinking skills. What it boils down to is this:

> *The more possibilities you can create and evaluate, the greater your likelihood of finding a good solution.*

You will discover that there are very few situations or problems that do not provide you with more than one possible course of action. You must use your creative thinkings skills to come up with them and your critical thinkings skills to evaluate them before deciding. Consider this situation.

▶ Angela and Rob have applied for part-time work in the library. The hours are Wednesday and Thursday from 6 p.m. to 10 p.m. and Saturday and Sunday from 12 noon to 4 p.m.

Angela says "I can't work on Saturday or Sunday, so I'll take Wednesday and Thursday."

Rob says "I was going to ask for the same hours."

The librarian says she will return in 15 minutes to see if they have resolved the problem.

Angela thinks, "The librarian should make her preference known and not make us decide. I'm not going to budge."

Rob thinks, "I'm not going to give up my Saturday basketball game. And my mother would be furious if I didn't see her on Sunday. Just because Angela spoke first doesn't mean she gets her choice."

Angela and Rob spend the time talking about their favorite courses. Both think that by standing firm they will get their own way. They refuse to think about how to solve their shared problem.

When the librarian returns and finds they have not made a decision, she says, "We have several choices. I could close the library on Saturday and Sunday afternoon. I could look for others to work then. Or you two could each agree to work one day on the weekend."

The librarian has thought creatively and in doing so gets Angela and Rob to open their minds also.

Rob says, "I think I could do that. What about you, Angela?"

Angela thinks for a minute, then says, "Yes, I could work Saturday but not Sunday."

Rob says, "I can take Sunday if I can start at 1 instead of 12. I'll ask the librarian if 1 to 5 would be okay."

---

The librarian helped Rob and Angela by making a ridiculous suggestion—to close the library. She also got them worried by suggesting she could look for two other applicants. Her third suggestion was quite reasonable. As a result, Rob could think of a solution to the problem of working on Sunday.

## SUMMING UP

The goal of thinking as an individual is to make yourself a free and independent person. The first step toward being an independent person is to know who you are. You need to make yourself aware of the people and experiences that helped mold your thinking.

Knowing what you value makes it easier for you to make decisions when faced with conflicting choices.

Thinking barriers can be divided into two broad categories:

- Fear of differences.
- Defensive reaction.

Fear of differences comes into play when you are reacting to a new situation, a new idea, or new people. It includes:

- Glorifying the group.
- Stereotyping.
- Conforming.
- Resisting change.

Defensive reactions occur when you unthinkingly defend a position, action, idea, or belief you have held. Defensive reactions include:

- Don't look at me—refusing to take responsibility.
- You're as bad—attacking the other person rather than considering the idea.
- Self-serving bias—exaggerating our own ability or conveniently forgetting ego threatening or unpleasant facts.

Being aware of your thinking barriers puts you well on the way to overcoming them.

## ▼ DEVELOPING YOUR SKILLS

Exercise 1

### Practice Thinking as an Individual

You are the manager of a local auditorium known as the Veterans Memorial Center. Half the money to build the center came from private donations, mostly through the efforts of veterans groups. The municipality, which owns the center, put up the rest of the money. Your salary and the funds to keep the center operating are raised by renting out the auditorium. Your responsibility is to look for organizations interested in renting the center. You decide whom to rent to, draw up the contracts, and collect the fees. Your job depends on being able to keep the auditorium rented and making money.

A nationally famous singing group approached you about renting the hall over the Fourth of July weekend. You are pleased because they want the auditorium for four days, and you know they will attract a large crowd. That increases the amount you can charge the group as well as ensures that the concession stands will sell a lot of food and drink.

As soon as the upcoming concert becomes known, objections arise. Many people, including members of veterans organizations, do not want this group performing in the Veterans Memorial Center. The group has refused to play the "Star Spangled Banner" at recent concerts. Furthermore, the group has played songs that some say are unpatriotic. The group's spokesperson says that the group really loves this country. It is objecting only to politicians and others who wave the flag and cheapen the ideal of patriotism to advance their own selfish interests.

You are caught in the middle of a controversy. On the one hand, many people, including community leaders and veterans, want you to cancel the contract. On the other, those who want to hear the group say cancelling the contract would violate the group's right of free speech. Also, of course, you must consider the money involved.

- As a first step in resolving this dilemma by independent thinking, identify those factors that might have influenced your values and attitudes that might have a bearing on your decision in this situation.

_____

_____

- **Assuming all statements given above are true, identify all the thinking barriers that might be at play in this controversy. Describe how any might apply to either of the sides and to yourself.**

Exercise 2

## Practice Creative and Critical Thinking Skills

Take the same problem discussed on page 41 and, using the skills for creative and critical thinking you have learned, reach and support a decision.

- Identify the problem.

_____

_____

_____

_____

- List possible solutions and evaluate them in terms of their pros and cons.

| SOLUTIONS | PROS | CONS |
|---|---|---|
|  |  |  |
|  |  |  |
|  |  |  |
|  |  |  |
|  |  |  |
|  |  |  |
|  |  |  |
|  |  |  |
|  |  |  |
|  |  |  |

Exercise 3

## Consider This Idea

Your school is planning to stay open 48 weeks a year, with a two-week winter break and a two-week summer vacation.

Use your critical thinking skills to evaluate this idea.

- List several ways this would affect your life and label each good or bad. Use a separate sheet of paper.

- List the immediate, short-term, and long-term consequences for you if you were in school 48 weeks a year.

| IMMEDIATE CONSEQUENCES | SHORT-TERM CONSEQUENCES | LONG-TERM CONSEQUENCES |
|---|---|---|
| | | |
| | | |
| | | |
| | | |
| | | |
| | | |
| | | |

- Write a brief evaluation of the plan, stating whether, on the whole, it is a good one, a bad one, or both.

_____

_____

_____

_____

Compare your thoughts with those of your classmates.

# UNIT 11
# PLANNING

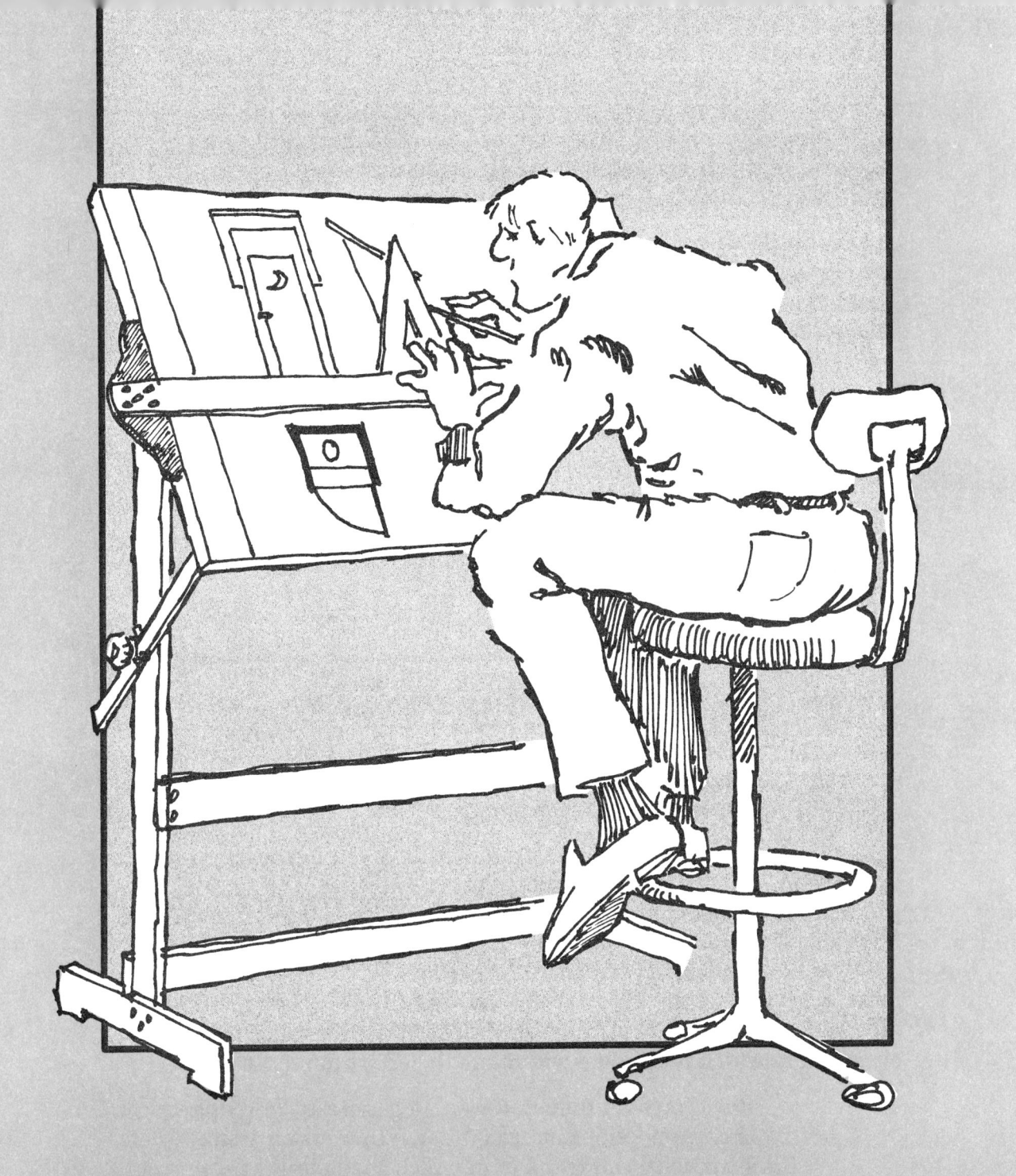

**After completing this unit, you will be able to develop a vision for your future and specify the steps and timeframe you will need to begin realizing it.**

> *No one can make you learn.*
> *You must want to learn.*

Unless you have a reason for doing something, you feel reluctant to do it. If forced, you will make an effort, but not an enthusiastic one. When you do have a reason to do something, you willingly work to do it well. Mortimer J. Adler in *How to Read a Book* (NY, Simon and Schuster, 1960) made this point. He was talking about reading. He believed that most of us do not take the time to read well. He also believed that we all could read well if we wanted to. He gave this illustration of a situation in which most of us will make the effort to read well:

> If we consider men and women generally, and apart from their professions or occupations, there is only one situation I can think of in which they almost pull themselves up by their bootstraps, making an effort to read better than they usually do. When they are in love and are reading a love letter, they read for all they are worth. They read every word three ways; they read between the lines and in the margins; they read the whole in terms of the parts, and each part in terms of the whole; they grow sensitive to context and ambiguity, to insinuation and implication; they perceive the color of words, the odor of phrases, and the weight of sentences. They may even take the punctuation into account. Then, if never before or after, they read.

## VISION AND MOTIVATION

People in love have a reason for carefully reading the love letters sent to them. They are motivated. Although Mr. Adler was speaking of reading, his point is equally true for any task we undertake. If we are motivated, we will make an effort to do well. Love is a powerful motivator, of course, but there are others.

People who have a positive vision of their future have a powerful motivator. A vision is your idea of what you want your career and life to be like. Having an idea of what career you want, where you want to be at a certain age, not only ensures your moving toward that goal, but makes it easier for you to tackle the sometimes boring or difficult tasks everyone faces from time to time.

In this unit, you will learn how your vision can be developed and how it relates to your self-image. You will learn what you can do to develop a vision or to change a negative one.

A vision can be a powerful tool to help you shape your future. A positive vision helps shape a positive future.

## VISION, GOALS, AND TO-DO LISTS

Vision—an overall view of life—provides direction and meaning to day-to-day activities. To make your vision a reality, you convert it into short- and long-term goals. These goals are the concrete steps you need to take to realize your vision. You must, in turn, translate your goals into specific things to do on a daily basis.

You might be thinking that this is all too structured. Who wants each day broken down into a series of to-do activities that must be done? Who wants to be locked into this kind of a routine? No one. And no one is.

Having a vision, supporting goals, and to-do lists does not mean you spend every waking moment striving toward your goals. It means, rather, that you will definitely spend a portion of most days in some meaningful activity that will help you realize your vision.

Having vision backed up with goals and to-do lists will result in your having more time to relax and enjoy yourself. You will not be wasting time wondering what to do. Being motivated, you will not put off doing what you need to do or do it reluctantly and slowly. When you do have free time, you will enjoy it more, knowing you have accomplished something. In this unit, you will learn how to set goals and make up to-do lists based on your vision.

## TIME MANAGEMENT

You may not think of managing time as a study skill, but it is. If you do not manage your time to attend the necessary classes, do the necessary study, take care of the cooking, cleaning, laundry, eating, sleeping, and, probably, work a part-time job, you will not do well.

Twenty-four hours a day is all the time anyone has. The person who is successful in life, who accomplishes many things, has no more time in the day than the person who drags along not doing much because "there isn't enough time." The successful person has a vision and knows how to manage time to get the most of what there is.

Having a vision defined by goals and to-do lists is the first step toward managing your time to get the most out of every 24 hours. In Chapter 4 you will learn some techniques to help you manage your time effectively.

## STRESS MANAGEMENT

Even if you have a clear, positive vision that you have translated into goals and to-do lists and are managing your time, you will still experience periods of stress. Everyone does. Stress can be helpful. It can stimulate us to perform at our best. Professional actors, singers, and athletes all experience stress when they perform, no matter how often they have done so. The sense of stress helps them to "get pumped up" so they perform well. Without a feeling of stress, they might not perform as well because they did not feel challenged.

Stress comes to us in two ways:

1. We invite it.
2. It is thrust upon us.

Yes, we invite it. Professionals invite it whenever they step up to perform in front of a crowd. We invite it by taking a dare, or postponing a paper until the last moment. More commonly, stress is thrust upon us. It comes with the unexpected accident, a demand from a boss or a parent, a difficult or unexpected school assignment.

However it comes, you must deal with it. As mentioned, some stress can be helpful. But, often stress can be harmful. You can control it so as to take advantage of stress to make yourself perform well while avoiding or minimizing the bad effects, as you will learn in Chapter 5.

# 3 Finding a Vision; Setting Goals

**After completing this chapter, you will be able to develop a positive vision of your future and set goals to make that vision a reality.**

You would not begin a journey without knowing your destination. If you did, you would wander aimlessly—waste time and money and have little joy. Your life is a journey through time as well as space. If you know where you are heading—if you have a *vision* of what you want to do—the more rewarding your life will be and the more direct your journey toward that end. You will do things, such as study, not because you are told to or because everyone else is doing them, but because doing them helps you realize your vision of the future—to get to where you want to be.

## THE IMPORTANCE OF A VISION

Successful people—those who know what they want in life—have a positive vision of their future. Having a positive vision motivates you. Without motivation, you are unlikely to study well, learn much, or enjoy the process. You will drift into jobs rather than enjoy a rewarding career. Having a vision, an idea of what you want to do with your life, is probably your single most important motivating factor. Developing the vision requires effort. But the effort is spent in a directed way and will pay off for you. Daily challenges will become easier to face and have more meaning.

### Positive or Negative Vision

Your vision must be positive. Some people develop a negative vision of their future, which is worse than having no vision. A negative vision drains energy and destroys motivation. Work and effort seem pointless.

No one can foretell the future. But anyone can influence and shape it. It is a fact that we subconsciously create the kind of person we are and, to a large extent, the kind of life we experience. People with negative visions overlook this simple truth. Because they have had tough times, met failure, been discouraged, or never were encouraged, they develop a negative vision. People who do so can change, though, reminding themselves that the future is unpredictable. They can decide not to let a negative vision shape a negative future, but develop a positive vision that will shape a positive future. Your vision operates as a self-fulfilling prophecy: what you expect, and work for, will occur.

### The Shape of Your Future

Having a vision means taking a long-range view of your life. It means having a sense of where you want to be in the future, what you want to do with your life, not just today or tomorrow but in the immediate and far future. Your vision of the future covers your whole life: where you live, how you live, and what you do.

> *Your vision could be as general as having a steady job, not having to worry about money, helping people, saving the environment.*
>
> *Some people have a vision of being rich and famous. Others want to run their own business. Others only know they want to live in the country or the city.*
>
> *A career vision could be to own a farm, have your own plumbing business, build boats, be a welder, teach, be a secretary, manage a supermarket, run a day-care center, or provide health care.*

Even a general vision of the future increases motivation. The more specific your vision, however, the greater its force as a motivator. Since your work will be a major influence in your life, having a vision of the career you want is particularly important. Consider how the different attitudes of these two people helped shape their future.

▶ Rich and Greg are friends who share a love of music and have vague ideas about a career related to music. Each reads this ad in the local paper.

**Position Open: Sales Service Assistant**
Need enthusiastic individual to assist sales manager. Will be responsible for providing information on music to customers over the phone and in person. We prefer one year of general office experience and some typing skills. Person in this position will learn all aspects of music business and have opportunity to advance.

Rich says to himself, "This sounds like the job for me! I have only six months office experience but they only say they prefer one year, not require it. My typing skills are pretty poor, but the ad said 'some.' With this job I can find out if I want a career in music. I'm going to send in my resumé today."

Greg's reaction to the ad goes like this. "Gee, I'd love a job like that, but I've never been good at talking to people, especially on the phone. I do have over a year of office experience, but my typing isn't great. I guess I won't bother to apply. They wouldn't hire me. I'm not qualified."

---

Greg will not be offered the job because he will not apply for it. His negative vision tells him he is not qualified. If he did apply, he might be offered the job because he has more experience than Rich. Rich, on the other hand, has a positive attitude. His attitude enables him to apply for the job, and he is hired. Rich takes a positive step toward achieving his vision.

## YOUR OWN VISION

There is no question about the value of having a vision. So, how do you get one? Do you say to yourself, "In the future I want to be . . . ." and in a few seconds hatch your vision? Does the vision come to you in a flash as you react to a book you have read, a movie you have seen, or a person you know? Does your vision simply develop out of your experiences?

You may suddenly decide one day what you want to do with your life or you may develop a vision over a period of time. Either way, it does not develop in a vacuum. Other people and your experiences play a part in its creation. Major influences include your family, friends, and teachers. What you hear on television or read in newspapers, magazines, or books also influence you. Other influences include political and religious leaders; people you like, admire, or who impress you; places and things you like. Your values affect your vision.

Your vision of the future directly relates to your self-image. To have a positive vision of the future, you must have a positive self-image. Your experiences and the reaction of others to you influence your self-image. If you have had a series of setbacks or no encouragement, your self-image will suffer. You may think, "Why try? I'll only fail." If this describes you, you must work to change your self-image. One of the most important things you can do in life is change a negative self-image to a positive one.

If you do not have a vision, the techniques and strategies you learn in this chapter will help you develop one. If you have one or have a negative one, they will help you refine it, clarify it, or change it. You will be encouraged to use your creative and critical thinking skills to think for yourself. You will want to overcome barriers to thinking that you read about in Chapter 2.

## STEPS TOWARD A VISION

Although your vision develops as a result of your experiences and the influence of others, you control what form your vision of the future will take. Here are specific steps for developing your vision of the future.

### Step 1: Develop a Positive Attitude

The first step is to develop a positive attitude. What can you do if your experiences have been mostly negative? Work to develop a positive attitude and self-image.

Everyone fails at some time or other, even those who seem most successful. Failing is part of growing and developing. Here are some things to do when you fail or stub your toe:

- Do not be too harsh on yourself.
- Try not to take it personally.
- Look at yourself as objectively as possible to identify what might have caused the problem.
- Look at all the circumstances that contributed to the problem.
- Do not just blame yourself.
- Look for outside reasons.

Successful people are ones who are not quick to blame themselves when things go wrong. They do not say, "Well, that's just me. I'm a failure." Rather they look for the cause and say, "Oh, that's why that happened! I'll fix that."

Yes, this is like pulling yourself up by your own bootstraps. It is difficult, but it can be done. Remember reading earlier about the self-fulfilling prophecy? What you expect to happen will, to a considerable extent, happen. Instead of saying, "Why try? I'll only fail," you might as well say, "Why not try? What have I to lose?"

Developing a positive attitude is easier said then done, of course. But it can be done. Consider the following example.

A man compiled this dismal record of failure:

> *Failed in business*
> *Defeated for state legislature*
> *Failed in business again*
> *Defeated in bid to be speaker of the House in state legislature*
> *Defeated in race for Congress*
> *Defeated in bid for reelection to Congress*
> *Defeated in bid for U.S. Senate*
> *Defeated in bid for Vice Presidential nomination*
> *Defeated in second bid for U.S. Senate*

Given this record, it would have been easy for the man to develop a negative image of himself, decide he was going to be a failure, and give up. Instead, he resisted having a negative image of himself or a negative vision of the future. Rather, he kept a positive image of himself that helped him to generate a positive vision of his future. He kept his vision and in 1860 was elected President of the United States. Today, this man, Abraham Lincoln, is known as one of the greatest presidents in the history of our country.

In developing your positive self-image and a vision of the future:

- Remind yourself that it is not what happens to you but how you react that really matters.

- Get into the habit of thinking positively. Whenever you find yourself thinking, "I can't . . ." "It won't . . ." "I never . . ." "I don't . . ." stop yourself. Convert those negative thoughts to positive ones: "I can . . . " "It will . . ." "I do . . . ."

Doing this will not change the world. But none of these thoughts reflects the world, just your attitude toward it. So you might as well make it a positive attitude. Despite all the evidence to the contrary, Abraham Lincoln kept telling himself, "I can." And he did.

## Step 2: Know Yourself

The second step toward creating a useful vision of your future, particularly of your career, is knowing yourself.

People who are unaware of themselves make unwise career choices. Self-awareness is the first step toward experiencing a successful career and fulfilling life. Two forces—biological and environmental—shape you.

**Biological.** You inherit your physical characteristics from your parents and other ancestors. These include such obvious ones as your hair, eyes, nose, mouth, feet, height, weight, and less apparent ones, such as your nervous system, brain, and spinal cord.

**Environmental.** Your surroundings, factors outside of you, affect your development and behavior. Your social environment has a big influence on you. Think about the people who have been most important to you. Who has encouraged you to stay in or return to school? Who wants you to earn good grades? Who are your idols? What do you particularly like about them? Could you accomplish similar things in your life?

Knowing yourself also means being aware of your talents and your values.

**Talents.** Everyone contains a unique combination of talents. Few, if any, of us realize the full potential of our talents. You must have the desire to develop your talents. The greater your desire, the greater your development and use of talent.

**Values.** You develop values—standards for deciding what is important to you—as a result of your experiences and the influence of other people, as you read in Chapter 2. Of the two, experience is the more powerful influence. Experiences in early years strongly shape the values you hold for life.

Knowing your values helps you form your vision. Read the following list and rank each item as being of high, moderate, or low value to you by placing a checkmark in the appropriate box.

| Value | High | Moderate | Low |
|---|---|---|---|
| Achievement | | | |
| Advancement | | | |
| Adventure | | | |
| Affection | | | |
| Competition | | | |
| Cooperation | | | |
| Creativity | | | |
| Financial security | | | |

| Value | High | Moderate | Low |
|---|---|---|---|
| Fame | | | |
| Family happiness | | | |
| Friendship | | | |
| Health | | | |
| Helpfulness | | | |
| Inner harmony | | | |
| Integrity | | | |
| Loyalty | | | |
| Order | | | |
| Pleasure | | | |
| Power | | | |
| Recognition | | | |
| Religion | | | |
| Responsibility | | | |
| Self-respect | | | |
| Wealth | | | |
| Wisdom | | | |
| Other (specify) | | | |

## Step 3: Know What Is Out There

The third step in building a positive vision is finding out what is available. You live in a complex, diversified society, and there are hundreds of different careers. The more careers you know of, the easier it is to develop a realistic vision that reflects your talents and values. Interviewing and reading are two ways of discovering what is out there.

**Interviewing.** An interview does not have to be a formal meeting in which you ask prepared questions. Interviewing can mean simply talking to people. You already know of some careers because of what your parents, other relatives, friends, and neighbors do. You can talk to such people to learn about their careers. When you have an idea of a career you would like, you could set up a formal interview.

**Reading.** This is an excellent way to learn what careers exist. Reading for fun, reading a novel, reading magazines, both professional and general, all forms of reading can be a potential way of discovering what careers exist.

In your town or school library, you can find two reference resources put out by the U.S. Government that provide information on specific occupations:

- *Dictionary of Occupational Titles* (referred to as the DOT).
- *The Occupational Outlook Handbook.*

The DOT is a listing and brief description of a huge number of specific jobs. Browsing through it can open your eyes to a wealth of possible careers. The DOT not only lists job titles, it identifies them as being in one of three categories according to whether they primarily require working with people, with data, or with things. The DOT also lists the type of skills required in each category.

The *Occupational Outlook Handbook* lists about 300 general occupations, as opposed to specific job titles. It describes the work, training required, earnings, and working conditions. It tries to predict the future for the occupations, whether the occupation will likely decline or grow. The handbook also describes the employment outlook for the different occupations—whether more openings are expected than candidates to fill them or more candidates than openings. Do not rule out a preferred career because the handbook predicts there will be fewer openings than applicants. This really suggests only that you must work harder to get the job you want, not that you will not get it.

### Step 4: Brainstorm

The first three steps set up a base upon which to build your vision. The fourth step is to begin building it. In this step, be creative. Let your imagination go. Remember what you read about creative thinking in Chapter 1. You do creative thinking at this step. Create several possible visions. Do not analyze what you are putting into your vision. Remember that to brainstorm is to think of as many options as you possible can.

Think about your life, where you are now and where you want to be in 10, 20, 30, or 40 years. Think of the kind of life you would like to have. Think about your values, your talents, and what interests you. Ask yourself questions such as these:

> *Do I like to work with people?*
> *Do I like to work alone with things or data?*
> *Do I like to work with my hands?*
> *Do I like to work outside?*
> *Do I want to be my own boss?*
> *Do I want to be near the water?*
> *Do I want to be in the mountains?*

Brainstorming is a tool to help you plan the kind of life you want. To ensure that your brainstorming is effective, follow these procedures.

- Give yourself a specific amount of time in which to brainstorm your vision of the future, say 15 to 30 minutes.

- Write down all the ideas that occur to you. Do not worry about being too specific. Rather than knowing that you want to be a doctor, nurse, or medical technician, your vision may not be any more specific than wanting to care for sick people. You can be even more general: "I want to serve people." You will narrow down the list later.

- Do not limit yourself or try to be practical. For example, imagine you love music and want a career as a singer. You know, however, you cannot carry a tune. Never mind. At this point write down the idea of a career as a singer.

Writing down an unrealistic vision is worthwhile. Writing it down can lead you to think of other ways to achieve your goal. For example, if you love singing but cannot sing, you may decide to be the manager of a band. You may write songs. You may work in a music store or sell recording equipment. There are often more ways than one to do what you want. Remember the thinking step of considering all possibilities.

After you are satisfied you have a complete list, or your time has run out, move to the fifth and last step in creating your vision of the future.

## Step 5: Refine Your Vision

The fifth step requires you to use critical thinking. You cannot be everything or do everything. Once you have developed a list of possible career and life visions, you must make choices. You must also make your career vision as specific as possible so you can base short- and long-term goals and day-to-day activities on it.

Your vision will change. Setting a vision is not a one-time act that you must get right or else. You will have many opportunities to rethink and revise your vision as you and your circumstances change. Your vision should be firm enough to provide direction and goals, but not so rigid that you cannot change it to meet new conditions.

When faced with choices and the need to make decisions, consider what *you* want in life. Do not be pressured by what others say you should do. It is your life and your vision. The better you are able to clarify and understand your values, the better you will be able to refine your vision. If you do not value working with people, you would not be happy as a travel agent no matter how much you like planning trips and traveling or how great your best friend tells you it is. Consider each possibility you have listed. For each one, ask yourself:

> *What really interests me about this?*
> *What is there about this that I might not like?*
> *What skill does this require that I might have or can learn?*
> *What skill does this require that I do not have and probably cannot learn?*

To clarify your idea of what you want, review your activities and jobs of the past year or two. Ask yourself what you liked or did not like about them. For example:

> *In that part-time job at the supermarket did I like meeting people at the checkout counter or did I find it annoying?*
> *Did I like keeping track of inventory and stocking shelves?*

Most careers combine elements that you will like with ones you dislike. You must know enough to determine whether the parts you like will offset the parts you do not care for. For example, you might like working with people and dislike paperwork. Yet, many people-oriented careers require paperwork.

When you have refined your vision, be sure to write it down. Put it in a safe place. Some people make a poster of their vision and put it up on the wall as a reminder and constant incentive.

## THE IMPORTANCE OF SETTING GOALS

By visualizing what you want in life, particularly in terms of a career, you have done a lot to ensure success. You can still do more, however, to convert this vision into reality. Even when you know the destination of an automobile trip, you use a map to pick the best way to reach it when the area is unfamiliar to you. The map you use on your journey through life—to realize your vision—is a list of goals and activities. To achieve your career vision, you take these three steps:

1. Set long-term, mid-term, and short-term goals.
2. Prioritize goals.
3. Make daily to-do lists related to your goals.

If you do not relate your vision to your day-to-day activities, you will not realize it. Vision, goals, and daily to-do lists work together to give direction and purpose to your life. Your vision provides the base upon which you build specific goals. These specific goals in turn help you plan your days to ensure that you take purposeful actions rather than simply drift through a welter of aimless activities.

This is not to say that you spend every moment of your days working toward your vision. On the contrary, having vision-based goals makes it possible for you to plan your days. You do what you plan in the allotted time. You do not waste time. Then you are free to relax and use the rest of the day as you want.

Realizing a vision, especially a life career vision, takes time. You get there, as you do in any journey, one step at a time—that is, goal by goal. Some goals require that you set still other goals. To become a paramedic, you have to learn first aid, take courses in medicine, and practice life-saving techniques, such as the Heimlich maneuver.

Goals should be measurable. They should not be vague or poorly defined. It should be clear to you when you have achieved a goal so you can enjoy the sense of accomplishment. This encourages you to go on to new and more challenging goals.

If you think about all the things you must do to reach your final goal, you can become overwhelmed. You begin having such thoughts as:

> *It's too much. I can't possibly do all that!*

So you break each goal down into doable portions and organize them:

- According to the time they will take.
- To reflect the order in which they should be done.
- In a way that makes most sense to you in your circumstances.

## LONG-, MID-, AND SHORT-TERM GOALS

Goals can be broken down into practical, doable portions based on time.

- **Long-term goals** are the articulation of your vision; they represent where you want to be in 10, 20, or 30 years.
- **Mid-term goals** are ones that you want to achieve within the next 5 years.
- **Short-term goals** are ones that you want to achieve in less than one year, maybe even tomorrow or next week.

Your vision is your starting point. Set your long-term goals first, then your mid-term goals, and, finally, your short-term goals. The reason for this order is that your key goals at each level should be related to your final goal—the achievement of your vision. Not all your goals, particularly short-term ones, will directly relate to your long-term goal.

▶ Dana has a vision about helping people. She wants a career, possibly in government, that would allow her to do this. She does not want a routine office job. She wants to live in a mid-sized city like the one she grew up in.

After reviewing the types of careers described in the *Occupational Outlook Handbook*, she decides she would like a career either as a police officer or as a parole officer. She decides to set a long-term goal of becoming a police officer in a mid-size city. She keeps the possibility of being a parole office as a secondary long-term goal in case becoming a police officer does not work out.

If your vision is not specific, now is the time to make it so. Then write it down as a long-term goal. Dana made her general vision of helping people into a specific goal of becoming a police office or a parole officer.

After setting your long-term goal, you must think of the mid- and short-term goals that will help you realize the long-term goal. Thinking about the effort you must exert to achieve a long-term goal will either reinforce your belief that this is what you really want or encourage you to reconsider your long-term goal.

▶ Dana sets a mid-term goal of getting a degree in criminal justice. She plans to get an associate's degree first, which takes two years. She cannot afford 4 years of college now. She reasons that she could begin working with her associate degree and eventually go to night school to get another degree.

She sets a short-term goal for next week to enroll in a course on criminal justice. Another short-term goal is to enroll in the summer intern program for next year in the local police department. Because her plans require money, she sets another short-term goal of getting a paying job. The police interns are not paid. She gets a job as a waitress with the understanding she can arrange her hours to attend school and, in the summer, be a police intern.

Still another short-term goal is to open a bank account and save a portion of her salary for education.

Some short-term goals will be accomplished in a few minutes or hours. Do not mix them up with routine tasks and short-term activities that you want to do. You have to eat, sleep, and find time to relax. You may have to get your car fixed or buy new glasses. These should not be considered short-term goals unless they are directly related to achieving your long-term goals and to your vision.

Not short-term goals:

> *Going to the movies with a group of friends just for relaxation.*
> *Cutting your study time to get your car fixed so you can go to the beach on the weekend.*
> *Finishing a novel you enjoy.*

Short-term goals:

> *Going to movies with a friend who has worked in a job related to your career choice, getting there early, and using the time to ask the friend about the job.*
> *(This combines relaxation and learning more about your goals.)*
> *Cutting your study time to get your car fixed so you can keep an appointment with your adviser about courses to take next year.*
> *Buying a necessary textbook.*
> *Taking time in the library to check a resource related to your goal.*

Below are some other techniques to help you select and refine your long-, mid-, and short-term goals.

## Be Practical

There is no point in setting a goal that you cannot possibly achieve or do not really want to achieve. Whether or not a goal is practical often depends on your status. As your status changes, so will your goals. If you are in your thirties, it is not practical to suddenly decide to become a professional basketball player. On the other hand, some goals that might not be practical for you now might become so later on.

▶ Dana could not afford more than two years of schooling at first. After getting her associate's degree and a job in the police department, continuing her education became practical and affordable. She is now studying nights for her bachelor's degree in criminal justice. She is also considering changing her long-term goal and is thinking of going on to law school to become a lawyer.

## Review Goals

Everyone's situation changes through time. As you reach some goals, you must make new ones. Old goals change. You should even look for ways to change them. Dana continually reviewed her goals. Originally, she thought she would be a police officer; now she is considering becoming a lawyer. Review your goals, particularly your long-term goals, from time to time. As you take steps to achieve a goal, you may change your mind about it.

### Put Your Goals in Writing

You have heard before of the value of putting things in writing. You definitely should put your goals in writing. When you write them, they become more real for you. You take them more seriously. You can review written goals. You cannot really review goals that you try to carry in your head. They are not definite enough unless written; they do not hold their form but change from day-to-day.

Another benefit of keeping written records is that over time you will be able to look back and see how your interests shifted, how you resolved conflicts, and, most important, what you have achieved.

## PRIORITIZED GOALS

To *set priorities* means to put your goals in order of what is the most important to you. This refers mostly to your short-term goals and, to a lesser extent, to mid-term goals. Setting priorities can be difficult because it may force you to see that you may not accomplish all your goals. At the same time, however, you will feel more confident about achieving those goals that are most important. To set priorities you need to recognize conflicts and resolve them in accordance with your goals.

### Resolve Conflicts

Taking a trip around the world and getting your degree at the same time could be conflicting goals if you do not have the time or money to do both. Living in a warm climate and working as a ski instructor clearly conflict. Identify conflicts. Then make a choice. This is part of the process of making your vision specific and realistic.

Sometimes you can resolve a conflict between two choices without having to give up one. You could reward yourself after getting your degree by taking a trip around the world. Or your long-term goal could be to live in a ski-resort six months of the year and in Florida the other six months.

Resolving conflicts when setting goals can be difficult. For example, when deciding to take a part-time job, you might have to weigh your need to make money against your desire for practical experience in a field related to your long-term goal. The better you know your mid- and long-term goals, however, the easier it is to make the right decisions.

## Use a Decision-Making Matrix

To help yourself make the right decision when faced with difficult choices, try using a *decision-making matrix*. This is a table or grid with your goals arranged down the side and current conflicting choices across the top. (See figure below.) You rate the choices on a scale of 1 to 3 as to how much or how little they help you achieve your goals. The choice with the highest score is usually your first choice.

▶ Kevin's vision was to help people live in harmony with the environment, to cut down on the creation of waste and the exploitation of our natural resources. His long-range goal was to become a city planner and eventually open his own business as a consultant in urban planning. This summer he has been fortunate in being able to choose between three jobs: a city planning intern, a truck driver, or the head of his own landscaping business. However, he cannot make up his mind about which is best for him to take. His instructor shows him how to make a decision-making matrix.

| Decision-Making Matrix |||||
|---|---|---|---|---|
| | | \multicolumn{3}{c}{Summer Jobs} |||
| | | City Planning Intern | Truck Driver | Landscaper |
| **Short-term goals** | Earn money for school | 1 | 3 | 2 |
| | Experience in planning | 3 | 1 | 2 |
| Subtotal | | 4 | 4 | 4 |
| **Long-term goals** | Degree in urban planning | 3 | 1 | 2 |
| | Job as city planner | 3 | 1 | 1 |
| | Have own business | 3 | 1 | 3 |
| Total | | 13 | 7 | 10 |

For moving toward his long-range goals, Kevin's clear choice is to take the position of intern in the planning department. For his short-term goals, all alternatives have equal weight, but for different reasons. If earning money is his most important short-term goal, he might need to take the position of truck driver because he would earn the most money at it. His second best choice, overall, is running his own landscaping business. He would not make as much money as he would driving a truck, but he will make more than being an intern and he

Chapter 3      Finding a Vision; Setting Goals—63

will get experience in running a business, as well as some environmentally useful experience in such things as composting yard waste.

Creating a career decision chart did not make Kevin's difficulties melt away, but it did make it possible for him to clarify his thoughts and to make an informed decision.

Kevin was forced to establish his own priorities when choosing a summer job. He had to decide whether earning money or getting experience in his chosen field had the higher priority.

Throughout life, Kevin will face choices and the need to set short-term goals. The priorities he sets will influence his choices. Factors influencing his priorities could include such things as where he wants to live, whether to have a family, and his general economic conditions. Kevin has control over some factors and not over others.

## TO-DO LISTS

In life you must do things every day that are not directly related to your goals. Preparing what is called a *to-do list* helps prevent the many daily demands you face from taking charge of your life. A to-do list is an enumeration of the activities you plan or must accomplish. To-do lists may apply to a day's activities, a week's, or even longer periods of time. We are discussing daily to-do lists. To-do lists will:

- Help you get done the things you *have* to do (those daily demands) as quickly and efficiently as possible.

- Help ensure that you do not lose sight of the things you *want* to do (move toward your goals).

Here are some strategies for making daily to-do lists.

### Check Your Goals

Make sure your to-do list includes a mix of goal-related and non-goal-related activities. If you have to spend time getting the car fixed (non-goal-related), be sure also to spend time on something that is goal related, such as studying for a course leading to your career goal.

Short-term goals help you decide your daily activities. During the day, you will have to respond to other demands, meet family needs, and deal with emergencies. Nonetheless, plan your day around *your* goals. You may not get to them all because of these other matters, but if you did not plan your day this way, you might not get to any of them.

▶ Gail's long-term goal is to be a computer programmer. She realizes she faces several years of schooling before getting a degree. She has a short-term goal of enrolling in the local computer school.

On her to-do list for today, she puts obtaining the school's catalog to see what courses are offered on programming. She also has a short-term goal of getting a job. She adds to her list making an appointment with the local employment office to ask about part-time jobs where she might learn about programming.

### Prepare a *Written* To-Do List Each Morning

The morning is a good time to make your to-do list. You are fresh from a night's sleep and are looking ahead. Use the previous day's list as a guide. Do not spend more than 5 to 10 minutes making the list. Be sure to write the list down. An unwritten list is not a list at all. You need a written list to review and help you prepare new lists. Furthermore, a written list gives you a record of accomplishments, which can give you a boost.

### Prioritize Your To-Do List

As with goals, prioritize the items on your to-do list. Identify tasks that are most important, those that are less so, and those that are relatively unimportant. Check priorities daily. An unimportant goal one day can become an important goal the next. Be realistic about your priorities. If you have to do something that is both high priority and time-consuming, do not set too many other high priorities for the same time. Be realistic about how much you can do in one day.

The method you use to keep track of your priorities is not important, as long as you understand it and find it easy to work with. You can use one of these methods.

- Use H for High, M for Medium, and L for Low.
- Use numbers: 1, 2, 3, or letters: A, B, C.
- Put a star next to the one or two most important activities.

Rank activities in relation to overall goals. Activities that move you toward your goal have high priority; those that do not, have a low priority. If you do not get to do any of the B or C items on your list, it will not be a disaster. The A's must be done.

Sometimes activities not related to your overall goals must become top priority. If your instructor announces a surprise quiz, studying becomes a top priority, even if you had thought your most important

**Chapter 3**            **Finding a Vision; Setting Goals—65**

activity for the day was going to be preparing a job-hunting campaign. Identifying clear priorities is often a task that requires thought.

### Review Your List in the Evening

In the evening review your to-do list. Cross out completed activities if you did not do so earlier. Some days you might feel you accomplished nothing until you look at the completed activities on your list. This should not take more than 5 to 10 minutes.

### Keep Your To-Do Lists Simple

Do not let listing tasks become a task itself. Preparing your daily list should take no more than 5 or 10 minutes. You can cross out and add activities as you go along. Do not list routine tasks. You know you will get up, get dressed, and have breakfast.

### Carry Your To-Do List with You

Do not keep to-do lists on bits of paper. Use a notebook, small enough to fit in your bookbag or pocket. By keeping the list in a notebook, you are less likely to lose the list, and you have a handy way of keeping your lists for the future.

### Accept Unfinished Business

Do not worry if some items on your to-do lists are undone at the end of the day. The idea is not to complete a lot of tasks, but to do the right ones. Change the list as necessary, but do not let every little thing get in the way of your main priorities. While not cast in iron, the list should not be written in sand. If you set realistic goals, prioritize well, and follow through, you will use your time productively. Tasks will get done, you will feel good, and you will move toward your goals.

## SUMMING UP

Having a positive vision motivates you. Without motivation, you are unlikely to study well or learn much or enjoy the process. You will drift into jobs rather than enjoy a rewarding career. Having a vision, an idea of what you want to do with your life, is probably your single most important motivating factor.

Your vision must be positive. A negative vision drains energy and destroys motivation.

You can influence and shape your future. A negative vision shapes a negative future. A positive vision shapes a positive one. Your vision operates as a self-fulfilling prophecy.

Having a vision means taking a long-range view of your life. It means having a sense of where you want to be in the future, what you want to do with your life, not just today or tomorrow but a few months, years, or decades from now.

Many outside influences affect your vision, but you can also consciously develop and alter it. Other people and your experiences play a part in its creation. Major influences include your family, friends, and teachers.

Your vision of the future is directly tied in to your self-image. To have a positive vision of the future, you must have a positive self-image.

Steps you can take to develop your vision include:

1. Develop a positive attitude.
2. Know yourself.
3. Know what is out there.
4. Brainstorm.
5. Refine your vision.

Three steps you must take to make your vision a reality are:

1. Set long-, mid-, and short-term goals.
2. Prioritize goals.
3. Make daily to-do lists related to your goals.

Vision, goals, and daily to-do lists work together to give direction and purpose to your life. Your vision provides the base upon which you build specific goals.

Your goals will be easier to achieve if you organize them according to the time they will take and the order in which they should be done. Goals can be broken down into three practical time groups:

1. Long-term goals represent where you want to be in 10, 20, or 30 years;
2. Mid-term goals are ones that you want to achieve within the next 5 years;
3. Short-term goals are ones that you want to achieve in less than one year, maybe tomorrow or next week.

Your vision is your starting point. You set your long-term goals first, then your mid-term goals, and, finally, your short-term goals.

Strategies to aid you in setting goals are:

1. Organize your goals.
2. Be practical.
3. Review goals.
4. Put goals in writing.

You should prioritize your goals. This refers mostly to your short-term goals and, to a lesser extent, to mid-term goals. Do this by resolving conflicts and using a decision-making matrix.

To-do lists relate your goals to your everyday activities. To-do lists help you get done the things you *have* to do and help ensure that you do not lose sight of the things you *want* to do.

Strategies for making daily to-do lists include:

Checking your list of goals.
Preparing written to-do-lists each morning.
Prioritizing your list.
Reviewing your list each evening.
Keeping your lists simple.
Carrying your list with you.
Accepting that you may not do everything on your list.

## ▼ DEVELOPING YOUR SKILLS

Exercise 1

### Assess Your Self-Image as a Learner

You have read that to have a positive vision, you must have a positive self-image. What is your image of yourself as a student? Remember that how you think about yourself can affect how you function. Read each statement below. Does it describe you and your image of yourself as a student? Give an example from experience to prove or disprove it.

I am a good student.

_____

_____

_____

I know my reasons for learning.

_____

_____

_____

Learning is central to my life.

_____

_____

_____

I am a positive thinker.

_____

_____

_____

Examine your answers. If you see evidence of a negative self-image, try to think of ways in which you can change negative answers to positive ones.

Exercise 2

## Refine Your Vision

Use the table below to refine your vision of the future. If necessary, use additional paper.

In column 1, list everything you can think of that you do now, would like to do in the future, think you should do, or have been told by others to do.
In column 2, check everything in column 1 that you enjoy or want to do.
In column 3, check off everything you do not enjoy or do not want to do.
In column 4, check those items you have talent or training for.
Ignore column 5 for now.

| 1. EVERYTHING | 2. LIKE | 3. DISLIKE | 4. ABILITY | 5. ACTION |
|---|---|---|---|---|
| | | | | |
| | | | | |
| | | | | |
| | | | | |
| | | | | |
| | | | | |
| | | | | |
| | | | | |
| | | | | |
| | | | | |
| | | | | |
| | | | | |
| | | | | |
| | | | | |
| | | | | |
| | | | | |

Exercise 3

## Develop a Positive Attitude

Carry around a notebook for a few days and make a note of every time you say or think, "I cannot do this." or "This can't be done." Try to analyze why you say or think this way.

- Is it because you do not want to do something or perhaps you do not have the skills? The time? The money?
- Is it because you have a negative vision?

Try to distinguish between things you really could do with a little more effort and things that would be unrealistic to try to do.


Exercise 4

## Identify the Source of Your Values

On a separate piece of paper, list four people whom you admire and look up to. They could be people you know, such as friends, coworkers, family members, or people you have read about or have seen on television or in a movie. For each describe as precisely as possible what it is that makes you admire him or her.

- Do the four people have similar characteristics?
- Which people would you like to be like?
- Are there any people you would not like to be like? Why not?

Exercise 5

## Set Vision-Related Goals

Now go through the steps of setting your goals.

**Step 1.** Refer to the table in Exercise 2, on refining your vision. Complete the final column by listing actions for items that you like (checked in column 2) and have an ability to do (checked in column 4).

**Step 2.** Use these items to set your goals. Suppose one of the things you like to do is groom your dog. Would you consider a long-term goal of working with animals, say as a trainer? Or do you simply like your dog and not want to work with other animals?

**Step 3.** Make a list of your long-term goals and label each one as a long-term goal, mid-term goal, or short-term goal.

Long-term goals

_____

_____

_____

Mid-term goals

_____

_____

_____

Short-term goals

_____

_____

_____

Exercise 6

## Resolve Conflicts

Use your goals developed in the previous exercise. Think of some possible conflicts you may face at some time in deciding what course of action to take. Your choices might be like Kevin's were regarding summer jobs. If no actual conflicts occur to you, make up a possible list of summer jobs and rate them using the decision-making matrix on the next page. Refer to the example on page 63.

| Decision-Making Matrix |||||
|---|---|---|---|---|
| | | | | |
| Short-term goals | | | | |
| | | | | |
| Subtotal | | | | |
| Long-term goals | | | | |
| | | | | |
| | | | | |
| Total | | | | |

Exercise 7

## Make a Daily To-Do List for a Week

Follow the techniques described in this lesson to make daily to-do lists for a week. Review the lists in the evening. At the end of the week, review what you have accomplished.

- Did the lists help you keep your priorities in focus?
- Did they remind you of what you needed to get done?
- Did they help you organize your time more efficiently?
- Did you feel a sense of accomplishment?

# 4 Managing Time

**After completing this chapter, you will be able to organize your time and meet your goals.**

Time is your major resource. It is the one resource you must have to do anything—work, study, or play. It is also the one resource that you cannot get more of once you run out of it. If you have not completed your term paper when the due date arrives, you cannot reclaim the wasted time. At the eleventh hour, of course, you can stay up all night and grind out a paper. This is a good way to exhaust yourself and have nothing to show for it except an inferior paper that does not reflect your true ability or knowledge.

The better you manage your time, the more effective you will be in whatever you try. You take a big step toward managing your time when you develop vision-based goals and then translate those goals into daily to-do lists.

It is impossible to add another hour to your day. Even those dynamo achievers who seem to do so much have only the same 24 hours you have. They do more because they schedule their time effectively. They do not have more hours than anyone else, but they get more out of the hours they do have. You can also, with some simple time-management techniques. It just requires planning, scheduling, and, yes, writing things down.

Do either of these scenarios sound familiar?

▶ Sam has to write a paper for his sociology course by November 1. In early October, he thinks, "I've got over three weeks to do the paper, so no big deal. I've got plenty of time." The weather is nice and it's great to be outdoors, especially since winter is coming. He thinks about the paper now and then, sometimes with a twinge of guilt. "I'd better get going on it tomorrow." As time goes on, it becomes increasingly difficult for him to find the time to work on the paper. He makes a few feeble starts. He worries more and more about it, but other interests constantly distract him. Suddenly it is the end of October, and Sam has made almost no progress on his paper. He has less time than ever to work on it because he is working longer hours in his job. Now he has a serious problem.

▶ Roseanne is more organized than Sam. She decides that she will get her paper done early. She plans to spend each Saturday working on it. The first Saturday arrives. She decides that since she has all day for the paper, she will start by rearranging her room to get her desk in a better place for working. This takes an hour. She settles down to work, and the phone rings. A friend suggests a movie that evening. "Great idea," says Roseanne. "I'll have earned it after working all day on my paper. Call me when you know the time and place. And, by the way, what should we see?" Three phone calls later, the movie question is settled. Roseanne works for 45 minutes and then breaks for lunch. It's a beautiful day, so she eats outside, after changing into her shorts. The second Saturday is a repeat of the first. And so the time goes by filled with good intentions, many interruptions, and little real progress on the paper.

Sam, secure in the knowledge that he has "plenty of time," makes no plans. Vaguely aware he must do something, he drifts along putting writing off until it is too late to do a decent job. He does not gain time to do other worthwhile things by not working on the paper. A sense of unease and guilt increasingly fill his days. He does not really enjoy the time he spends on outdoor activities.

Roseanne started on the right foot. She made a plan to begin working on her paper early. Then everything fell apart. Although unlike Sam, she did plan time to write the paper, she did not use her time well. Also, she did not write her plan down, so it was never real to her. Now, you will learn some ways to avoid wasting time the way Sam and Roseanne did.

# KNOW YOURSELF TO MANAGE TIME

What does knowing yourself have to do with managing time? Well, when you think of it, you realize that what managing time boils down to is managing yourself. If managing time is really managing yourself, the more you know about yourself, the better equipped you are to manage time well. Because that is so, this chapter will help you:

- Become aware of how you perceive and use time now.
- Identify and end your time-wasting habits.
- Develop and use scheduling techniques.
- Develop a time-use policy.

## Are You in Charge?

Speaking of knowing yourself, would you say you are in charge of your life, or does time run away with you? Try this simple test for a suggestion of how you handle time. As honestly as you can, state whether each of these five statements is true or false. (Enter a T for true and an F for false on the lines at the end of the statements.)

1. I always underestimate how much time a project will take.____
2. I rarely have enough time to do what I want.____
3. I never have time for planning.____
4. I feel strongly that time limits me.____
5. I frequently postpone important assignments, waiting until I have enough time.____

Give yourself a 0 for each F you entered and 1 for each T. Add them up and circle your score on the sense of time scale.

**SENSE OF TIME SCALE**

| 1 | 2 | 3 | 4 | 5 |
|---|---|---|---|---|
| In charge | | | | Not in charge |

This simple scale only suggests your tendencies to perceive and handle time. If your answers were all *false*, your total is zero. You probably have a relaxed feeling about time and an idea of how to manage it.

If you answered all *true*, you probably have difficulty in scheduling your time to accomplish all you wish. Most of us fall somewhere in between the two extremes.

## Habits Help or Hurt

Knowing your tendencies can lead you to a further awareness of yourself that is essential to managing time. This means knowing your strengths and weaknesses and your good and bad habits.

Read the following list. As honestly as you can, rate the items as *Never*, *Sometimes*, *Often* and place a checkmark in the appropriate column. Do this quickly. First impressions are best. The purpose of this exercise is to make you think of how you use your time so you can work to eliminate weaknesses and increase strengths.

| Habits | Never | Sometimes | Often |
|---|---|---|---|
| I write down my goals. | | | |
| I keep a daily to-do list. | | | |
| I identify short- and long-range goals. | | | |
| I prioritize my lists. | | | |
| I set aside a special time for planning. | | | |
| I allocate a quiet time for uninterrupted study. | | | |
| I deal effectively with interruptions. | | | |
| I am punctual (work, class, appointments). | | | |
| I finish assignments before their deadlines. | | | |
| I keep my work area uncluttered. | | | |
| I have a place for everything. | | | |

If you answered *often* 8 or more times, you already have control of your time. If you answered *often* only between 5 and 7 times, you have some control, but can use more to be fully effective. Fewer than five *often* entries indicates you need to work to make better use of your time.

**Habits** are what we have conditioned ourselves to do. We execute our habits almost without conscious thought. We do not need to force ourselves to do what has become a habit for us. Habits are big time-savers when they are good and big time-wasters when they are bad. In a sense, habits are the basic building blocks of time management. The only person who can develop them, obviously, is you.

To develop good habits and drop bad ones, you must be aware of those you have. Rate the following list of habits as either *G* for good or *B* for bad. Put the correct letter only after those habits that represent a habit you have. On the blank lines at the bottom, add any habits, either good or bad, you think you have that are not on the list.

| HABIT | RATING |
|---|---|
| Write down goals | |
| Allow reading matter to pile up | |
| Make "to-do" lists too long | |
| Often do not finish priority items on my "to-do" list | |
| Allow work area to become cluttered | |
| Put things off to the last minute | |
| Extend breaks, lunch hours | |
| Put everything promptly in its place | |
| Start an important task even when there is not enough time to finish | |
| Use travel/waiting time to do work | |
| Always use small bits of time for routine tasks | |
| Usually do several small tasks instead of part of one big important task | |
| Am firm about not letting people interrupt me | |
|  | |
|  | |
|  | |

How did you do? Following are two lists identifying good and bad habits. Add to the right lists any habits you thought of that are not already on the lists. Make copies. Keep them around to remind yourself of what you do that is good and what you need to work at to change.

Good Habits to Reinforce

- Write down goals.

- Put everything promptly in its place.

- Start an important task even there is when not enough time to finish.

Chapter 4  Managing Time—79

- Use travel/waiting time to do work.
- Am firm about not letting people interrupt me.

Bad Habits to Get Rid Of

- Allow reading matter to pile up.
- Make to-do lists too long.
- Often do not finish priority items on my "to-do" list.
- Allow work area to become cluttered.
- Put things off to the last minute.
- Always use small bits of time for routine tasks.
- Usually do several small tasks instead of part of one big important task.

## SCHEDULE YOUR ACTIVITIES

Do you remember reading in Chapter 3 that you have activities related to achieving your goals and activities not related to goals? Both kinds of activities go on your daily to-do lists. Now you must schedule those activities to make sure you really do them and so that the unavoidable pressures of each new day do not sweep you away. Such daily to-do lists are the start of scheduling and managing your time.

Before putting an activity on your list, ask yourself, "Do I have to do this at all? What would happen if I did not do it?" You use your critical thinking skills to make this evaluation.

### Essentials of Scheduling

Three simple rules sum up effective scheduling:

1. Keep it simple.
2. Keep it realistic.
3. Write it down.

You can apply these rules to develop any one of four types of schedules to manage your time. The four types of schedules are:

1. A general time-use schedule.
2. A long-term schedule.
3. A weekly schedule.
4. A daily schedule.

You may not need all four schedules, and two are really tools to help you prepare the other two. They all fit together and overlap. You are studying them separately to understand the basic rationale of each.

You may feel at this point that planning and scheduling will take up all your time. Not so. Planning and scheduling will actually help you free up time. But until you have done so, nothing is more important to you than planning and scheduling.

## General Time-Use Schedule

A general time-use schedule is a guide. It represents how you plan to use your time in a typical week. To create one is simple, but it takes a little thought. If you keep a log of what you actually do for about a week, that will help you develop a time-use schedule.

A time-use schedule simply blocks out the chunks of time when you will do certain things. Some, such as the hours for sleep and those for meals, are more or less set for you. Also, of course, are those hours you must attend class or be at your job. The other hours of the day, and there are many left, are yours to command. Decide in general what you will do with them: establish certain hours for study, others for research, others for recreation, and so on.

**Forming Habits.** The value of setting a time for doing important tasks daily is that you will more likely do them. If you make it a habit to do the same things at the same times each day, they become easier to do. Experience has shown that we are more effective if we carry out the same mental activity at the same time each day.

Developing the habit of studying at a certain time increases your ability to do it well. Studying always at a set time conditions your mind to be ready as soon as you begin. You can concentrate better than you do when you study at different hours.

The first thing you do to develop a time-use schedule is to block out required activities. Then you decide what you will do in the other hours you have.

**High- and Low-Energy Periods.** When deciding what to assign to the different hours, consider when are you most energetic: When you first get up? Late in the day? Assign important tasks, such as studying, to those times. Also, be aware of when you are less energetic: After meals? After class or work? Schedule less important tasks and free time then.

Try not to fool yourself. Do not schedule difficult tasks for periods when you usually feel tired, thinking you can force yourself to work.

This is a general schedule to give you an idea of when it is best to do things. It is not a scheduling of your specific activities, but a guide to help you schedule activities effectively.

| Time-Use Schedule | | | | | | | |
|---|---|---|---|---|---|---|---|
| | MON | TUES | WED | THURS | FRI | SAT | SUN |
| 6A-8A | | | | | | | |
| 8A-12N | | | | | | | |
| NOON-1P | | | | | | | |
| 1P-2P | | | | | | | |
| 2P-4P | | | | | | | |
| 4P-6P | | | | | | | |
| 6P-7P | | | | | | | |
| 7P-10P | | | | | | | |

## Long-Term Schedule

A long-term schedule shows you not only when you will start doing something but also how long you will continue to do it. It shows what has to be done at a specific time, such as attend a class. It also shows where you have time for studying, eating, and so on. A long-term schedule allows you to see a period longer than a day or a week and to spot potential problems and busy periods. You refer to it when preparing your daily to-do lists. See the example on the next page.

Use your long-term schedule to plan. For example, if you need five weeks for a term paper, the task "begin research on paper" should appear on the chart five to six weeks before the due date. When you are a new student, it is hard to estimate how much time you need for a task. With experience you will soon have a good idea of how long it takes to do book reports and term papers. Other points to know:

- Your circumstances will determine the length of your long-term schedule. For a student, the schedule could cover one semester.

- Plot test dates, term paper dates, special projects, field trips, final exams, or anything with a deadline.

- If you have a job or other responsibilities requiring you to do something by a certain date, include these.

- List all the tasks to be done from the top down.

- Divide the period—for example, a semester—into monthly and weekly segments shown along the top.
- Use X's to show ending or deadline dates.
- Use lines to show times when you are working on a task.

▶ Rosemary is a new student at her school. She has her class schedule, however, and a list of assignments for the term that she received after attending her first classes. She has a part-time job as well and wants to be involved in extracurricular activities. She knows she has a tough semester ahead and prepares a long-term schedule to help her plan her time. Shown below is an example of a long-term schedule she has prepared based on her first semester.

| | September | | | | October | | | | November | | | | December | | | |
|---|---|---|---|---|---|---|---|---|---|---|---|---|---|---|---|---|
| | 1 | 2 | 3 | 4 | 1 | 2 | 3 | 4 | 1 | 2 | 3 | 4 | 1 | 2 | 3 | 4 |
| **Course 1** | | | | | | | | | | | | | | | | |
| Bk Report 1 | | ——— | ——— | ——— | ——— | X | | | | | | | | | | |
| Bk Report 2 | | | | | | | ——— | ——— | ——— | X | | | | | | |
| Term Paper | | | | | | | ——— | ——— | ——— | ——— | ——— | ——— | ——— | X | | |
| **Course 2** | | | | | | | | | | | | | | | | |
| Field Trip | | | | | X | | | | | | | | | | | |
| Field Trip | | | | | | | | | X | | | | | | | |
| Rdng Asgn | | | | ——— | ——— | ——— | X | | | | | | | | | |
| Mnthly Quiz | | | X | | | | | | | | X | | | | | |
| Term Paper | | | | | | ——— | ——— | ——— | ——— | ——— | ——— | X | | | | |
| **General** | | | | | | | | | | | | | | | | |
| Midterms | | | | | | | X | | | | | | | | | |
| Play | | | | | | ——— | ——— | X | | | | | | | | |
| Finals | | | | | | | | | | | | | ——— | X | | |
| Extra Wk Hrs | | | | | | | | | | | ——— | ——— | ——— | ——— | ——— | X |

Chapter 4      Managing Time—83

A glance at her long-term schedule shows Rosemary that she has some problem times. The last week of October is particularly busy as she takes midterm exams, and starts two term papers, finishes a reading assignment, and rehearses for a play. With extra hours at work and finals in December, Rosemary knows she will have to use her time wisely. She cannot afford to put things off and she prepares her daily to-do lists accordingly.

## Weekly Schedule

Develop a weekly schedule in which you translate your time-use and long-term schedules into specific activities for each seven-day period. At the same time each week—a Friday or Sunday night, for example—review what you have done in the past week and prepare for the coming week. Take about 10 or 15 minutes to do this.

Your filled-in weekly schedule should allow enough time for you to complete all your top-priority tasks. It should be realistic with respect to how long you can work in any given day. If you need eight hours of sleep to function well, do not plan to start work at 6 a.m. and not stop until the following midnight. Your time-use schedule will help you resolve conflicts such as this.

Your weekly schedule, as all schedules, must be realistic in projecting how long it will take you to complete tasks. Some people have the habit of always underestimating how long a task will take or how fast they can work. Furthermore, there is always the unexpected. Schedule your activities loosely enough to accommodate the unexpected. Realistic schedulers know that the unexpected is about the only thing they can really expect.

Follow these simple guidelines for preparing a weekly schedule.

- Consult your goals and to-do lists.

- Use your time-use and long-term schedules as guides.

- Do not list routine tasks, but do make sure to allow yourself time for doing them—getting to classes, eating meals, and so on.

- Do schedule periods of recreation. You must take time to relax, have fun, do what you want. You will work and study more effectively if you take breaks. Exercise and personal time are necessary for your health and general well-being. Allow time for them in your schedule—no matter how busy you are.

- Write it down.

Here is a typical weekly schedule form.

| Weekly Schedule | | | | | | | |
|---|---|---|---|---|---|---|---|
| HOURS | MON | TUES | WED | THURS | FRI | SAT | SUN |
| 7A | | | | | | | |
| 8 | | | | | | | |
| 9 | | | | | | | |
| 10 | | | | | | | |
| 11 | | | | | | | |
| 12 | | | | | | | |
| 1P | | | | | | | |
| 2 | | | | | | | |
| 3 | | | | | | | |
| 4 | | | | | | | |
| 5 | | | | | | | |
| 6 | | | | | | | |
| 7 | | | | | | | |
| 8 | | | | | | | |
| 9 | | | | | | | |
| 10 | | | | | | | |

## Daily Schedule

Your daily schedule is nothing more than your to-do list with the activities you need to do slotted into appropriate times of the day. You create your daily schedule when you create your to-do lists.

Making a daily schedule helps you keep your to-do list realistic and forces you to prioritize. Your time-use and long-term schedules should help you avoid facing too many daily scheduling jams.

You should carry your daily schedule with you. It is a good idea to have a small calendar in which to keep all your schedules. When preparing your daily schedule:

- Consider your goals.
- Use your time-use, long-term, and weekly schedules as guides.
- Be realistic in estimating the amount of time required for each activity.
- Be sure to allot time for routine tasks not listed.
- Be sure to allot some free time for yourself.
- Schedule similar tasks together. Avoid single-purpose errands. As you prepare your list, try to think of related tasks to group together. For example, if you know you must go to the library to do some research, schedule returning or getting books at the same time rather than making separate trips.
- Write it down.

Here is a typical daily schedule form.

| \  | Daily Schedule |
|---|---|
| HRS | TASKS |
| 7A |  |
| 8 |  |
| 9 |  |
| 10 |  |
| 11 |  |
| 12 |  |
| 1P |  |
| 2 |  |
| 3 |  |
| 4 |  |
| 5 |  |
| 6 |  |
| 7 |  |
| 8 |  |
| 9 |  |
| 10 |  |

It is almost certain that events will often cause you to make changes in your daily schedule. That being the case, you may wonder why you should bother making a detailed schedule. The reason is the difference between being in charge and not being in charge of your time. When you have prepared your schedule and circumstances force you to make a change, you are aware of it. You make the change and whatever other adjustments are necessary. You are aware of what was not done, so you can schedule to do it later. Further, having a schedule helps you resist potential changes. The schedule will encourage you to distinguish between unavoidable changes and avoidable ones.

## Keep a Log

Every so often, it is a good idea to see how much time routine tasks are taking. Keep a log for a week and put down everything you do. This is not a list of things *to do*, but a list of things you *actually do*. This log will give you an idea of how you are spending your time.

You might decide you need to do routine tasks faster or stop doing some of them. Keeping a log is important if you find you continually are unable to complete the items on your to-do list or daily schedule.

# GET STARTED; KEEP GOING

You have set your goals and written your to-do lists and your schedules. Now you have to do the work. Here are some tips and techniques to get you started and keep you going, especially when faced with tough tasks.

- Do *first* that high-priority, difficult task that you *least* want to do. When it is done, you will feel relieved and ready for other tasks. When you find yourself delaying the start of a high-priority task, remind yourself that only one thing happens when you do this: The difficult task becomes more difficult.

- Look for easy ways to start difficult tasks. All big tasks can be broken down into parts. Nothing is done all at once. Use creative thinking to match how you feel at the moment with what you have to do. You sit down to write a report, but do not feel like writing. You would rather be talking with someone, or reading. So, review your notes, check your outline, check facts with a classmate. Let your mood help you as long as it gets you started on some aspect of your Number One Activity.

- When breaking down that big task into manageable pieces, set meaningful deadlines. Do not spend 30 minutes on a 15-minute task.

- Do not put off large tasks until you "have more time." You will never have more time. In fact, you will have less time later. Today will be gone. Even if you cannot complete it in the time allotted, start it. There are parts of every large job that can be done quickly. Maybe you need to write a term paper that will take hours. Organizing your notes and preparing an outline could be a quick way to get started.

- Be aware of your low- and high-energy periods.

- Do put off low-priority activities if doing them prevents you from completing high-priority activities.

- Reward yourself when you finish a difficult task.

- Work where you will not be disturbed.

Be prepared to take advantage of found time. Found time is what would otherwise become wasted time. There is no need to waste time, especially the time that is spent waiting or commuting. Be prepared to take advantage of the gift of unexpected time: a delay in the doctor's office, a postponed appointment, a traffic jam, a late train or bus. To be ready for such gifts of time you should:

- ✓ Always have a copy of your to-do list with you.
- ✓ Always have some essential reading material.
- ✓ Find portions of your Number One task you can do.
- ✓ Keep a notebook or blank index cards to note ideas.
- ✓ Think up little tasks related to Number One goals that can be done in odd moments.

The following quote from the German poet Goethe sums up good time management.

*It is better to be doing even the most insignificant thing than to consider even a half-hour insignificant.*

This does not mean you should be working every second. You have read more than once of the importance of taking breaks, having fun. Relaxing, especially after completing a task, is not an insignificant thing. It is important.

If you do not have good study habits, all the time-management skills in the world are useless. Four good study habits to develop are:

1. Set regular hours to study alone.

2. Find a suitable study area.
3. Keep up with assignments.
4. Have the necessary study tools.

### Set Regular Hours to Study Alone

Establish a specific time for studying alone. This is not to say that you should not study at other times when the need and the opportunity arise. Nor is it to say that you should not study with others at times. Studying with a partner or in a group can be productive and, sometimes, even necessary. It is to say, however, that you should always do a serious amount of studying at a set time by yourself. You should block out this time on your time-use schedule.

### Find a Suitable Study Area

Find a suitable place that is quiet and well lighted. It should be a place where you will not have your concentration broken by interruptions, either by visitors or by phone calls.

### Keep Up with Assignments

If you have set a regular time to study and a place to do it, you will more likely keep up with your assignments. It is important to develop the habit of keeping up. Sometimes keeping up requires extra effort. But any extra effort you use to *keep up* will be less than the stressful effort required to *catch up*.

Playing "catch up" is neither productive nor fun. This is as true for studying as it is for any ball game. When you fall behind, you find yourself trying too hard and achieving less. If you are constantly battling a deadline—writing a paper or preparing for a test—your concentration will be focused on meeting the deadline rather than on learning.

If you keep up with assignments, you will find you learn more and will actually have more time for doing other things.

### Have the Necessary Study Tools

A simple way of ensuring your effectiveness as a student is to arm yourself with the necessary tools for studying. Here is a brief list of essentials:

- *Pen and paper* are so taken for granted that they are often forgotten. Make it a habit to check these simple things before you leave for class. Have an adequate supply in your study area. Always have at least two pens, especially in class. You should also have blank, unlined paper of standard letter size (8 1/2 inches by 11 inches), particularly if you want to type your papers.

- Reference books, such as a *dictionary*, are essential. Have a standard dictionary for your study area, and a paperback version to carry with you. An *almanac*, listing world information and an *atlas*, a collection of maps, are also useful.

Other study tools you may find helpful are:

- A *highlighter* pen to mark important points in notes and your own books.

- A *tape recorder* to use when studying alone. Read your notes and other information into it. Reading aloud helps fix the material in your mind, and you can play the material back for additional study. Do not, however use a tape recorder at a lecture. Using a tape recorder at a lecture is NOT a good practice.

- A *typewriter* to type or retype notes to make certain they can be read later and to help organize and remember them.

- A *personal computer* for word processing is an excellent tool for storing and sorting notes and preparing papers. Many schools have them available. Budgeting time to learn to use them will be worthwhile.

- A *calculator* is useful for courses involving math. (Wallet-sized ones can be hard to use because the buttons and display are small.)

- Additional tools and material that you might need include pencils, erasers, correction fluid, pencil sharpener, paper clips, scotch tape, a stapler, and a ruler.

## SUMMING UP

Time is your major resource. It is also the one resource that you cannot get more of once you run out of it.

Managing time boils down to managing yourself. The more you know about yourself, the better equipped you are to manage your time well. Be aware of how you perceive and use time.

Habits are the basic building blocks of time management. Habits are what we have conditioned ourselves to do. Our habits are so much a part of us that we do them almost without conscious thought. We do not need to force ourselves to do what has become a habit for us. Habits are big time-savers when they are good and big time-wasters when they are bad.

Three simple rules sum up effective scheduling: keep it simple, keep it realistic, write it down. Use your critical thinking skills to evaluate activities and only schedule those that you must do.

These are four types of schedules you can use to manage your time: a general time-use schedule, a long-term schedule, a weekly schedule, and a daily schedule.

To ensure you do your priority tasks, you should:

- Do first those priority tasks you least want to do.
- Look for easy ways to start difficult tasks.
- Be aware of your low- and high-energy periods.
- Do not put off large tasks until you "have more time."
- Do put off low-priority things if doing them prevents you from completing high-priority things.
- Reward yourself with something you enjoy when you finish a task.
- Work where you will not be disturbed.
- Be prepared to take advantage of found time.

If you do not have good study habits, all the time-management skills in the world are useless. Try to work on these four good study habits:
1. Set regular hours to study alone.
2. Find a suitable study area.
3. Keep up with assignments.
4. Have the necessary study tools.

## ▼ DEVELOPING YOUR SKILLS

Exercise 1

### Keep a Log

Keep a log of how much time you spend on one routine activity. Pick one from the list below or pick one of your own. Just be sure that what you pick is something you do quite often and that you might be spending too much time on. Keep the log for one week. Every time you do the activity you will record the amount of time you spend on it. Either carry the log with you or keep it in the place where you do the activity. For example, you could keep the log in the car or taped to the TV.

> Eating
> Watching TV
> In the car
> On the bus or train
> Talking to family
> Hanging out with friends
> Cleaning up the house or apartment
> Shopping
> Playing sports
> Reading for pleasure

Exercise 2

### Make a Weekly Schedule

Construct a weekly schedule. Look at the sample on the next page, and use the chart below it for your own schedule. You may also devise your own form. Break the day into hours or even smaller blocks of time if that is better for your purposes. Create a schedule that reflects the realities of your life, and put in your hours for study. Put down the activities you know you must do, and carve out those special hours you will put aside for studying.

## SAMPLE

| Hours | Mon | Tues | Wed | Thurs | Fri | Sat | Sun |
|---|---|---|---|---|---|---|---|
| 8:00 | breakfast | → | → | → | → | | |
| 9:00 | class | → | → | → | → | breakfast | → |
| 10:00 | study | class | study | class | study | → | visit friends |
| 11:00 | study | → | → | → | → | → | and |
| 12:00 | lunch | → | → | → | → | study | family |
| 1:00 | chores | → | → | → | → | lunch | → |
| 2:00 | job | class | job | class | job | job | racquet |
| 3:00 | ↓ | ↓ | ↓ | ↓ | ↓ | ↓ | ball |
| 4:00 | | racquet | ↓ | racquet | ↓ | ↓ | free time |
| 5:00 | ↓ | ball | ↓ | ball | ↓ | ↓ | ↓ |
| 6:00 | dinner | → | → | chores | dinner | free time | dinner |
| 7:00 | class | → | → | dinner | free time | | study |
| 8:00 | study | study | study | study | | | |
| 9:00 | ↓ | ↓ | ↓ | ↓ | ↓ | ↓ | ↓ |
| 10:00 | | | | | | | |
| 11:00 | ↓ | ↓ | ↓ | ↓ | ↓ | ↓ | ↓ |

## YOUR SCHEDULE

| Hours | Mon | Tues | Wed | Thurs | Fri | Sat | Sun |
|---|---|---|---|---|---|---|---|
| | | | | | | | |
| | | | | | | | |
| | | | | | | | |
| | | | | | | | |
| | | | | | | | |
| | | | | | | | |
| | | | | | | | |
| | | | | | | | |
| | | | | | | | |
| | | | | | | | |
| | | | | | | | |
| | | | | | | | |
| | | | | | | | |
| | | | | | | | |
| | | | | | | | |
| | | | | | | | |

Exercise 3

## Use a Long-Term Planning Schedule

Create your long-term planning schedule like the one shown below to use for the rest of the semester. Review it weekly. Your schedule will help you to set up and prioritize your daily to-do lists.

|  | September |  |  |  | October |  |  |  | November |  |  |  | December |  |  |  |
|---|---|---|---|---|---|---|---|---|---|---|---|---|---|---|---|---|
|  | 1 | 2 | 3 | 4 | 1 | 2 | 3 | 4 | 1 | 2 | 3 | 4 | 1 | 2 | 3 | 4 |
| **Course 1** | | | | | | | | | | | | | | | | |
| Bk Report 1 | | | | | | | | | | | | | | | | |
| Bk Report 2 | | | | | | | | | | | | | | | | |
| Term Paper | | | | | | | | | | | | | | | | |
| **Course 2** | | | | | | | | | | | | | | | | |
| Field Trip | | | | | | | | | | | | | | | | |
| Field Trip | | | | | | | | | | | | | | | | |
| Rdng Asgn | | | | | | | | | | | | | | | | |
| Mnthly Quiz | | | | | | | | | | | | | | | | |
| Term Paper | | | | | | | | | | | | | | | | |
| **General** | | | | | | | | | | | | | | | | |
| Midterms | | | | | | | | | | | | | | | | |
| Play | | | | | | | | | | | | | | | | |
| Finals | | | | | | | | | | | | | | | | |
| Extra Wk Hrs | | | | | | | | | | | | | | | | |

Long-Term Schedule

Exercise 4

## Rearrange Weekly Schedule

Alan has planned his schedule for the week like this. He and his wife Jan take turns taking their three-year-old daughter Candy to the day-care center in the morning. This week is Alan's week to take her.

Alan has to put in 2 hours each week in the computer lab for his computer programming course. This week the lab will be closed in the afternoon, which is when Alan usually works there, and open from 7 a.m. to 11 a.m. Write on the lines below your suggestions for how Alan should rearrange his schedule to fit in 2 hours in the lab.

|  | MON | TUES | WED | THUR | FRI |
|---|---|---|---|---|---|
| 7A | study for exam ↓ | study for exam ↓ | appt. w/ adviser ↓ | study ↓ | take car to service station ↓ |
| 8 |  |  |  |  |  |
| 9 |  |  |  |  |  |
| 10 | class | class | class | dentist |  |
| 11 | class |  | class |  | class |
| NOON | buy books | exam | lib | lib | lib |
| 1P | lunch w/ Phil |  | lib |  | lib |
| 2 |  | comp. lab | lunch | comp. lab | p/u car |
| 3 | job ↓ | job ↓ | job ↓ | job ↓ | job ↓ |
| 4 |  |  |  |  |  |
| 5 |  |  |  |  |  |
| 6 |  |  |  |  |  |
| 7 |  |  |  |  |  |
| 8 | dinner |  | dinner | dinner | dinner |
| 9 | study for exam | | study ↓ | watch basketball game | w/ Alicia and Carlo |
| 10P |  |  |  |  |  |

_____

_____

_____

Chapter 4      Managing Time—95

# 5 Managing Stress

**After completing this chapter, you will be able to apply strategies for using helpful stress and reducing harmful stress.**

Being able to handle stress is an important life skill. For many reasons, modern society puts considerable pressure on people. Ironically, while jobs are safer physically than they once were, job-related stress has increased. This increased stress has occurred in part because of new technologies.

We live and work at a faster pace than our ancestors did. Simply driving to work on traffic-filled highways can cause stress even before we begin to face the demands of our job. At work, we face complex machines and, often, competition. Also, increased financial needs might force us to accept longer work hours.

School has its own stress-producing situations. Simply being in school and trying to learn something new can generate stress. There are common high-stress producers, such as taking exams, preparing papers, or making oral presentations in class.

## WHAT IS STRESS?

Everyone experiences stress. Some people feel it often, others less often. Stress is present during your finest hours—when you achieve your highest goals, when you make a breakthrough, when you perform at your best. In these instances, stress is positive, helping you achieve on a higher level.

On the other hand, stress can interfere with your ability to cope. When you face a demanding task, have to speak before the class, take a test, or face a report deadline, you experience stress.

In these situations, stress can be harmful unless you know how to reduce it and turn it to your advantage.

### Two Ways of Defining Stress

Different experts define stress differently, depending on how they view it.

- Some describe it in physical terms: your bodily response to a stressful situation. Physical signs of stress include:

    *Feeling of tiredness*
    *Shaky hands*
    *Dizzy spells*
    *Cold or sweaty hands*
    *Rapidly beating heart*
    *Headache*
    *Sleeplessness*
    *Weight loss or gain*

- Other experts define it in psychological terms: how your perception of a situation determines whether you see it as stressful. Psychological signs of stress could be:

    *Short temper, irritability, or impatience*
    *Edginess*
    *Aggressiveness, hostility*
    *Excessive competitiveness*
    *Inability to concentrate*
    *Inability to sit still or relax*
    *Inability to become interested in anything*
    *Fingernail biting*
    *Butterflies or knots in your stomach*
    *Feeling of insecurity*
    *Confusion*

A reason for the differing definitions is that a situation that causes stress to one person may not affect another in the same way. In general, stress is individually determined and is both a physical reaction and a mental perception.

### Short- and Long-Term Stress

Stress may be *short term* or *long term*. For example, after a near miss in a traffic accident, you will experience short-term stress. You are shaken. You take it easy until your nerves calm and, after a while, return to normal. You can experience short-term stress in any number of circumstances—having a job interview, going on a first date, experiencing your first day on a new job, speaking in public.

Long-term stress results from on-going problems, which you might or might not be aware of. These could include such things as an overloaded schedule, a persistent medical problem of a person close to you, or some other continuing condition in your life. It could even be your diet. You must exert effort to cope successfully with long-term stress and work to find out what causes it.

Long-term stress can be more difficult to deal with than short-term stress because it might involve several aspects of your life. Also, it can sneak up on you without your realizing it. Here is an example of what can happen.

> In the fall Joanna says good-bye to her family and moves into an apartment near campus, eager to start the new school year. She has signed up for a full course load. She is confident she will be able to handle it plus a part-time job as a waitress on Friday and Saturday nights. Life is going well for Joanna; she has lots of friends and is busy. By October, however, she and her roommate are having disagreements about when to watch TV, about sharing household chores, and about letting friends stay overnight. Further, her roommate keeps telling her how easy the accounting course is that Joanna is struggling with.
> 
> The waitressing job is fun, but Joanna tends to stay out late afterwards. She is increasingly tired during the day. She spilled coffee on a customer one night, and her boss yelled at her. When she goes home at the end of the semester, her irritablity and short temper surprise her family. She complains of being tired and having headaches all the time.

Joanna is showing signs of long-term stress. If she stops to look for the causes, they seem fairly obvious—her job, her roommate, the accounting course. Now, she is unable to control her life to make it less stressful. As a result, her course work and her social life suffer.

Here is another example of a person's life gradually becoming more stressful without his fully realizing it.

> Greg has a summer job doing highway work. When fall comes, he starts school but agrees to continue the job for another month. During the summer the job was fine. Greg, although tired at the end of the day, could go home, relax, go for a swim, and get a good night's sleep. Now he has to go home and study.
>
> Two days a week he works in the morning and goes to class in the afternoon. His boss does not want him to leave until 1 p.m. This gives him little time to clean up, eat, and get to class.
>
> Yesterday Greg was working on the highway when a motorist passed by so close he knocked Greg over. Although Greg was not hurt, he felt increasingly angry as the day wore on. When he arrived at his last class that evening, he was so tense that he was rude when the instructor asked a simple question.
>
> After class the instructor said to Greg, "You don't seem to like this class much, Greg. Maybe you should consider dropping it."

Greg's situation may improve when he leaves his job. Now he is not successfully juggling two different parts of his life—working and going to school. The sooner he resolves the conflict, the better off he will be. Joanna and Greg both showed signs of being under stress. Joanna was irritable, short-tempered, tired, and had headaches. Greg felt angry and was rude. The person under stress may feel other signs of stress, which no one else notices.

### Constant Stress

A few people feel stress about things in general. They have free-floating anxieties. They convince themselves that something will go wrong. This constant stress is not long-term stress resulting from an identifiable cause. A person experiencing constant stress, for which no apparent cause can be found, might need professional help.

One example of this stress, only recently recognized, is stress caused by a traumatic experience in one's past. Often the person who experiences this kind of stress does not even remember the traumatic event. It has become buried in the person's subconscious. Nevertheless in subtle ways it affects behavior. Soldiers who have experienced terrible events in wars have suffered from this kind of stress.

The ordinary stress you will face—either short- or long-term—is something you can learn to control and to make work for you.

### Good Stress

Some stress is necessary for you to perform well. Without stress, according to some theories, you would not be energized to perform as well as you can. Some experts refer to the *optimum level of* stress by which they mean that an individual is stimulated to perform well. You need a *medium* or *moderate* level of stress to perform at your peak. Too little stress or too much stress will lead to poor performance.

The optimal level of stress depends on the individual and the nature of the task. Performance of complex tasks that demand concentration (writing, speaking publicly) requires a lower level of stress for best performance than does the performance of less complex tasks. With the optimal level of stress, a person will perform better on the complex task, however, than a person who feels no stress at all.

Good stress is stress that has a positive rather than negative effect. Think of athletes in the final round of a competition. Stress can give them greater strength, powers of concentration, quicker reactions.

Similarly, entertainers thrive on the stress of being in the spotlight, risking boos or accepting applause from hundreds or thousands of people. If you must give a public speech, a degree of stress will improve your presentation. Stress helps you meet challenges.

## WHAT CAUSES STRESS?

The introduction to Unit II states that stress comes to us in two ways:

1. We invite it.
2. It is thrust upon us.

### Invited Stress

You invite stress whenever you accept a challenge. In that sense, you invite stress by enrolling in school. You are challenging yourself to learn. Anyone who decides to make a living working or performing in front of others—athletes, actors, lawyers, doctors, teachers—is inviting stress. It is part of the daily lives of such people. To succeed, they must learn to make the stress they feel function as a positive influence in their lives. Simply by the fact of facing it daily, people in these positions gain a degree of immunity to stress. Their experience hints at a basic truth about stress and coping with it: If you accept and face it, you can control stress and make it work for you.

### Uninvited Stress

Change is most often the cause of uninvited stress. Change can be frightening. It requires adjustment on your part. You experience stress as the result of inevitable changes, either good or bad: new schools, new jobs, getting married, having children, deaths in the family. At times, unexpected events occur, such as being robbed, being in an accident, losing a job. Unpredictable events are the more stressful.

## You Set Degree of Stress

Two factors determine your degree of stress:

1. What happens outside—actual events.
2. What happens inside—your emotional and physical reaction.

What is happening inside you is more important in determining how stressful a situation is than the actual event itself. You decide what is stressful. Certainly some situations are in themselves stressful. If you are accosted on the street by someone with a gun or knife demanding your money, you are in a stressful situation, no doubt about it. Even here, however, you control the extent of the stress to some degree.

Keeping yourself calm, for example, can help you think coolly so as not to make a bad situation worse. A sense of stress can be communicated. By controlling your level of stress, you keep others from becoming too stressed. That can be helpful in many situations.

In the more common, although less obviously threatening, stressful situations—public speaking, meeting a deadline, facing a difficult assignment—the degree of stress you experience is controlled more by your own mind than by the outside event. We know this because the same situation will cause different degrees of stress in different people.

> Jayne and Morgan walk into class one day to find that the instructor is giving a surprise exam. It will count for 20 percent of the final grade. Jayne does not think twice about it. This is a class in her favorite subject. She loves this class. She likes it so much that she has read the entire textbook already. She knows that she is going to sail through this test. She feels only the stimulating stress of meeting a challenge.
>
> Morgan is not prepared. He panics, his palms become sweaty, his thoughts get all jumbled up. He feels great stress and as a result forgets what he does know that would help him on the test.

The event is the same. The perception is different. So is their reaction. One is calm. The other is stressed. Many events or tasks are *not* stressful in and of themselves. Much of the stress you feel is generated in your own mind. Realizing this can help you control stress. A further proof that the cause of stress is in yourself, not in events, is your own changing reaction to the same situation. As you become more self-confident, a task that at first caused you stress can become routinely unstressful.

# CONTROL OF STRESS

Your goal is not to eliminate stress, which would be impossible. Your goal is to take advantage of positive stress and to reduce the negative effects of harmful stress. You control stress in one of two ways:

1. You change your situation (what is happening to you).
2. You change yourself (how you react).

Here are some techniques for reducing stress.

## Develop Realistic Goals

You have already taken a major step toward reducing harmful stress if you have set goals based upon a vision of what you want your life to be. People who know what they are doing and know where they are going experience less stress than those who do not. If you have used your critical thinking skills, you will have set yourself realistic goals. If your goals are unrealistic, they will be a cause of stress.

Why do realistic goals reduce stress? The answer to this is clear to anyone who has ever become lost while traveling. As long as you know where you are and where you are going, you feel relaxed and comfortable. As soon as you realize you are lost, that you do not know where you are or how to get to where you are going, you begin to experience stress. Having clear goals in your life and a map in the form of to-do lists to help you achieve them can keep harmful stress out of your life.

## Organize Your Time

You further reduce your chances of experiencing harmful stress when you learn how to manage your time. If you manage your time well, use schedules and prioritize activities as you learned in the previous chapters, you will less likely encounter stressful situations. On the other hand, if you fail to manage your time well, you can easily end up constantly stressed as you frantically race from one unscheduled activity to another.

## Recognize What You Can Do

Make a list of situations you know cause you stress. Divide the list into things you cannot avoid or control and things you can hope to avoid or control. An old prayer goes:

*Give me the courage to change what I can change.*
*Give me the strength to accept what I cannot change.*
*And give me the wisdom to know the difference.*

You might not always be able to do this, but, to the best of your ability, direct your efforts toward stressful situations you can change. Do not waste time trying to change what you cannot control.

## Avoid What You Can

Certain situations you can avoid without running away from your problems. People in your class or at work who cause you to feel stress are examples. Avoid sitting near them in class or getting into conversations with them at work beyond what is required for doing the job. If you hate cold weather, find a way to exercise indoors in winter. Avoid climbing ladders if you fear heights.

## Confront Stress You Cannot Avoid

If you cannot avoid a situation you find stressful, confront it. Deal with it head on. Do not try to ignore a situation you cannot avoid. Do not postpone thinking about it or acting on it.

One of the most harmful tactics is to use mood altering substances—drugs. Use of drugs, including alcohol, prescription, and nonprescription drugs, alters a person's mood temporarily and makes stressful situations appear to go away. The stress producing situations do not go away, of course, and the person is ultimately worse off.

There are five things you can do to confront stress:

1. Force yourself into the situation.
2. Learn all you can about the situation.
3. Examine your reactions to the situation.
4. Do not put things off.
5. Exercise and have a proper diet.

Depending on the nature of the situation, you will use some or all five approaches in confronting your stress. Following are some situations people commonly find stressful along with some ways of coping with them.

**Public speaking** is a common cause of stress, either giving a prepared talk or responding to questions in a classroom discussion. You might always be able to avoid doing this if it is stressful, but if you do, you will pay a price. Consider this example.

> ▶ "Fred, we're promoting you to head our new training program for computer operators. You learned the system faster than anyone else. You have an excellent grasp of it, and you seem to have a way of explaining it to coworkers."
>
> Fred was flattered. His promotion was completely unexpected.

He was pleased with the large pay raise that went with it.

"Now you're part of management, Fred," the general manager continued. "You'll attend the biweekly managers' meetings. I'll introduce you and announce your new position at this week's meeting. At the next one, I'd like you to make a short report about the new department and your general plans."

When he heard this, Fred's initial glow began to fade. "Uh, you want me to make a report to all the managers?"

"Oh, just a general outline, Fred. There won't be time for a detailed report. That can come later. Just speak for 10 or 15 minutes. Talk about what you'll be teaching."

Fred felt a cold knot forming in his stomach. He dreaded speaking before groups. In school he had avoided speaking in class. Because he worked hard, he managed to get good grades anyway, but he never conquered his fear of public speaking.

The general manager continued. "I want you to visit all our branch offices to set up programs. I think the best approach will be for you and me to visit them first. We'll get all the employees together at each, even those who may not be working on computers. That way everyone will know what's going on. There are only 40 people in each branch. I'll introduce you and you can talk about your training program. Plan a 30-minute talk. You'll give the same talk at each branch so it will be easy."

By now Fred was dismayed. Although he could explain and teach well in one-on-one situations, he felt he could not talk before groups. He decided to reject the promotion, saying that family needs made it impossible for him to do any traveling that kept him away overnight.

The general manager was unhappy. He pointed out that the promotion was a big one that opened up a new avenue of career advancement. Fred declined. Just the thought of making speeches caused him stress. Another person received the promotion.

---

Many people would rather do almost anything than speak in public, so Fred's anxiety is understandable. His failure to confront his fear is not. Here are some things you can do to avoid Fred's problem.

- **Prepare**. The greater your understanding of your subject, the more confident you will be when you stand up. As part of preparing, imagine yourself speaking before a group.

- **Practice**. Give talks to yourself. Do it in front of a mirror. Do it with a friend. Tape yourself if you have the necessary equipment. Watch out for nervous tics and distracting habits, such as saying "um," "like," and "y'know."

- **Pretend**. Think of the audience as one person. Pretend that the person to whom you are speaking is your best friend. He or she thinks highly of you and is eager to hear what you have to say. There is no reason to be nervous when speaking to such a friend. Pick out one person in the audience to be your "friend." Talk to that person.

- **Puncture your fear**. Consider why speaking in front of a group causes so many people stress. One cause is the fear of being judged or appearing a fool. If we stumble over a word, we think that the audience will be critical of us. If we forget for a few seconds what we were about to say, we fear the audience will think we are stupid. In reality, nobody in the audience is going to judge you as harshly as you will judge yourself. Remind yourself that it is more likely that they are watching and thinking, "Gee, I'd be really nervous if I were standing up there."

- **Just do it**. The best way to overcome fear of speaking in public is by doing it. Each time you speak in public, it becomes easier to do. Anticipation is almost always worse than reality. As long as you avoid the experience, your imagination will make you fear it. Classroom discussion is a good place to get experience. Any experience you gain communicating your thoughts in an organized manner adds to your self-confidence and poise.

As with Fred, you might have a career in which you will be called upon to make presentations to colleagues or customers. Outside of a career, if you wish to participate in community or church organizations or local government, you will need to express yourself orally before others.

**Learning**, as you read, is another common source of stress. Being a student can be stressful. Suppose you are experiencing stress over having to learn to use computers. You never cared for them, do not know anything about them, and really do not want anything to do with them. Yet, you know that everyone is using them and that computer skills are a requirement for many jobs. This is a case in which you should learn all you can about the situation. Ask yourself questions:

> *What have I done to get computer skills?*
> *Should I take a course to learn how to use them?*
> *What use will I most likely have for computers—word processing, data processing, or something else?*

If you are not sure how to answer this last question, get some ideas from the descriptions of computer courses in the catalog. Talk to friends who use computers as well as those who do not. Become knowledgeable about computers and software.

So, to confront a particular cause of stress, learn all you can about it. Answer questions yourself and also find someone who is knowledgeable and can give you answers. In going through this question-and-answer process, the stress you felt starts to diminish.

**Test taking** is a common source of stress. Obviously true in school, it is equally true in the workplace, where taking tests is often necessary to get jobs and promotions. To conquer your feelings of stress in such situations, examine your reactions. Try to understand the real source of your stress. Are you worried about a test because you think it will affect your grade? Make sure you know the real value of the test in the overall grade—and the real value of the grade in your life. You will learn specific strategies for coping with test anxiety later in this course.

Do not blow things out of proportion, which we often do when feeling stress. Have you already decided you will fail? Give yourself a chance—do not decide anything until you have tried. Make sure your reactions have a basis in fact. Besides keeping you from overreacting, examining your feelings helps you calm down and overcome stress.

## Change Yourself

Until now, you have been studying ways to change the situation you are in as a way of handling stress. Some of those tactics, you may have noticed, would result in changing yourself. But the focus was on changing the situation. Now consider some ways to change yourself to handle stress effectively.

**Examine Your Response**. Examining your response is different from examining your reaction. Your reaction is how you feel. Your response is what you do. When some people encounter stress, they tend to respond always in the same way even when the response does not solve their problem or diminish their stress. Psychologists call this *fixation*.

> ▶ Rita was eager to be a good student. She was so eager that she felt considerable stress. Because English was a second language for her, she was particularly concerned about understanding everything she heard in her lecture course. To be sure she really learned the material, she tried to write down everything the lecturer said. This is impossible, and the effort to do it caused Rita to lose track of the main points being made. Furthermore, her notes, which sometimes did not even include essential points she had missed, were so long and her rushed handwriting so bad, it was difficult for her to review them for exams. The result was poor performance and increased stress.

Rita must examine her response and realize that taking down everything is impossible. She should train herself to listen for and make notes only of major points so she can concentrate on listening and not on note taking.

**Take Some Action**. Approach stressful situations as problems to be solved and take some action. For example, if you are worried about how you are doing in a course, make an appointment to talk to the instructor. If your feelings are correct and you are not doing well, you are better off finding out before the final exam. The instructor may have specific suggestions to help you.

Suppose the source of your stress is a full schedule. You are always rushing from class to job. Look for ways to slow down. Consider asking your employer if you could change your hours. Even a 15-minute change in when you start or leave could make a difference. Do you have to fight a lot of traffic? Try starting a little earlier or changing your route. Look at your written weekly schedule to find ways to relieve the pressure.

**Do Not Procrastinate**. Do not procrastinate on stressful things, especially if they are important. Suppose you have a term paper to complete within six weeks. Just thinking about it causes you to feel stress. Start researching it now. Force yourself to schedule time to work on it. Keep progress reports to be sure you will complete it on time. By tackling the job head on instead of worrying about it, it immediately becomes less stressful.

**Exercise**. Tension stored in muscles contributes to feeling stress. A good way to get rid of stress is physical exercise. Exercise reduces the tension in muscles and helps clear your mind. It also reduces fatigue and creates a sense of well-being. People who exercise regularly usually feel more self-confident and creative than those who do not. Regular exercise will help you sleep better and, surprisingly, eat less. A result will be more energy during the day.

Other benefits of exercise include improved physical appearance, increased strength and endurance, and reduced blood pressure. Altogether, these benefits help you combat stress.

- Think about the type of exercise you like to do—riding a bicycle, playing a game of basketball, or just going for a long walk.

- If you are out of shape, start exercising three times a week for 10 minutes at a time. Gradually increase the amount as you build up your stamina.

- Find a companion to exercise with. Another person can increase your motivation to stick to an exercise plan.

**Find Relaxing Alternatives**. You can relax and reduce stress by engaging in enjoyable activities other than physical exercise. Listening to music, reading a novel, or playing a game can take your mind off the day's worries. One simple relaxing alternative is to soak in a hot bath or stand in a hot shower for a while. Hot water relaxes muscle tension.

**Consider Your Diet**. What you eat and drink is a possible source of stress. Being healthy and feeling well reduce stress. Simple, nutritious food creates good health and good feelings. Some food contains caffeine, which can cause stress. Caffeine is a stimulant. It gives an artificial burst of energy, but too much can make you tense. Too much refined sugar or foods containing it give a burst of energy quickly followed by a let down. Alcohol leads to stress. Alcohol is a depressant. It leaves you feeling bad physically and psychologically. Here are some ways to reduce stress caused by diet.

- Learn about nutrition and evaluate your own diet.
- Try to reduce the amount of fat intake.
- Get sugar from fruits and vegetables, not from refined sugar.
- Eat whole grains instead of refined ones, fresh fruit and vegetables rather than prepared foods.
- Eat fewer portions of red meat, which is high in fat, and more portions of chicken and fish, which have lower amounts of fat.

Changing a diet will not bring overnight results. Take your time to find things to eat and drink that you enjoy, but that are also better for you and will help you control stress.

**Use Deep Breathing and Meditation**. People have used deep breathing and meditation to help reduce stress for a long time.

*Meditation* is a systematic, practical method for increasing self-awareness and reducing stress. It gives a sense of tranquility that often lasts, no matter what the day brings. To experience meditation in a small way, get into a relaxed position. Make sure you are in your most comfortable clothes. Think of a peaceful scene and try to let the concerns of the day flow out of you. Let your hands lie limp; do not clench your fists. Turn your head from side to side, slowly, being aware of any tension in your neck muscles. Let the tightness in those or any other areas of your body flow out of you. Done regularly, meditation can help you maintain a feeling of calm.

*Deep breathing* can be an effective way to get control in a stressful situation. Remember Morgan's stress when he walked into his class to learn there would be an unexpected test. He did not remain calm. He panicked, which only worsened matters and made him do poorly on the test. The simple act of breathing slowly and deeply, in through the nose and out through the mouth for a few moments, could have helped him relax enough to clear his mind and improve his performance.

**Seek Help**. If you cannot control your stress and feeling of anxiety yourself, seek help. Talk to a friend or someone in your family. Talk to a school counselor, if there is one. Speak to an instructor you particularly like. Check to see if there are any stress-management classes either at your school or in the community. Many organizations, such as the YMCA, YWCA, and community centers, have such courses.

When feeling stress, it may help you to think about these words of the late U.S. President Franklin D. Roosevelt,

> *The only thing we have to fear is fear itself.*

He was speaking to rally the nation out of a severe economic depression, but his words speak to anyone facing any stressful situation. Work to minimize harmful stress, but be ready to face and accept inevitable stress. To have a life without stress would mean your never trying anything new, never accepting risks and challenges, never working toward goals, and never realizing your potential.

## OVERCOMING TEST STRESS

Most people taking tests experience stress—a perfectly natural reaction. Here, as in other situations, stress can work for you by increasing your motivation to do well, improving your concentration, and sharpening your performance. On the other hand, if stress distracts you, it works against you.

Taking tests can be an ordeal. Even thoroughly prepared students, who are aware of the instructor's goals, sometimes stumble when actually taking the test. They become victims of test stress or of not having good test-taking skills. You will learn techniques for taking objective and essay tests in Chapters 10 and 11. Here are some strategies to cope with test stress.

### Strategies to Use Before a Test

You can act to control anxiety that you might start to feel in the days and weeks before the test. Here is a checklist of those techniques.

**Acknowledge Feeling Stress.** Remember that most people taking tests experience anxiety—a perfectly natural result of what is called the *fight-or-flight* instinct under stress. Remind yourself that feeling some stress is helpful.

**Take the Initiative.** Most instructors want tests to be learning tools and will often discuss them ahead of time. Use these discussions to ask questions to find out what is important. Talk with classmates to learn what they expect the test to emphasize. If you and your classmates disagree, make a note of it and in the next class ask for clarification.

**Keep Things in Perspective.** While there is no denying that tests are important, they are rarely a life-or-death matter. Ask yourself how much this test will really affect your life one year or five years from now.

**Be Prepared.** Being prepared is one of the best ways to reduce test stress. Try to study well in advance so you have time to cover all the material. If the test is upon you and you find you only have time to cram, then cram. After all, cramming will be better than nothing.

**Recall Your Last Test.** On your last test did you experience test stress? How did it effect you? Did your anxiety make it hard for you to read instructions carefully? If so, tell yourself that it is important to read instructions and therefore all right to take the time to do so.

**Do Not Be Too Hard on Yourself.** Whether you have studied in advance or are cramming at the last minute, do not be too hard on yourself. You cannot undo the past. If you skipped classes, did not start studying soon enough, did not use classroom discussion to your advantage, now is not the time to chastise yourself. It will only make matters worse. Make a list of the things you wish you had done. Then, put it aside to look at after the test. Right now, focus your attention on studying for the test.

## Strategies to Use During the Test

In addition to helping yourself deal with stress before a test, these are things you can do to control stress during a test.

**Arrive Early.** You do not want to be rushing in at the last minute, looking for a place to sit while the instructor is passing out the test and giving instructions. Give yourself extra time on the day of the test to arrive early. If you have a favorite seat, foolish as it may seem, it will annoy you if someone else takes it.

**Do Mental Warm-Ups.** While you are waiting for the rest of the class to arrive, do mental warm-ups. Think about the things you studied, drum up facts, dates, figures. Get your mind focused on the subject of the test.

**Listen to Instructions**. Listen carefully to any oral instructions and be sure you understand. If you do not understand, ask. Do not start the test wondering what you are supposed to do.

**Read Instructions Carefully**. Read the instructions and the questions carefully. A brilliant response that does not answer the question will not count for much.

**Take Time to Relax**. If you feel your mind going blank or your handwriting is becoming unreadable, pause. Use the relaxation techniques described earlier. Think of yourself taking a test with a successful confident attitude.

**Use All the Time Allowed**. When you finish that last question, you may feel tempted to leave the room right away. It is better to stay until the end of the time allowed and use it to advantage. Reread the instructions to be sure you followed them. Look at your answers. Do not impulsively change answers but if you are sure that something is wrong, change it.

### When the Test Is Over

Do not create post-test stress by second-guessing yourself. Wait until you have more perspective on the test and it has been graded and handed back. Then, review the test. Analyze your preparation and determine what you need to do next time. Write your ideas down. If you need to, change your study habits, note-taking techniques, or reading habits for the next test. To remind yourself, look at your test review notes occasionally, and again just before the next test.

## SUMMING UP

Stress is felt as anxiety and fear. When encountering a stressful situation, your body prepares to fight or flee. Everyone experiences stress. Some people feel it often; others less often.

People react to stressful situations both physically and psychologically.

Stress may be *short term* or *long term*. Long-term stress results from on-going problems, which you might or might not be aware of. Long-term stress can be more difficult to deal with because it might involve several aspects of your life.

Some stress is necessary for you to perform well. Too little stress or too much stress will lead to poor performance.

Stress comes to you in two ways: (1) you invite it and (2) it is thrust upon you.

You invite stress whenever you accept a challenge. More commonly, stress is thrust upon you. Although change may be a factor in stress you invite, it is most often the cause of uninvited stress.

What is happening inside you is more important in determining how stressful a situation is than the actual event itself.

Essentially, you control stress in either one of two ways:
1. You change your situation (what is happening to you).
2. You change yourself (how you react).

Techniques for reducing stress by changing the situation include:

- Develop realistic goals.

- Organize your time.

- Recognize what you can do.

- Avoid what you can.

- Confront stress you cannot avoid by:
    1. Forcing yourself into the situation.
    2. Learning all you can about the situation.
    3. Examining your reactions to the situation.
    4. Not putting things off.
    5. Exercising and having a proper diet.

Some anxiety is not only natural but is helpful. It increases your motivation to do well, improves your concentration, and sharpens your performance.

Indications that you are feeling anxiety include a knot in your stomach, sweaty palms, or fear of failure.

There are strategies you can use to control test stress before taking tests, during tests, and after tests.

Before-test strategies include:

- Acknowledge feelings of anxiety.
- Take the initiative to find out more about the test.
- Keep things in perspective.
- Be prepared.
- Recall your last test.
- Do not be too hard on yourself.

During-test strategies include:

- Arrive early.
- Do mental warm-ups.
- Listen to instructions.
- Read instructions carefully.
- Take time to relax.
- Use all the time allowed.

Do not create post-test stress by second-guessing yourself. Wait until the test has been graded and handed back. Then, review it, analyze your preparation, and determine what to do next time.

## ▼ DEVELOPING YOUR SKILLS

### Exercise 1

### Identify What Causes Stress for You

Do not assume that something, for example a test, is a source of stress for you, just because it is for others. List below four causes of stress for you.

_____

_____

_____

_____

### Exercise 2

### Recall an Experience When Stress Helped You

Describe a time in your life when you were under stress, but the stress had a positive effect, not a negative effect on you. Write your description on a separate sheet of paper.

### Exercise 3

### Recognize How You React to Stress

Look at the list of physical symptoms of stress in this chapter. Have you ever felt any of these? Describe an episode in your own life when you were under stress and how you felt. Write your description on a separate sheet of paper.

### Exercise 4

### Use a Stress Control Method

Over the next week, be aware of when you feel stress. Use one of the stress control methods described in the chapter. Afterwards, review whether the method worked.

Exercise 5

## Recall Your Last Test

**Right after you had completed the test, how did you think you had done? Write your answer on the lines below.**

_____

_____

_____

_____

**When the graded test was returned to you, was the result what you had thought it would be? Write your answer on the lines below.**

_____

_____

_____

_____

**Think about how you prepared for that test, and list some things you wish you had done differently to prepare for it. Write your answer on the lines below.**

_____

_____

_____

_____

# UNIT III
# LEARNING

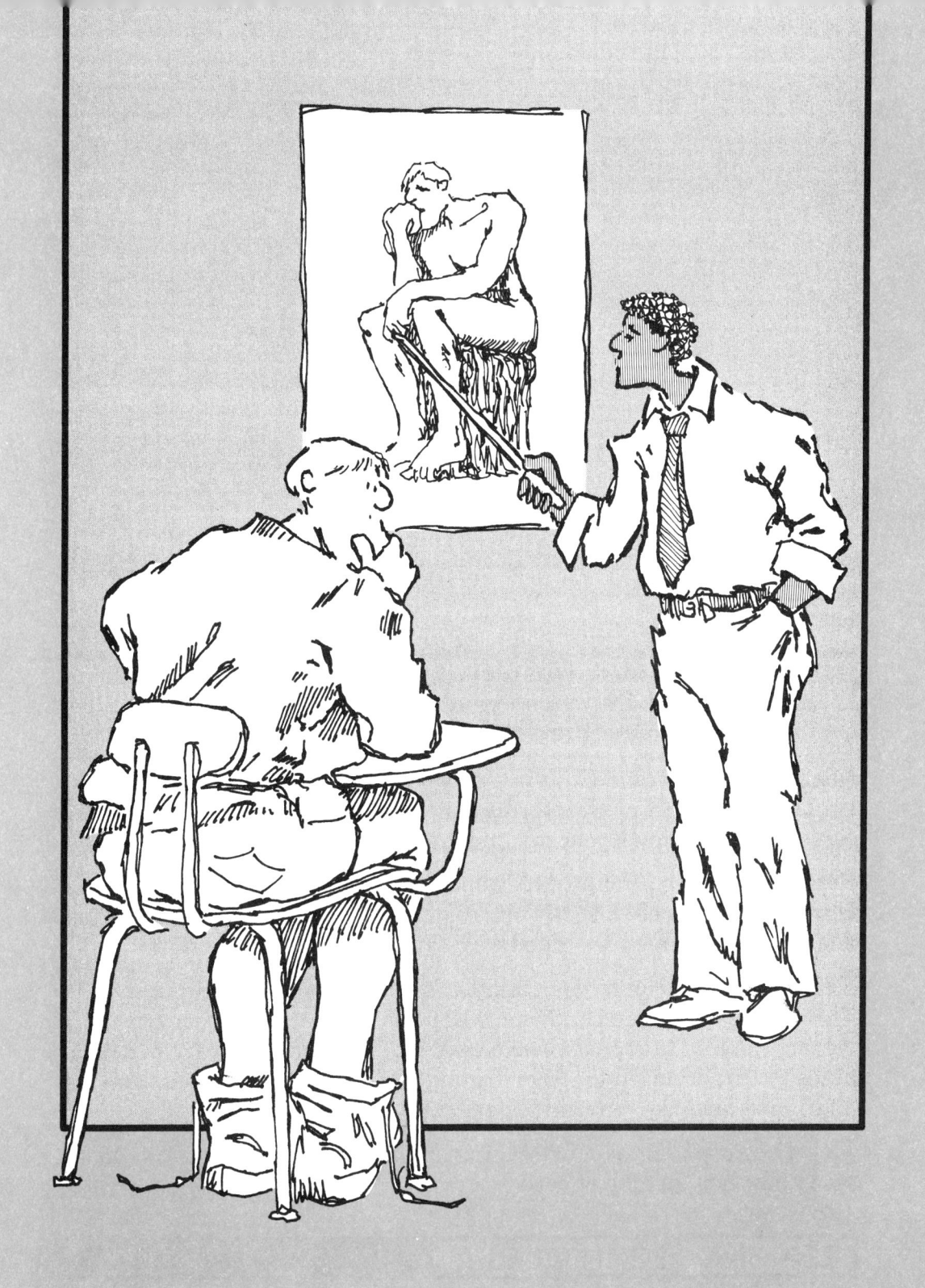

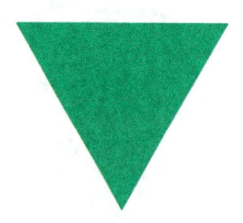

**When you have completed this unit, you will be able to use improved reading and listening skills to organize, summarize, and evaluate concepts.**

Reading and listening skills are your two most important learning skills. A large part of all information, all learning and understanding, comes to you through reading and listening.

Personal observation and experience are other ways of learning. However, if you relied solely on personal experience, you would waste a lot of time learning the hard way what others already know.

Reading skills alone have no limitation beyond your ability to read. Through reading, you can learn what others already have learned without having to repeat their mistakes. Through reading you have access to experienced teachers throughout the ages. And you can call on them whenever you want by opening a book.

To get the most out of your reading and listening in school, you must also know how to take effective notes.

## READING TECHNIQUES

There are many purposes for reading. Most of your reading, however, broadly fits into one or another of the three following types:

1. Reading for pleasure or entertainment.
2. Reading for directions—to find out how to do something.
3. Reading to gain basic knowledge of a topic or a concept.

Chapter 6 focuses on the second and third types of reading—reading for directions and reading to gain basic knowledge. However, reading for pleasure is also valuable. Whether you enjoy science fiction, mysteries, poetry, romance novels, or historical novels, reading expands your mind. Reading something you enjoy is a great way to relax and at the same time improve your reading skills. The more you read—whatever kind of reading—the more effective you will become as a reader. That is because reading is a skill and like any other skill, the more you practice or use it, the more capable you become.

In all types of reading, even for pleasure, you acquire information. Information you get when reading for pleasure will usually not have an immediate practical impact on you. It could, however, have a subtle, long-term impact.

## Reading for Directions and Specific Information

Sometimes when you read directions, you have an immediate, practical need for the information. For example, you may have to read directions for putting paper in the copy machine. This is not a particular skill, the steps are simple, and if you do not remember them next time, you need only glance at the manual again.

When you read directions to learn a skill, you need to understand and remember. For example, turning on a computer and starting the software are things you will be doing often in your courses and in the workplace. You do not want to have to refer to the manual or your notes every time you work at the computer. You are reading not only to get information, but also to understand it. The better you understand the basic directions for using the computer, the more likely you will be able to learn new ways to use it.

Reading for directions or specific information is selective reading—reading to get an isolated piece of information. You do not need to read an office supply catalog from cover to cover to find the cost of a ream of copy paper. You do not read reference books, such as dictionaries or telephone directories, comprehensively. With selective reading you need to locate desired information quickly and to read it correctly.

## Reading to Gain Basic Knowledge

Much of your reading in school is to gain knowledge, to develop an understanding of basic concepts. First, you learned basic concepts of math (addition, subtraction, multiplication, division) and later how to apply them to figure percentages and convert fractions and decimals.

Later you can apply this knowledge in a wide range of jobs from bookkeeping, to marketing, to technical troubleshooting.

In psychology courses you learn about internal and external influences that shape you and others and about stages of development that all humans experience. You will use this basic knowledge later in life whether you become a paralegal, a police officer, a child-care worker, or something else.

When you read to gain understanding, you should read thoroughly and carefully. Look for ways that will help you remember and understand what you read. You need to read effectively to discuss the material in class, to prove mastery on a test, and to get knowledge to use on your job and in other aspects of your life.

This and the following chapter will help you improve the efficiency and effectiveness of your reading ability. You will learn techniques to prepare you to read material in depth and techniques to apply while you are actually reading.

## LISTENING TECHNIQUES

Because you spend so much in school listening to lectures and class discussions, the ability to listen well is important. You want to be as effective a listener as possible.

In Chapter 8, you will learn about specific listening skills. Some of the skills are similar to those you learn for reading effectively. This is understandable. Reading and listening are your two major ways of acquiring new knowledge. Your need to listen does not end when you leave the classroom. Learning is a lifelong demand. Good listening skills allow you to meet that demand successfully.

Listening may seem so basic and commonplace that you may be surprised to discover that you can acquire and develop listening skills.

Listening, as you will learn, is different from hearing. You can get a sense of the difference between listening and hearing by asking out loud the following question using the two different verbs,

> *Did you* **hear** *the lecture last week on troubleshooting in electronics?*

> *Did you* **listen** *to the lecture last week on troubleshooting in electronics?*

*Listening* suggests that you took in or understood what was said. *Hearing* suggests only that your ears picked up a sound. Consider these two versions of a sentence:

*Oh, yes, I* heard *her.*

*Oh, yes, I* listened *to her.*

Which version implies that the person speaking really took note of what was said?

As with reading, preparation is important when you are going to have to do serious listening. How you prepare for listening, the techniques you practice, and what you do after listening all affect your ability to understand and remember. Chapter 8 covers techniques to help you prepare physically and mentally to listen.

Once you are in the class, the lecture room, or shop, there are other techniques you can use to be sure you get the most out of what you hear.

There are many obstacles, external and internal, that can prevent you from listening effectively. It helps to spend some time thinking about what they might be and asking yourself what you can do to remove them. To be a good listener, you must be aware of the obstacles that prevent you from actively listening. If you are aware of these obstacles, you can counter them and make yourself an active listener. There are five common types of listening roadblocks. You will learn about them in Chapter 8.

As you read the following chapters you will become more aware of what you do and do not do as you listen. You will get a better of idea of how to change your habits so you get more out of your listening. However, do not let assessing your habits become an obsession. We have all had the experience of concentrating so hard on how to do something that we cannot actually do it. If you think too much in class about how to listen, you will not be able to listen.

## NOTE-TAKING TECHNIQUES

It is not enough that you read and listen well and have a clear understanding of what has been said or written. You also want to be able to take good notes. Taking notes while listening or reading will improve your ability to remember and understand. Also, of course, you will have the notes for later study and review. Chapter 7 will teach you how to take effective notes when reading, and Chapter 9 will do the same for when you are listening.

# 6 Reading Strategies

*When you have completed this chapter, you will be able to use techniques to prepare yourself to read and strategies to improve your understanding.*

A wealth of knowledge is available in print. From great literary classics to instructional manuals for the fax machine—virtually any information you want or need is in print. Books, magazines, and newspapers contain the accumulated knowledge of the human race. All this information is useless, however, if you cannot read and remember what you read. Reading is central to learning. The more effectively you read, the more effectively you learn.

## PREPARE YOURSELF TO READ

To read effectively and efficiently, you should prepare yourself for reading. The following are four techniques for preparing to read:

1. Clarify your reading purpose.
2. Motivate yourself to read.
3. Use the knowledge you already have.
4. Preview what you are going to read.

### Clarify Your Purpose

You will get more out of what you read if you clarify your purpose for reading. Before reading, ask yourself, "What is my general purpose for reading this?" As a student, your immediate answer might be that you are reading a text because your instructor assigned it. That might be the external purpose, but it should not be the only one. Your purpose may be to gain knowledge or to learn how to do a specific task.

For example, you might be taking a course in accounting, and your instructor has assigned the reading of Chapter 2. Certainly, your reason for reading Chapter 2 is that your instructor told you to. You know that if you want a passing grade, you must read at least some of what is assigned.

These reasons for reading reflect your general purpose. If you want to get all you can out of your reading, however, you must go beyond that. The more specifically you can state your purpose, the more effective your reading will be.

In the case of the accounting class, you see that Chapter 2 is about the accounting cycle. You know that your goal is to become an accountant. An accountant must know what the accounting cycle is. You have clarified your purpose for reading this assignment by recognizing that it is related to your career goal.

Stating your purpose in a specific way before reading helps focus your attention. You can focus your attention more sharply by narrowing your purpose even more. To do this, you might ask yourself such questions as:

> *Am I reading to gain knowledge to pass a test?*
> *Am I reading to gain a second viewpoint on a topic?*
> *Am I trying to gain specific knowledge or learn a new skill? If so, what exactly is it?*

For example, say you are reading to learn word processing. You are preparing to read a chapter that covers moving text within a document. You tell yourself that your purpose for reading is to learn how to do this. Knowing a specific purpose makes it possible for you to determine if your reading is productive. When you are finished reading, you can ask yourself,

> *Did I learn to move text within a document?*
> *How do I move text?*

Another approach to clarifying your purpose for reading is to ask yourself why the instructor assigned this particular material. Has the instructor given any clues as to why this assignment is important? Usually assignments relate to what the class has discussed or will discuss soon.

> Carrie was taking a psychology course. The instructor introduced the topic of human development and explained that this is a major field of study within psychology. The instructor named four areas of human development. He gave the class an assignment to read about cognitive and mental development. Carrie does not know what cognitive development is, but she can guess at the meaning of mental development. She defines her purpose for reading this assignment like this.
> 1. To learn about an aspect of human development, one of the major fields in psychology. Future assignments will probably cover others.
> 2. To find out what cognitive means and how cognitive and mental development are related.
> 3. To find out if mental development means what she thinks it means.

Of course, once you finish a reading assignment, you will understand even better what the purpose was for reading it.

## Motivate Yourself to Read

You might be like many people who enjoy reading for its own sake. If so, you will not have much of a problem with motivating yourself to read, most of the time anyway. Not all reading material, however, is equally stimulating, interesting, or entertaining. Sometimes you must read something that is difficult or that you find uninteresting. In such situations, regardless of how much you might usually enjoy reading, you find yourself putting off the chore.

When you do this, you make the reading assignment increasingly difficult to begin. What little positive motivation you had at first declines each time you delay starting the task. Eventually, the only motivation you will feel is the negative motivation that comes from guilt, desperation, and anxiety. These feelings are really irritants rather than motivators. You will perform worse when reacting to irritants than when reacting to motivators.

If you have clarified your purpose, you have taken a big step toward motivating yourself to read even those difficult assignments. Whatever you do, you must have a good reason for doing it. The clearer and more specific the purpose, the higher your motivation. And the more difficult the reading assignment, the greater the need for a clear purpose. Having a clear purpose for reading will make the task seem easier.

In addition to clarifying your purpose for reading, you can take other steps to motivate yourself.

**Challenge Yourself to Read Every Day.** Last-minute reading is frustrating and not rewarding. If you have all week to finish reading a difficult assignment that you have been dreading, make yourself read a little of it each day. The accomplishment of having read one day will motivate you to read again the next day. Near the end of the week, instead of looking desperately at an increasingly difficult reading task, you will be looking triumphantly at an almost completed difficult task.

**Work with a Classmate.** Set a date with a classmate to discuss the assignment or to quiz each other before the class or test. This early deadline will give you extra motivation. Also, knowing that someone else expects you to complete the reading by a certain time will encourage you to study.

**Alternate Your Reading Material.** If focusing your attention is a problem, read one thing for a while and then stop and read something else. For example, read a few pages of material you find difficult or uninteresting. Summarize it for yourself, then switch to another assignment. Just be sure to keep returning periodically to the difficult assignment until it is completed.

**Reward Yourself.** Promise yourself a reward for whenever you complete a demanding reading assignment ahead of time. Think of some of the things you do to put off reading—taking a walk, snacking, making phone calls. Use these as rewards for completing an assignment.

As you become more effective, reading may very well become its own reward.

## Use Knowledge You Already Have

Take a few minutes before you start a reading assignment to think about your existing knowledge of the subject. If you do this, you will understand and remember the material you read.

Say that you have been studying word processing, and you have read about moving text within a document. Now you are beginning a chapter on copying text. Remembering the steps involved in moving text will help you more easily understand what you read about copying text.

> ▶ Andy was dismayed when he looked at his reading assignment for his course on using electronic spreadsheets. Just thumbing through the textbook, he saw so many new terms and concepts that he felt he could never understand what he was reading. "I'll never master this," he complained to his friend Brett. "Look at all these terms and concepts, range format, logical operators, cell

addresses, macros, @ (at) functions. What the heck is an @ function? It's too much!"

"Take it easy," Brett said." I don't know what an @ function is either, but we'll find out. But we do know what a paper spreadsheet looks like. It has all those rows and columns. I bet a cell is where a row and column meet."

"Hey, you could be right," Andy said. "And the address could be row and column numbers, like row 2, column 3."

"Sure, something like that," Brett agreed. "And we have learned to create macros in word processing. A macro is just a bunch of commands you put together to run automatically. I bet spreadsheet macros work sort of the same way."

"Now that I think of it," Andy said, "we talked about logical operators once in a math class. They're things like the greater than and less than symbols. Do you suppose they are used in electronic spreadsheets?"

"I bet they are," Brett said.

"You know, quite a bit of this stuff does look familiar," Andy said. "I don't think it will be that difficult after all."

---

By reviewing what he already knew, Andy identified several things that helped him to understand what he was reading as he began to study electronic spreadsheeting.

When you review what you already know, you help yourself to identify what it is you do not know and need to learn. In his case, Andy knew he still must learn about the @ functions as well as what a range format was. Thinking about what you do know in relation to what you are learning will give you a base upon which to build an understanding of the new material.

## PREVIEW YOUR READING

Before jumping in and reading every word, take a few minutes to preview the material. You preview reading material to obtain an idea of the topics covered, their relative importance, and where each is found in the text. Previewing is an important step when reading. Previewing prepares you to understand the material when you read it later in depth.

Previewing involves two steps:

1. Preview the organization to learn the presentation of the material.
2. Skim the content to familiarize yourself with the points that are covered.

### Preview the Organization

Whether you are going to read an entire book, just a chapter, or an article in a magazine, knowing how the topic is organized helps you understand what you read. If you are going to read a chapter or part of a chapter, then preview only that section. Look at the headings within the section to get an idea of what topics you will be reading about.

If you are going to read most or all of a book, then you have more to preview. At the beginning of each course, you should get in the habit of previewing the entire textbook for the course.

Look over the textbook. Pick it up. Look at the cover. Turn it around. Look at the back cover. Thumb through it. How many pages does it have? How many chapters? Are there a lot of illustrations? You cannot judge a book by its cover, but taking a few seconds to familiarize yourself with the book's appearance gives you a rough idea of what to expect. Think about the title and, if there is one, the subtitle.

### Know the Elements of the Book

Next look at the other elements of the book. The table of contents shows you if the chapters are grouped into larger units. Are there other helpful elements, such as a glossary, bibliography, or index? Knowing the elements of a book will help you to preview effectively. The following sections describe the elements of a book. Look at these elements when previewing a book.

**Title page**—This tells you the title, subtitle, and the name of the author or authors of the book.
**Copyright page**—This shows you the copyright year, the year the book was published.
**Table of contents**—It gives chapter titles and the page numbers on which they start. Sometimes chapters are grouped in parts or units by themes, which have their own titles. Textbooks often have detailed tables of contents. In addition to titles, they list headings and subheadings that appear in chapters. Look at a table of contents to get an idea of the topics covered.
**Introduction or preface**—Most books have an introduction, and many have a preface. They are essentially the same. In them, the book's purpose is explained. Both these elements come in the front of the book. Often only a few pages long, they are worth a quick review.
**Body of the book**—This is the main text.
**Illustrations and tables**—Illustrations could be photographs or drawings, with captions to explain something about them. Tables are used to present figures or text in columns so that they can be easily understood and relationships easily seen.

**End-of-chapter material**—End-of-chapter material is some form of activity at the end of chapters. These activities may be questions or review material. Many textbooks have a section called a *summary* at the end of chapters. A summary briefly reviews and lists the main points of the chapter.

**Glossary**—A glossary is a list of unfamiliar or specialized words used in the text with their definitions. In textbooks, words to appear in the glossary are usually in boldface **like this** in the body of the book so they stand out. When you spot an unfamiliar word, check the glossary, which usually comes immediately after the last page of text.

**Index**—An index is an alphabetical list of all the topics in the book and the numbers of the pages on which they are found. The index is often the last element in the book.

**Appendix**—Some books will have an appendix (or several appendixes) containing additional information about some matter the book touches on. The author did not consider the material of primary importance, but felt it could contribute to one's understanding. Appendixes appear before the index.

**Bibliography**—A bibliography is a list of reference materials, such as books or magazine articles, that the author used in preparing the text. It can be a useful source for additional research. Bibliographies may appear at the end of each chapter or at the end of the book.

**Footnotes**—Books often have footnotes carrying either additional information or the source of the information. They are at the bottom of the page on which the material appears, or they are grouped at the end of the chapter.

**Typographical clues**—Textbooks use *typography* to help you understand the material. Typography refers to the appearance of the words. You read above that words in the text that appear in the glossary are in **boldface**. That is a typographical clue. Foreign words or those with special meaning are often in **italics**, which look *like this*. Another typographical clue is underlining like this. Using all CAPITAL letters is another typographical clue indicating importance. These are all ways the author has of calling your attention to a point. Be aware of them.

## Use Skimming Techniques

Skimming is an easy way to familiarize yourself with the content of the material you are about to read: what it has to offer, how it is organized, what its main points are. You can learn a lot from skimming, and it will enrich your understanding when you do your in-depth reading. Here is how to skim effectively.

**Look at the elements of the material you are about to read.**
Note chapter titles and headings. Develop an idea of where things are—how the material is organized. Do this for the whole textbook the first time you prepare to read it even if your assignment is to read only the first chapter. Skimming helps you to see how each chapter fits into the overall picture.

**Next, skim the assigned chapters**. Read only headings within the chapter: section titles, paragraph headlines, and so forth. Then read the first and last paragraphs or the summary. First paragraphs usually give an overview of what the chapter covers. Last paragraphs often sum up the major points of the chapter. You might also skim again the chapter you read last to see how it relates to the one you are about to read.

**Now look at elements set off from the text.** These are graphs, charts, photographs, art, tables, and lists. In textbooks, this material provides you with information as well as making the pages look interesting.

**Look for clues of importance and relationships**. What seems important? (One topic gets a page, another one only a paragraph.) Look for relationships. (Why does the author talk about the discovery of oil in this chapter on whaling? Because when petroleum came along, people stopped needing whale oil.) Look for the typographical clues—**boldface**, *italics*, and underlining—to discover important words and ideas. Look for familiar words or ideas to relate to lectures or other reading.

**Take brief notes while skimming**. As you skim, write down questions that occur to you, points that seem important, key words to suggest facts that you need to learn. The things you jot down can become lists of facts to learn. As you skim, begin an outline for study purposes. You will learn about making outlines later.

**Avoid spending too much time skimming**. About 15 or 20 minutes should be enough for every two hours you expect to spend on careful reading. While skimming, do not get bogged down in details. Do not try to answer every question that occurs to you. Do that as you read and study. By skimming first, you will know *what* to study, and that will make your reading more profitable.

## FOCUS YOUR ATTENTION

You focus your attention on reading by identifying and overcoming reading obstacles. Common reading obstacles include inattention, procrastination, and distractions. You can apply specific techniques to overcome these obstacles.

### Overcome Inattention

Have you ever read a book that was almost impossible to put down—a mystery, or thriller, or an exciting biography? When you read for pleasure, you choose books that interest you. Perhaps most of your school reading will also be of interest to you. Unfortunately, you may also have reading assignments you find uninteresting.

The temptation is great to let your mind wander while you are reading something that is not interesting to you. When you feel your mind beginning to wander, think of your purpose for reading. If you have clarified your purpose before beginning to read, as you learned in the previous chapter, you have done a lot to motivate yourself.

The greater your motivation, the less likely your mind is to wander. When your mind does begin to wander, it is relatively easy to bring your attention back if you know what your specific purpose for reading is. If necessary, write your purpose on a piece of paper and keep it near as you read. Before beginning to read, ask yourself the same questions you could ask when clarifying your purpose:

> *Am I reading to gain knowledge to pass a test?*
> *Am I reading to gain a second viewpoint on a topic?*
> *Am I trying to gain specific knowledge or learn a new skill? If so, What knowledge? What skill?*

Then focus your attention for the time it takes to locate and record the information you need to achieve your purpose.

---

▶ Marta was having difficulty focusing her attention on the chapter on electronic office procedures. She enjoyed the course overall, but this week the class was studying information management systems, which did not interest her. Her mind kept wandering as she tried to read about procedures for storing and retrieving files. "Why am I reading this?" she wondered idly. But the idle question made her think seriously about her purpose for reading.

Although her career plans did not include managing information systems, she sees herself as an administrative assistant and perhaps someday an office manager. She realized that the more she knew about how an office operates, the better she could do her work. Thinking further, she knew she wanted to get a good grade in this course because it was a basic one in her field of study. She knew the instructor gave quizzes on the assigned reading, and the results were a considerable portion of the overall grade for the course.

"Right," she told herself as she recalled her purpose for reading. "I'm going to concentrate on the main points to be sure I understand and remember them so that I will do well on the quiz."

She used her preview and skimming skills to determine the main points and was able to focus her attention to achieve her purpose.

When a task does not interest you, it looms as an unending chore. By having a goal and a purpose, you know the task will end when you achieve your purpose. The "unending" task becomes less overwhelming.

### Overcome Procrastination

Putting off a task never makes it easier. Students who procrastinate leave themselves less time to read and review. The technique of previewing or skimming will often help you get started. If, after previewing or skimming, you still find it hard to begin, try this:

- Read and highlight the first sentence of each paragraph in your assignment. This will help you to break a long assignment into smaller chunks. When you have done this, you have also completed part of your assignment. You have, in a sense, tricked yourself into beginning.

- Tell yourself you will spend just 10 minutes to get started. At the end of the 10 minutes, think about when you will work on this material again. You might find yourself becoming interested in the material and moving ahead with it.

### Overcome Distractions

Focusing on a reading assignment is difficult while other things compete for your attention. It is hard to concentrate on a text if the television is on, the radio is blaring, or you are uncomfortable.

- Remove or limit distractions as much as possible while reading. Turn off the TV and the radio. If you study better with the radio on, tune in to a nondistracting station.

- Sit in a place where you are comfortable and where your study tools are available.

- Be sure you have adequate light for reading.

### Create Mental Images

Create a mental image of the words on the page as you read. If you are reading about computers, picture working at the computer, performing the functions you are reading about. If you are studying telephone techniques, imagine yourself in an office situation using those skills.

### Highlight Your Text

Highlighting means to mark key words, phrases, and main ideas by underlining, using a marker pen, or circling. (Do this only if you own the book, of course.) Do not get carried away and mark everything—just the most important information. If you repeatedly refer to a section, highlight the page heading and information.

### Take Notes While You Read

As you read, jot down the important points of the text. If you are reading for specific information, such as a date or a name, make a note of it when you have found it. If you are reading for more information, use notes, outlines, and diagrams to help you retain it. Diagrams could be simply words and connecting lines arranged to show relationships clearly. (For more on effective note taking, see Chapter 7.)

## MONITOR YOURSELF

You have now focused your attention and have settled into your reading. But are you really involved in what you are reading? How good is your comprehension of what you are reading? When you have completed the assignment, will you be able to remember the important parts of it? Here are some strategies to help you do this.

Monitor your progress as you read. You can do this by developing and following a procedure for reading. The procedure builds upon and is a continuation of the steps you took to prepare yourself for reading. Those steps were clarifying your reading purpose, motivating yourself, using knowledge you already have, and previewing and skimming.

Having prepared yourself to read, follow these strategies to monitor yourself to ensure that you are achieving your purpose.

### Make Connections

As you read, think of how what you are reading relates to your past knowledge of this subject. If you are learning how to move a block of text in word processing, you must remember how to select or highlight the text you want to move. Quickly review what you know about selecting or highlighting text.

Is the subject completely new to you, one that you have never read about or heard of before? The chances are that even if you have never read about it, you have heard something about it on TV, in a movie, or from a friend. If this is the case, you may have remembered incomplete or incorrect information. Do not ignore what you think you know. It is better to bring it forth. You can then compare it to what you are now reading and decide whether it is correct or whether it is wrong and should be discarded.

If you have a conflict between what you thought you knew and what you are now reading, seek a solution. Ask your instructor about it. Learning involves not only acquiring new ideas and information but discarding wrong information and clarifying unclear information.

### Summarize and Paraphrase

During reading, take advantage of natural breaks in the material to summarize what you have just read. Paraphrase, or repeat to yourself in your own words, the main ideas of what you have just read.

### Make Up Questions

You know from experience that instructors use tests to determine how much students have learned. You do not need to wait until the instructor gives you an exam to determine how much you have learned. Give yourself tests as you read. You can create minitests for yourself easily in one of two ways.

1. After previewing and skimming the assigned reading, change some of the titles and headings into questions. Titles and headings usually suggest what the main points are.
2. As you read, write down at least one question for each major section.

So you can use the questions later and know what section they refer to, always identify the reading assignment, section heading, and page number on the paper with your questions. Number your pages also.

After reading the assignment, see if you can answer the questions you have raised. Asking good questions in itself is a good learning technique. You may discover you have asked yourself the same questions that appear on an exam.

▶ Roberta was studying WordPerfect. Her assignment this night is to read the chapter on Search and Replace. Some headings she sees are *Search and Replace, Search and Replace Options, Case Agreement*. She turned these into questions: *What does search and replace do? Why is search and replace useful? What are the search and replace options? How many are there? What does case agreement mean? What does it have to do with search and replace?*

By asking these questions, Roberta is building on the steps she took when she was preparing to read. She is more sharply focusing her purpose.

Roberta also jots down questions as she reads. She reads these sentences in her textbook: *When you use the Search and Replace feature, the text you key in at the Search prompt is considered a string. WordPerfect will search for the string, no matter what comes immediately before or after. In some situations, searching for a string can cause problems; in others, it can reduce the number of search and replaces required.*

As she reads this, Roberta writes down the questions, *In what way can searching for a string cause problems? How can it help?* When she can answer the questions without looking at the text, she knows she has mastered the material.

### Recite Aloud

As you read, talk to yourself, preferably out loud if you can. Ask yourself questions, and answer them out loud. Actually speaking the words makes you think more clearly about them. Hearing yourself say the words helps you realize whether you have in fact mastered the material or just have a vague idea about it. Only thinking the words sometimes fools you into believing you have mastered the material.

### Reread

Unless what you are reading is very simple or is something you are already familiar with, you will often have to reread. The more difficult the material, the more essential rereading or reviewing is. Review your notes and your questions. Reread sections that remain unclear.

### Predict What the Author Will Write Next

After summarizing, think ahead to what the author will write next about the topic. Your preview and skimming techniques give you the tools to predict what will come next as you read.

## OVERHAUL YOUR READING

If you seem unable to grasp what you are reading, you might need to make some adjustments in how you read.

### Adjust Your Reading Speed

Reading either too fast or too slowly can prevent you from understanding the material. It is pointless to read something fast if afterward you have not retained anything. If you have been reading quickly and find you are not understanding or retaining the material, slow down. Take time to practice the techniques above.

If you have been reading too slowly, on the other hand, you may lower your understanding level by losing track of the main idea from one sentence to another. Do not dwell on every word or sentence. Sometimes you may need to push on even if you do not fully understand. Rereading and reviewing are important in this situation.

The point is for you to find your natural reading speed.

### Read Creatively

When reading difficult material, you will have to read creatively. One way to do this is to break the material down so as to examine its parts to see what each part does and how it contributes to the overall meaning. Here is an illustration of reading creatively. First, read the following paragraph, which defines creative thinking.

The *Longman Dictionary of Psychology and Psychiatry* defines creative thinking in this way:

> *The mental processes leading to a new invention, solution, or synthesis in any area. A creative solution may use preexisting objects or ideas but creates a new relationship between the elements it utilizes. New mechanical inventions, social techniques, scientific theories, and artistic creations are examples of creative thinking.*

Now break down the paragraph into its sentences to get the meaning of each and to see how each relates to the others. It has three sentences. The first provides the definition of creative thinking. The second builds on the basic definition by further defining *creative solution*. The third sentence gives examples of outcomes of creative thinking.

The first sentence tells you something you already know: creative thinking is a mental process. It also tells you that creative thinking leads to new inventions, solutions, or synthesis. This more or less repeats—in different words—the definition of creative thinking you read in the Unit 1 introduction.

If you do not understand a sentence, break it down into its individual parts—phrases and words. One word—*synthesis*—in this sentence may be unfamiliar to you. When you meet an unfamiliar word, try to determine its meaning from the other words and sentences. If that does not work, refer to a dictionary. Always confirm your understanding of the word by checking a dictionary.

The second sentence makes an important point: you may use "preexisting objects or ideas" in creative thinking. Thus, you relate the facts and knowledge you already have to each other and to newly acquired facts to reach a conclusion. Use existing knowledge to help you understand new information. In this example, you used the knowledge you had of the definition for creative thinking given in the unit introduction. You realized both were saying essentially the same thing in different words. This is an important insight that will help you read creatively: different authors say the same things in different words.

The third sentence gives examples of conclusions of creative thinking. As noted, this definition of creative thinking is from a dictionary used by professionals and is precise and narrow. It focuses on new inventions and artistic creations, such as a novel or a painting, as examples of creative thinking.

After deciding that you understand what you have read, try to restate it in your own words.

## Continue Reading

If you continue to have trouble with a particular section, go on to the next section. The next section might clear up your confusion. You may also find it helpful to read about the topic in another book.

## Seek Help

Finally, if you cannot master a section, talk it over with a classmate. Write down questions about what you do not understand to ask the instructor. Often, you will find that writing down what puzzles you will help you to understand it.

## SUMMING UP

To read effectively and efficiently, you should prepare yourself for reading. The four techniques for preparing to read are:

1. Clarify your reading purpose.
2. Motivate yourself to read.
3. Use the knowledge you already have.
4. Preview what you are going to read.

Once you know your general purpose or reason, you should clarify your specific purpose for completing a reading assignment. The more specifically you can state your purpose, the more effective your reading will be. By clarifying your purpose, you take a big step toward motivating yourself to read even difficult assignments.

You can motivate yourself to read by challenging yourself to read every day, working with a classmate, alternating your reading material, and rewarding yourself.

Before you begin a reading assignment, think about what you already know about the subject. This will help you understand and remember the new material you read.

Before beginning to read, take a few minutes to preview the material. Look over the material to see how it is organized, and then skim the contents. Previewing is an important step when reading textbooks. Previewing a book prepares you to understand it.

Skimming is an easy way to familiarize yourself with a book's content: what it has to offer, how it is organized, and what its main points are.

To skim effectively you read the material's title, heads, and the first and last paragraphs. Look at the illustrations and for clues of importance and relationships, such as typographical clues. Take brief notes while skimming. Do not spend too much time skimming.

Strategies for focusing your attention include overcoming inattention; overcoming procrastination; overcoming distractions; creating mental images; highlighting your text; and taking notes while you read.

To monitor yourself while reading, make connections; summarize and paraphrase; make up questions about what you are reading; recite your questions and answers out loud; reread, and try to predict what the author will write next.

If you have difficulty in reading, you may need to adjust how you read. Reading either too fast or too slowly can hurt your ability to understand what you are reading. The main thing is to find your natural, comfortable reading speed.

Read creatively by breaking down sections of difficult text into smaller pieces to make them understandable.

Finally, seek help if you cannot master a section. Talk it over with a classmate. Write down your questions to ask the instructor. Simply writing down what puzzles you might help you understand it.

## ▼ DEVELOPING YOUR SKILLS

Exercise 1

### Define Your Purpose For Reading

Look at your reading assignment for your next class. On the lines below, write your general purpose for reading the assignment and one or two specific purposes.

_____

_____

_____

_____

_____

_____

Exercise 2

### Motivate Yourself to Read

Evaluate your own levels of motivation by answering the following questions. Write Yes or No on the lines at the end of each question.

- Do I begin reading assignments as soon as they are assigned?____

- Do I complete reading assignments before the class or the test day?____

- Do I read until I have accomplished my purpose?____

- Do I read every day?____

- Do I discuss my reading with a classmate?____

Have you answered No to any of these questions? If so, consider what you must do to change your answer to Yes. On the lines on the next page, write down motivation strategies to practice this week.

_____

_____

_____

Exercise 3

**Prepare to Read a Textbook**

Look at your reading assignment for your next class. What do you already know about this topic? Review your class notes, your reading notes, or the highlighting you did in the text. Write down two facts that you already know about the topic before you read the assignment. After reading, go back to these facts. Did you expand on this knowledge? Did making these connections in advance help you understand and remember your reading?

Exercise 4

**Know Your Textbook**

Examine one of your textbooks from another class, and write your answers to the questions on the lines provided. If a question is not applicable, write NA.

1. What is the title?

   _____

2. Who wrote this book?

   _____

3. What is the copyright year?

   _____

4. How many main parts does this textbook have?

   _____

5. How many chapters are in this textbook?

   _____

6. Which part has the most chapters?

   _____

7. Which part has the fewest chapters?

   _____

8. About how long are the chapters?

   _____

9. Does the textbook have an introduction or preface?

   _____

10. Can you identify the main purpose of the textbook from the preface? What is it?

    _____

11. Do the pages in the body of the book have illustrations, photographs, or diagrams?

    _____

12. Are the chapters divided into sections or lessons? How long are these sections?

    _____

13. Do the section titles give you clues to the content?

    _____

14. Are there questions for discussion and review at the end of each chapter?

    _____

15. Using the questions at the end of one chapter, describe a specific purpose for reading that chapter.

   _____

16. If there is a glossary, list six terms from it that are new to you. Find where these six terms are discussed in the text by looking in the index for their page numbers. List the page numbers.

   _____

   _____

17. Now look in the text for these six terms. On what page is each one first mentioned? Does the text give you a typographical clue that this is a new, important term?

   _____

   _____

18. Skim the bibliography of the textbook. Have you read any of the books or periodicals? If so, list them.

   _____

   _____

   _____

   _____

## Exercise 5

### Skim a Book

Find a book on a topic you would like to learn more about. It may be a topic you are already familiar with, but the book should be one you have not seen or used. Relying on your knowledge of your own reading speed, select a portion that you think would take you about two hours to read. Use a timer or an alarm clock; set it for 15 minutes. Skim the part you selected using the methods described in this chapter. At the end of your 15 minutes, review your notes.

- What elements did you identify?

___

- Do you have a sense of what you just read and how it fits with what you already know about the subject? Describe briefly what you learned.

___

- Did you identify the basic ideas? What are they?

___

Exercise 6

## Overcome Reading Obstacles

In the left column, list five obstacles to reading you face most often. In the right column, list strategies to overcome these obstacles.

| Obstacles | Strategies |
|---|---|
| _____ | _____ |
| _____ | _____ |
| _____ | _____ |
| _____ | _____ |
| _____ | _____ |
| _____ | _____ |
| _____ | _____ |
| _____ | _____ |
| _____ | _____ |
| _____ | _____ |
| _____ | _____ |
| _____ | _____ |
| _____ | _____ |
| _____ | _____ |
| _____ | _____ |
| _____ | _____ |

Exercise 7

## Apply Reading Techniques

Apply these reading techniques to the paragraphs below on telemarketing.

- Highlight the key words and phrases.

- Briefly describe a mental image you created while reading. Write your description on a separate sheet of paper.

- Relate the passage to other information you know about this topic.

- Summarize, in your own words, the main idea of the selection. Write your summary on a separate sheet of paper.

- Predict what the next section of text might be about. Write your prediction on a separate sheet of paper.

### In-House Telemarketing

Any company whose telemarketing operation calls for repeated, ongoing phone contact with the same customers will usually choose to set up its telemarketing operation in-house. This allows management to supervise the telemarketing project firsthand.

Some types of companies that would be likely to use an in-house operation would be insurance companies, banks, mail-order firms, manufacturers of appliances, and credit card companies.

In-house telemarketing operations are sometimes called **inside sales**. This term distinguishes them from **outside sales**, in which people make sales and service calls on the outside. The term "inside sales," however, includes other salespeople besides those in telemarketing, for example, retail sales clerks. Therefore "in-house telemarketing" is used for activities exclusive to telemarketing.

An in-house telemarketing operation may not have a specific location and separate department within a company, but does have a specific telemarketing operation plan and organization.

In-house telemarketing operations vary in size, from one person making and/or receiving calls at a desk in a general office, to a special telemarketing department with its own room(s) filled with people in sound-proof telemarketing stations (also called **telemods**) using the latest telecommunication equipment.

Adapted from *Basic Telemarketing* by Mary D. Pekas, Paradigm Publishing International, 1990, page 7.

Exercise 8

## Practice Reading Strategies

Read the following selection, applying the techniques you have learned in this lesson. When you are finished, answer the questions that follow.

**CHAPTER 27: MERGE DOCUMENTS**

Have you ever received a letter from a company marketing a new product? The letter seems to be addressed to you personally. Your name and address are listed on the letter, the salutation includes your name, and the body of the letter may mention something about you—the city in which you live, the state, or other information. Even though the letter seems to be addressed just to you, it was probably sent to hundreds or thousands of other households.

**Creating A Personalized Form Letter**

Creating a personalized form letter requires two documents. One document contains the form letter with identifiers showing where variable information (information that changes with each letter) is to be inserted. WordPerfect calls this the *primary file*. The other document, which WordPerfect calls the *secondary* file, contains the variable information.

The first thing to do is design the letter, a task which includes determining variable information.

The date, body of the letter, and the signature block are standard. The variable information—information that will change with each letter—is the name, address, city, state, zip code, and salutation.

**Determining Fields**

In a form letter, the variable information must be broken into sections called *fields* and identified with a special command. To determine the variable fields, you must decide how the information will be used and in what form. As an example, let's look at a family that belongs to the PTA.

> Mr. and Mrs. Jon Johanssen
> 124 East Main
> Selma, WA 98344

The name, "Mr. and Mrs. Jon Johanssen," could be identified as an entire field, but the salutation for this family should read "Dear Mr. and Mrs. Johanssen." If the name is left as one field, the salutation would read "Dear Mr. and Mrs. Jon Johanssen" (which isn't bad, but not completely correct). In this example, then, the name should be broken into three fields: title ("Mr. and Mrs."), first name, and last name. There is no need for the street address to be broken into smaller parts. Therefore, it can be identified as one field.

The city, state, and zip code can also be considered as one field. However, if you decide that you need the city or state name separated, you would need to make separate fields for each item.

After all fields have been determined, the next step is to determine field numbers. WordPerfect inserts variable data based on field numbers. Let's look at one way the field names in this example can be assigned numbers.

| | |
|---|---|
| Title | Field 1 |
| First name | Field 2 |
| Last name | Field 3 |
| Street address | Field 4 |
| City, state, zip code | Field 5 |

You may want to write this information on a piece of paper. When you create documents with a large number of fields, it becomes difficult to remember what is contained in each.

*A Mastery Approach to WordPerfect Version 5.0*, by Nita Hewitt Rutkosky, Paradigm Publishing International, 1989, pages 355 to 357.

Were there unfamiliar words in the text? List them and their definitions on a separate sheet of paper.

On a separate sheet of paper, summarize the main points of the selection.

List below the reading strategies you applied most often.

_____

_____

_____

_____

_____

List below the reading strategies you need to practice.

_____

_____

_____

_____

_____

# 7 Taking Reading Notes

**When you have completed this chapter, you will be able to take notes that organize and help you remember what you have read.**

You remember and understand more of what you read when you take notes. This happens because, by taking notes, you actively involve yourself in the reading. You are not reading passively. You use your critical thinking skills to select the important points and your creative thinking skills to put them into your own words. In this chapter, you will learn strategies for taking notes when reading textbooks and supplemental material. These represent the two kinds of reading you do as a student.

Your note-taking strategies as well as the kinds of notes you take will vary according to the type and purpose of the reading you do. You will learn of five different types of notes.

## NOTE TAKING FROM TEXTBOOKS

Information in textbooks is organized to aid the reader in learning. Thus, you often can take fewer notes when reading a textbook than when reading reference books or books written for professionals. Your main goal as you take notes while reading a textbook is *understanding* what you read. Your goal is not simply copying main points and facts for the sake of remembering them, although that is part of it.

To understand something, you must remember the facts about it. Memorization without understanding, however, is not learning. Without understanding, you cannot put to use facts you have memorized. A goal of learning is to be able to put what you know to use. This is true when you read and study a manual on automotive mechanics. It is equally true when you read and study a textbook on office procedures. Taking notes is part of the process of developing understanding. Here are strategies for taking notes that will help you understand as well as remember.

- **Rephrase the points**. As you write points down, put them into your own words.

- **Make note of questions**. Get answers to these questions by figuring them out yourself or by asking a classmate or the instructor.

- **Look for relationships or apparent contradictions**. Look for relationships among bits of new information as well as between them and what you have learned in class. Look for contradictions, such as "this goes against our instructor's information about . . . ," which you can clear up in class.

- **Prepare an outline for classroom discussion**. (See the section on outlining later in this chapter for how to do it.)

## NOTE TAKING FROM OTHER SOURCES

Supplemental material includes magazine articles or chapters from other books, usually reference or professional books. These materials can usually be found at the library. This additional material supports topics covered in the textbook and lectures. Often instructors will assign selected pages, not entire works.

Note taking from supplemental readings can be more demanding than note taking from texts because of the absence of the study-tool features that are found in textbooks. Unlike textbooks, supplemental reading often will be organized and written for someone already familiar with the subject. It is unlikely that you will find review questions. There usually will be headings and subheadings to help you locate important points. And there may be footnotes, a bibliography, and an index. Here are strategies for note taking while reading supplemental material.

- Be sure to read all assigned pages. Ask yourself why those pages were selected and how they add to what you are reading and studying in the textbook and learning in the classroom.

    *Do they present another point of view?*
    *Do they give another illustration or example?*
    *Do they go into greater detail on certain topics?*

- Take enough notes. Be sure you have covered the main points and will understand them later. This is important because the source might not be easily available for a second reading.

- Mark all your notes clearly with their sources. Include title, author, and page number at least, and possibly publisher and copyright date in case you have to find something again.

## USING DIFFERENT TYPES OF NOTES

The notes you take as you read can fall into five main groups.

1. Summaries and paraphrases of reading material.
2. Lists of key words or phrases.
3. Outlines.
4. Picture notes (diagrams, charts, and so forth).
5. Questions in the margin.

There is no one right type of notes for any given reading assignment. Use the one that suits your purpose and abilities. If listing a few key points is all you need to help you to remember and understand what you read, fine. If you find putting the material into your own words is necessary for understanding, do so. You will probably use all five types of notes in combination.

When reading new, difficult material, you will benefit most by summarizing and putting material into your own words. When reading for a general idea or preparing for a discussion, you will most likely jot down main points and questions. When looking for relationships, especially among many thoughts or items, using outlines and diagrams is most helpful.

### Summary Notes

To take summary notes, you review each major section and then write the major point mostly in your own words. Summarize major sections and secondary points if your major summary does not include them. Summarizing means to paraphrase and use a combination of your own words and those in the book. Do not write word for word what you read. Doing so is not as effective for understanding and remembering as is analyzing and interpreting while reading, and then summarizing.

Use creative thinking to summarize in your own words and use critical thinking to compare your words with the original text to be sure your words accurately reflect the meaning.

Summarizing provides immediate feedback. If you are unable to paraphrase points in mostly your own words, you know right away that you are not understanding the material. So you reread and write questions to ask the instructor or a classmate for clarification later. When summarizing, write down complete ideas, not just key words. Read the passage below and the example of summary notes.

> **Alienation**
> A kind of dissatisfaction characteristic of our industrial society is called alienation. Two kinds of alienation have been identified: alienation from work and alienation from fellow human beings. Alienation from work, a concept popularized by Karl Marx, is a product of modern assembly-line production processes. Assembly-line methods break work down into small, efficient tasks, but these tasks are meaningless and boring to the workers, who do not see the end result of their efforts. Not seeing or feeling part of the end result of their labors causes workers to feel alienated from their work. This situation was graphically shown by Charlie Chaplin in his classic film *Modern Times*. It is difficult for most workers to use their full potential when their work consists of tightening up 16 nuts on an assembly line or slapping labels on bottles hundreds of times a day. Workers cannot experience a sense of accomplishment when they feel like insignificant, replaceable cogs in a machine.
>
> The other kind of alienation, a concept popularized by Sigmund Freud, is also a by-product of industrialization: alienation from fellow human beings. The average worker changes jobs once every 4 years, and in any given year, a fourth of all workers change jobs. As a consequence, relationships with fellow workers, friends, neighbors, and even family are lessened and fleeting.
>
> Adapted from *Psychology: Human Relations and Work Adjustment*, 7th ed., by Rene V. Dawis, Rosemary T. Fruehling, and Neild B. Oldham, McGraw-Hill, 1989, pages 293-294.

**Summary Notes on Alienation**
Alienation: dissatisfaction felt in industrial society.

Two kinds of alienation:
1. Alienation from work. This happens because workers do not see the end result of their efforts.
2. Alienation from fellow people. Because people move around a lot, they have weaker relationships with family, friends, and neighbors.

As you see, these notes record the two kinds of alienation with a brief definition of each. If your instructor stresses major figures in the field, then it would be a good idea to record the names of Karl Marx and Sigmund Freud next to the concepts with which they are associated. Notice that the notes paraphrase, not repeat word for word, the passage. Also see how complete ideas are recorded, not just key words.

## Key-Words Notes

You do not need to summarize or take notes on every sentence you read. Some sentences contain essential information; others consist of secondary information, helpful to illustrate a point or clarify an explanation. While reading, you must make conscious decisions on what is essential information. In other words, use your critical-thinking skills. To help yourself do this, list what you think are the main points. Summarize when you think it is necessary.

Listing key words and phrases helps you remember and understand. When you have summarized material, these lists will be excellent to study when you prepare for exams or class discussions. Here is a passage from the same text, followed by notes using key words.

> JOBS AND TEMPERAMENT
> The *Handbook for Analyzing Jobs* defines 10 categories of temperaments that can be associated with particular kinds of work.
> **Directing and Planning.** This temperament accepts responsibility for the activities of others. People with this temperament are found in the ranks of professionals such as architects, teachers, business and project managers.
> **Influencing.** The temperament to influence others is right for jobs that require motivating, convincing, or negotiating with others, such as salespeople, lobbyists, and group leaders.
> **Performing Under Stress.** People with this temperament are able to handle emergencies and critical, unusual, or dangerous situations. These people are found in such careers as deep sea divers, flight attendants, fire fighters, animal trainers, and racing car drivers.

> **Key-Words Notes on Jobs and Temperament**
> 10 temperaments associated with specific kinds of work:
> Directing and Planning
> Influencing
> Performing Under Stress

The complete notes will include all 10 temperaments described in the text. The note taker decides not to list examples of work associated with each temperament. It is not difficult to think up appropriate work suited for each temperament. For example, movie directors could be people with temperaments that like to direct and plan; fire fighters with temperaments that perform well under stress.

## Outline Notes

The ability to outline is a useful study skill. Outlining helps increase your understanding of the material by organizing it in a visual way. There are two kinds of outlines: key-word outlines and sentence outlines. A good key-word outline identifies essential points and shows their relationship. To develop a key-word outline, you do this:

- Identify the main points of the material.
- State each point in one or two key words.
- Identify the secondary points.
- State the secondary points in one or two key words.
- Show relationships and the relative importance of points.
- Use roman and arabic numerals and letters. (See the table on the next page for examples of the kinds of numerals.)
- Indent secondary points.

Follow the same steps for a sentence outline in which you write out the main and secondary points. You use one sentence for each point.

**Identifying main points and related secondary points** is the core of outlining. Textbooks are usually easy to outline because you can use the headings and subheadings as a guide. On average, a textbook chapter has four to six major points, each with two to four secondary points.

The lists below are the same except that in the list to the right related secondary points have been indented under major points. The indents tell you that these items are related to and part of the major heading just above them. The simple act of indenting makes the relationship and relative importance of different items stand out clearly.

<u>Office Procedures</u>
Communication
Dictation
Spoken Word
Written Correspondence
Secretarial Work
Handling Mail
Organizing Meetings
Arranging Travel
Airline Reservations
Hotel Reservations

<u>Office Procedures</u>
Communication
   Dictation
      Spoken Word
   Written Correspondence
Secretarial Work
   Handling Mail
   Organizing Meetings
   Arranging Travel
      Airline Reservations
      Hotel Reservations

**Use numbers and letters to help you see relationships.** Below is a sample key-word outline using roman and arabic numerals and letters. It is the most common outline.

    I. Communication
      A. Dictation
      B. Spoken Word
        1. Interoffice
        2. Telephone
          a. Incoming calls
          b. Outgoing calls
        3. Presentations
      C. Written Correspondence
   II. Secretarial Work
      A. Handling Mail
      B. Organizing Meetings
      C. Arranging Travel
        1. Airline Reservations
        2. Hotel Reservations
        3. Car-Rental Arrangements

The standard roman numerals indicate major points.

Capital letters indicate secondary points.

Arabic numerals indicate the next subcategory.

The fourth level is indicated by small letters.

The fifth level would be indicated by small roman numerals.

| Roman (Standard) | Roman (Small) | Arabic | Decimals |
| --- | --- | --- | --- |
| I | i | 1 | 01.00 |
| II | ii | 2 | 02.00 |
| III | iii | 3 | 03.00 |
| IV | iv | 4 | 04.00 |
| V | v | 5 | 05.00 |
| VI | vi | 6 | 06.00 |
| VII | vii | 7 | 07.00 |
| VIII | viii | 8 | 08.00 |
| IX | ix | 9 | 09.00 |
| X | x | 10 | 10.00 |

Numerals Used in Outlines

Major points are not indented. Each sublevel is indented farther than the level immediately preceding it. The width of the indentation should be the same for similar levels. You should have at least two entries in each level. Each entry represents a different thought or aspect. Having only one entry at a level suggests you should either eliminate it or make it equal to the entry above. If it represents something different, it should be a new entry and not be included in the first entry. The first outline below is not good. The second is better.

    A. 19th century occupations
        1. 19th century tools
    B. 19th century clothing

    A. 19th century occupations
    B. 19th century tools
    C. 19th century clothing

Some outlines use only numbers with decimals. You would find this system used in technical manuals or in books about computers.

```
01.00  Communication
   01.10  Dictation
   01.20  Spoken Word
      01.21  Interoffice
      01.22  Telephone
         01.221  Incoming Calls
         01.222  Outgoing Calls
      01.23  Presentations
02.00  Secretarial Work
   02.10  Handling Mail
   02.20  Organizing Meetings
   02.30  Arranging Travel
      02.31  Airline Reservations
      02.32  Hotel Reservations
      02.33  Car-Rental Arrangements
```

## Picture Notes

Picture notes—diagrams, drawings, and charts—are effective study aids. They are not as familiar as outlines; hence, you may never have considered using them. Perhaps you have been in courses in which instructors drew diagrams on the chalkboard to illustrate an idea.

Once you try them, you will find that they help you to see relationships, connections, patterns, and sequences. A drawing can show clearly something that you did not recognize when you read the textbook or took notes. A diagram helps you see associations and put your thoughts in order. A chart helps you analyze and classify information. Diagrams, drawings, and charts are similar and the terms are often used interchangeably. They can serve somewhat different purposes and they differ from outlines in the ways shown in the table that follows.

| Outline | Key words or sentences show relative importance and relationships.<br><br>*Linear approach*—start at the top of the paper and proceed down, listing main points in succession. |
|---|---|
| Diagram | Graphics, such as straight lines, circles, and arrows, with key words, show relationships and how things work.<br><br>*Nonlinear approach*—begin at the top, in the middle, at the left side or the right side of the page. |
| Drawing | *Illustrative* representation.<br><br>*Key words* label parts. |
| Chart | *Major categories* organize information.<br><br>This is an example of a chart. |

The following explains different ways of creating various kinds of diagrams, drawings, and charts. Give them a try.

**Making a Drawing.** In creating a drawing, it is not necessary to be a prize-winning artist. Proportions do not have to be exact. Just make sure that you have illustrated the ideas you want to remember. If you draw a flower to help yourself remember the various parts, do not be concerned about whether it looks like a real flower. The main thing is that you can identify the parts.

- **Center it**. A good way to look at and study something with several important characteristics is to write the name of the item or the person in the center of a sheet of paper. Then write characteristics around it. If you are studying the features of a computerized office phone system, you might center the word *telephone* and surround it with the different features you are learning.

- **Sketch it**. A drawing of the parts of the computer will help you to visualize their relationship to each other. Much of the information you need to recall will be easier to remember if you have a picture of it.

**Making a Diagram.** Make diagrams that show the relationships between objects. If you are studying astronomy, make a diagram that *shows* the planets—with a bigger circle for the sun in the center. If you are studying business procedures, make a diagram with the president at the top and the lower levels of management positioned below. This form of diagram, shown above, is known as an organizational chart.

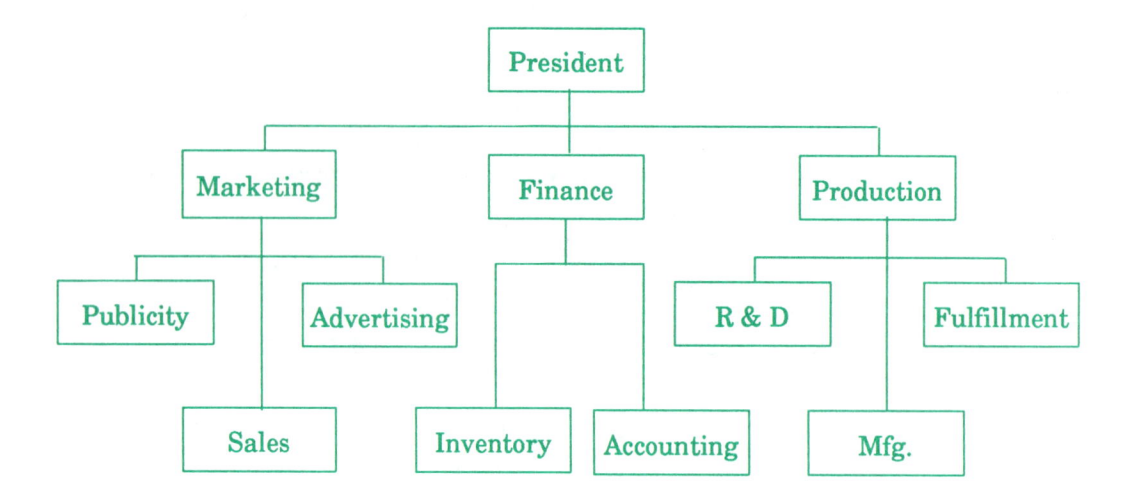

Different connecting lines, arrows, equal signs, X's, can illustrate different types of relationships.

Arrows in a diagram show sequence—the order in which things happen. In the diagram below, the arrow, the circular pattern, the

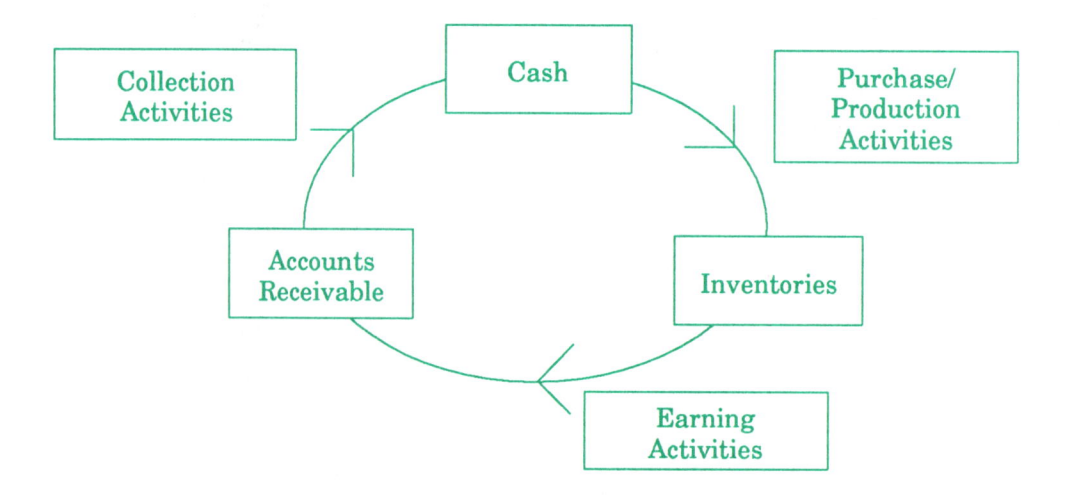

three rectangles with the notes outside the oval all help to illustrate the basic flow of finances in a business. Cash leads to inventories, which lead to accounts receivable, which lead back to cash.

Diagrams showing sequence and relationships are helpful in anything with an element of history. What came earlier; what came later? Many people have mental blocks about dates and remember them with

158—Studying Smart                                    Unit III difficulty. A diagram tracing the development of the typewriter, for example, could start with inventor Christopher Sholes in the 1800s and show each technological change in chronological order up to the typewriters used today. It would be much easier to remember all the facts and numbers if they were not buried in several long paragraphs of notes. The act of preparing a diagram also helps you clarify sequence and relationships.

Color can add another dimension to your drawings and diagrams, highlighting specific relationships. On an accounting flowchart, all collection activities could be highlighted in yellow, earning activities in blue, and so on.

Sometimes diagrams are called maps. These are not road maps, but loose, free flowing diagrams that list main points, the relation between them, and your reactions. They can be helpful in writing essays or papers.

**Making a Chart**. In creating a chart, as in making an outline, you must first decide the main points or categories, and then the secondary points and their relation to one another. Charts do not use numerals and letters but boxes, with possibly connecting lines, to set off information. The organizational chart is one example. You can use a ruler to make boxes or a computer program. Charts are usually used to compare information, while outlines usually show chronological succession.

## Questions in the Margin

Another note-taking technique is to write questions to yourself in the margin of your notes or your textbook. After reading a few paragraphs or pages, you stop and identify the most important points that you want to remember.

Then you write a question to test your knowledge about each point in the margin. Later, go back and, covering up the text or your notes, try to answer the questions that you wrote. Here is an example of how it works.

Suppose you are taking a course on forms of government and have just read this passage on socialism.

> In a socialist system of goverment most of the major industries are owned and controlled by the government. Although many businesses and industries are privately owned, the utilities, health care, transportation, and communications are publicly owned.

First you summarize the most important point to remember and write it down like this:

> *In socialist system major industries controlled by government.*

Next you write this summary as a question in the margin:

> *What does the government control in a socialist system?*

Or you might pose the question this way:

> *In what kind of system does the government control most of the major industries?*

The questions you write to yourself serve two purposes.

1. They strengthen your understanding of the important points to remember. You do not want to waste your time asking yourself unimportant questions.
2. They help you anticipate questions you will be asked on tests.

A further step in this technique can be to highlight the answers to your questions by circling them, underlining them, or using a marker pen. This helps you review more quickly because you do not have to search for the answers.

## USING A TAPE RECORDER

You will read in Chapter 9 why using a tape recorder to take notes during a lecture is a bad idea. However, using a tape recorder for taking notes when you are reading can be a good idea. Do not jump to the conclusion that using a tape recorder for taking reading notes will save you time and effort. It might, but that is not the point. And the effective use of the recorder could increase your work.

If you are in a situation where recording your notes this way is useful, try it. You will then have a tape you can listen to when reading notes is not possible, such as when riding in a car, or going to sleep . Listening to your notes just before going to sleep is a good way to learn the information.

When you record notes from reading you can apply many of the techniques used when writing them. That is, you can paraphrase, just record major points, and put the ideas in your own words. You can also record word for word what is in the text you are reading. Later, when you review and study these notes, you should try to put them into your own words. At some point after recording your notes, you must write them down when reviewing and studying.

## WORKING YOUR NOTES

Taking the notes is only the first step in effective note taking. There are two other important steps: organizing your notes and studying them.

The techniques for organizing and studying your notes are the same for both reading and listening. You will read about how to do this in Chapter 9. Do not wait until the night before the exam to work your notes.

As a final point, remember the three Bs from Chapter 1—the bus, the bath, the bed—and let your subconscious mind help you to think creatively. As you write and organize your notes, do not be afraid to let your mind wander from time to time. You may be surprised at what comes bubbling up. After struggling for hours to understand and make connections among important pieces of information, things may suddenly become clearer to you. Relaxing and letting your mind wander sometimes frees your mind for creative thinking. You must, however, first put in the effort to understand at the conscious level. Nothing comes without work.

## SUMMING UP

Taking notes makes you an active reader and helps you to retain more information. As a student, you read textbooks and supplemental material. You use both critical and creative thinking to take notes.

Taking notes is part of the process of developing understanding. Strategies for taking notes to help you remember and understand include:

- Rephrase the points.
- Refer to your lecture notes.
- Make note of questions.
- Look for relationships or apparent contradictions.
- Prepare an outline for classroom discussion.

Supplemental reading is done in sources other than your textbook. These sources include magazine articles or chapters from other books, usually reference or professional books. This additional reading supports and increases your understanding of topics covered in the textbook and lectures.

Strategies for note taking for reading supplemental material include:

- Be sure to read all assigned pages.
- Take enough notes.
- Mark all your notes clearly with their sources.

The notes you take as you read fall into five main groups:

1. Summaries and paraphrases of reading material.
2. Lists of key words or phrases.
3. Outlines.
4. Picture notes (diagrams, charts, and so on).
5. Questions in the margin.

Using a tape recorder to take notes when reading can help you study. You will have a tape to listen to at times when reading notes is not possible. When recording notes from reading, you will sometimes record word-for-word. But also use the techniques used when writing notes: paraphrase, record major points, and put the ideas in your own words.

## ▼ DEVELOPING YOUR SKILLS

Exercise 1

### Practice Paraphrasing

Read the selection below and, on a separate piece of paper, write a brief summary paraphrasing it.

> Telephoning, in a way, is a half-step between oral communication and written communication. It gives you the oral communication advantages of being able to hear vocal inflections and to respond immediately to what is said. It has the written communication disadvantage of not allowing you to observe body language. But it does enable people to communicate over great distances, just as the mail does.
>
> In addition, using a telephone means that you can demand attention without asking for it in advance. This is an advantage if you are doing the calling, but a disadvantage if you are the receiver. Perhaps you have done business with a person who is constantly interrupted by other customers calling. The telephone has thus gained a reputation of being a troublesome source of interruptions.
>
> Keeping these things in mind, when you plan to make a phone call, think through what you want to say (just as you would for any other medium); try to organize well enough that you can do all your business in one call. When you reach the person you want to talk with, ask, "Is this a good time to call?" or "Do you have a few moments now to talk?" Providing an opportunity for them to call you back later when they are less distracted will improve the chances that your message will be received clearly. Once you proceed, keep to the point and conclude your business promptly.
>
> *Psychology: Human Relations and Work Adjustment,* 7e, by Rene V. Dawis, Rosemary T. Fruehling, Neild B. Oldham. McGraw-Hill, 1989, page 238.

Exercise 2

### Practice Listing Main Points

Read the following text. On the lines at the end of the text, list the three main points of the selection.

> A **feasibility study** takes into consideration all the office tasks and includes an analysis of procedures, equipment, and productivity in regard to time, costs, and benefits. Through such a study—which can be used to examine any number of possible changes, not just those related to automation—a business can determine if specific changes in office methods and equipment are desirable.
>
> Basically, a feasibility study is concerned with people, procedures, and equipment—the three elements that make up an office system. For example, in a feasibility study devoted to studying automation, the human issues would involve the perceptions and reactions of the office staff and the necessary training of personnel. The procedural issues would involve productivity, security, and the new procedures

that would be needed with the new equipment. And the technological issues would involve decisions about which functions and tasks to automate, how to effect a transition to automation, and how to ensure compatibility of equipment.

*Electronic Office Procedures* by Rosemary T. Fruehling and Constance K. Weaver, McGraw-Hill, 1987, page 85.

_____

_____

_____

At your local or school library, look up the entry for *Industrial Revolution* in an encyclopedia. On a separate sheet of paper, make a list of the main points. Compare your list with a classmate's.

- Did you use the same source? Write your answer on the lines below.

_____

_____

_____

_____

_____

_____

- Are your lists of main points the same or similar? Explain why or why not on the lines below.

_____

_____

_____

_____

_____

Exercise 3

## Practice Outlining

Read the following passage. On a separate piece of paper, write an outline showing the major points and related secondary points.

**MANUAL TIME MANAGEMENT SYSTEMS**
Electronic calendaring systems have many advantages. However, even with them, you may still need to use manual calendars at times.

**Keeping Desk Calendars**
Write calendar entries neatly with a pencil so you can change them easily. If your notes are clear and your calendar is conveniently placed, your supervisor and coworkers can get information about your schedule when you are away from the office. Don't make confidential notes on this calendar. A combination of the types listed below may work best for you.

**Daily Calendar.** You may have a daily calendar on your desk. This kind of calendar has one blank or ruled page, or pair of pages, for each day. The pages may divide the workday into segments of an hour or less, which can help you schedule appointments and tasks.

**Weekly Calendar.** Some calendars display a week's schedule at once. Days may be divided into segments, and there may be blank areas for general entries. A weekly calendar allows you to see what you have planned for an entire week in one glance.

**Monthly Calendar.** You would use a monthly calendar to schedule events such as vacations or long-term projects. These calendars, which must be large enough for a month's worth of entries, generally hang on the wall. Sometimes people color code wall calendars. For example, blue lines could indicate when you will be out of the office and red lines the same for your boss.

**Yearly Calendar.** A yearly calendar is a master calendar for events that always occur at set times during the year. Holidays, annual budgets and reports, employee evaluations, and conferences are some of the things that might be listed on a yearly calendar. A yearly calendar is especially helpful to new staff members.

**Tickler Files**
Another daily reminder system is the tickler file, which stores reminders and other notes until you need them. One such method uses index cards and divider guides in two colors. Guides in one color are labeled by months; one in the same color is added for "Future Years." Those in the other color are numbered 1-31, for the days of the month. The divider guide for the current month is at the front with other months behind it. To use this kind of tickler file, you file notes behind the appropriate dates.

*Electronic Office Procedures* by Rosemary T. Fruehling and Constance K. Weaver, McGraw-Hill, 1987, pages 353-355.

Exercise 4

## Practice Making Picture Notes

No matter what career you choose, you will almost certainly encounter computers being used for various purposes. The following article, "Computers in the Office," tells you a little bit about the differences between how offices process information without computers and how they do it with computers.

Read the article. On a separate sheet of paper, make two diagrams—one that illustrates the traditional method and one the computerized method of information processing. Also, make a chart comparing the differences between the traditional office and the electronic office.

**Computers in the Office**
In traditional, noncomputerized offices, information is handled in a straight-line, or **linear**, manner. You start from scratch—raw data—work your way through a series of steps, and end with the finished product—a memo, report, letter, or whatever you are writing. The steps are:

*Input* (generate material by dictation or typing)
*Processing* (make changes and corrections; retype)
*Outputting* (generate the finished product)
*Distribution* (make copies; send to destination)
*Storing* (file material for reference and later use)

In a computerized office the steps are the same, but they can be taken almost simultaneously, and each one leads to all of the others. When you input material you also store it immediately by telling the computer to save it as a file. When you want to look at it or include it in a new document (the later use mentioned in the fifth traditional step), you call it up again and make any necessary changes. Retyping is not necessary, so you always have a finished product, even after you change it.

Once you have written the material, you can send it immediately if you have the right equipment. Or, you can print it out and mail it when you are ready. Or you can mail computer disks with the information on them.

As you can see, new, computerized offices have an overlapping process in which you can go from any step to any other. You could, for example, generate material and then distribute it immediately, without even storing it first. Or you could begin with old data, process it, store it, and not distribute it until much later.

Exercise 5

## Practice Writing Questions in the Margin

Read the material below. In the margin of this book, write four questions that ask about the most important points. Write each question next to where the answer can be found. This is the information you think you should know if you are going to take a test on this material.

> Many successful exporters first started selling internationally by responding to an inquiry from a foreign firm. Thousands of U.S. firms receive such requests annually, but most do not become successful exporters. What separates the successful exporter from the unsuccessful exporter? There is no single answer, but often the firm that becomes successful knows how to respond to inquiries, can separate the wheat from the chaff, recognizes the business practices involved in international selling, and takes time to build a relationship with the client. Although this may seem to be a large number of factors, they are all related and flow out of one another.
>
> Most, but not all, foreign letters of inquiry are in English. A firm may look to certain service providers (such as banks or freight forwarders) for assistance in translating a letter of inquiry in a foreign language. Most large cities have commercial translators who translate for a fee. Many colleges and universities also provide translation services.
> A typical inquiry asks for product specifications, information and price. Some foreign firms want information on purchasing a product for internal use; others (distributors and agents) want to sell the product in their market. A few firms may know a product well enough and want to place an order. Most inquiries want delivery schedules, shipping costs, terms, and, in some cases, exclusivity arrangements.
>
> *A Basic Guide to Exporting*, U.S. Department of Commerce, January 1992, page 9-1.

Now cover the passage and try to answer each of the questions.

# 8 Listening Effectively

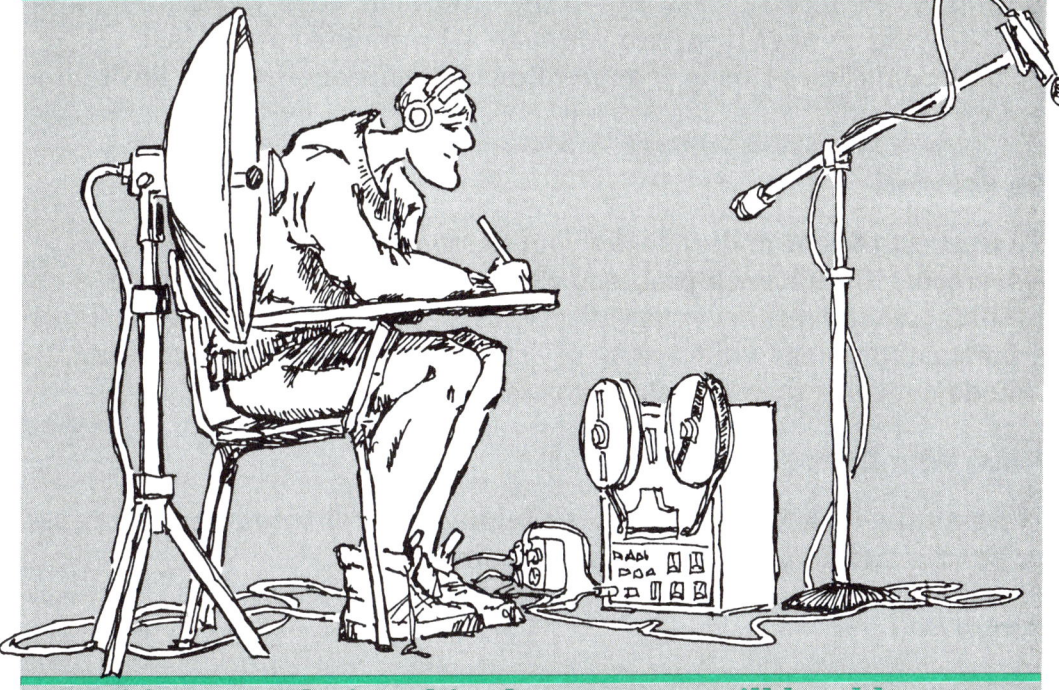

*After completing this chapter, you will be able to prepare yourself mentally and physically for listening and to use strategies to listen effectively.*

The ability to listen effectively is important. The more effectively you listen to what your instructor says and to the questions and answers from other students, the more you will learn and understand.

Effective listening begins before you enter the classroom. If you are physically and mentally ready to listen, you will get more out of a lecture or a discussion.

## PREPARING PHYSICALLY

You can easily prepare yourself physically to listen. The preparation is so simple that you may not even think about it or think that it is unimportant. That would be a mistake. A student prepared physically to listen has taken the first step toward making the best use of classroom or lecture time. The next four sections describe some simple preparations for preparing physically.

### Be Rested

Although you will not always have complete control of this, always make the effort to arrive at class rested. Forget about late night TV shows. Schedule your studying and work so that you can get a good night's sleep. Restrict your late hours to the weekend. A sleepy, tired listener is a poor listener.

Do you have a lecture class late in the afternoon when you have a hard time staying awake? If so, can you take a 15-minute catnap just before? Sometimes this is enough to restore your energy for a few more hours.

### Be Relaxed

To the best of your ability, leave your personal worries outside the classroom. If you have a problem, remind yourself that you can do nothing about it while in class. Drive it from your mind. Fretting about a personal problem while trying to listen and learn achieves nothing. You do not solve the personal problem, and you do not learn.

### Have Your Tools

Have all the tools you need for note taking—two or three working pens or pencils and an adequate supply of notepaper.

### Arrive on Time

Arrive at class in time to find a seat where you can see and hear well. This will help you to avoid inattention and distraction. Also, you cannot listen as you step over or on people as you find a seat after the class starts.

## PREPARING MENTALLY

Here are four steps you can take to prepare mentally for listening:

1. Clarify your listening purpose.
2. Motivate yourself to pay attention.
3. Activate the knowledge you already have.
4. Be aware of the lecture method.

If these steps sound familiar, it is because they are similar to the techniques for preparing to read.

### Clarify Your Purpose

To present an effective lecture, the instructor must spend time in preparation. He or she must clarify the purpose of the lecture, identify the main topics to present, and decide how to present them. As the lecturer must clarify his or her purpose before speaking, you must clarify your purpose before listening. To do so, ask yourself questions before the lecture, such as:

*How will this lecture relate to my reading?*
*How interested am I in this topic?*
*Will I be tested on this lecture material?*

It helps to identify both your *general* purpose and your *specific* purpose for listening as well as for reading. In a course on microcomputers, your general purpose for listening to a lecture could be to learn how to use electronic databases. Your specific purpose may be to clarify and reinforce facts you have found in reading about relational databases.

## Motivate Yourself to Pay Attention

It would be wonderful if the subject matter of the lectures we attend always interested us. Unfortunately, not all subjects interest us equally. One student may find accounting interesting. Another may find accounting boring, but selling exciting. To motivate yourself regardless of your level of interest, you can:

- Remind yourself of your general and specific purposes.

- Relate the topic to your goals. You may be unenthusiastic about a lecture on double-entry bookkeeping. Your goal may be to own a franchise for a fast-food restaurant. A knowledge of bookkeeping will be essential. Knowing this can stimulate your interest.

- Look for specific parts that excite your interest.

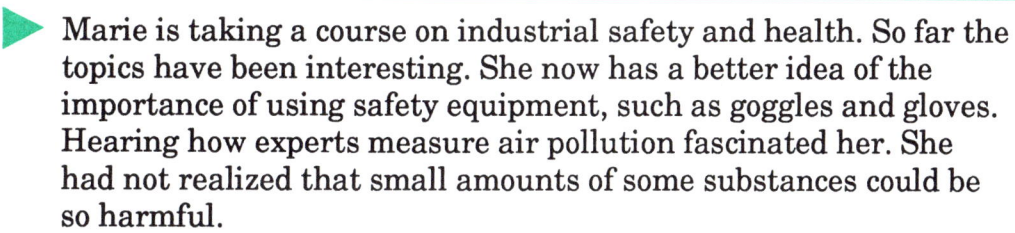

▶ Marie is taking a course on industrial safety and health. So far the topics have been interesting. She now has a better idea of the importance of using safety equipment, such as goggles and gloves. Hearing how experts measure air pollution fascinated her. She had not realized that small amounts of some substances could be so harmful.

The next lecture is on noise pollution. Marie says to her friend Tom, "A whole class on noise? There can't be that much to say. I'm going to sit in the back and study for the quiz."

Tom replies, "After that concert last week, my ears rang for an hour. I wouldn't want to work in a factory without a way of protecting my hearing. Maybe the lecturer will discuss using earplugs and headsets."

Marie has never found headsets comfortable and wonders what it would feel like to have to wear one on a job. Tom says, "I read about some new materials that they put on walls and ceilings to absorb noise." What Tom says interests her. Marie decides to get to the lecture early to get a good seat and listen, rather than take a back seat and study for a quiz.

By talking with Tom, Marie motivated herself to take an interest in a lecture on noise pollution that, at first, she thought would not interest her.

### Activate the Knowledge You Already Have

Picture the process of learning as an inverted pyramid. You begin with one fact, which leads to more facts and then even more facts, until you have gained a wide area of knowledge. Many lectures you will listen to will include or build on previously presented facts. Reviewing these facts prepares you to listen effectively.

Two practical steps to take to prepare yourself to listen are:

1. Completing your assigned reading.
2. Reviewing your related reading and previous lecture notes.

### Be Aware of the Lecture Method

As you review your notes and do background reading, think of the ways your instructor might present the topic.

> *Will the lecture restate facts from your reading?*
> *Will the instructor present an opposing viewpoint?*
> *Are there questions on this topic that your reading raised but did not answer?*
> *What topics covered in earlier lectures and readings may the instructor enlarge on?*

## LISTENING OR HEARING

As with reading, listening is not a passive act. The ability to listen actively and well is important for anyone wishing to learn, whether in a formal or an informal situation. Furthermore, listening well is a skill that will pay dividends for you throughout your life. Before examining ways to listen effectively, consider the difference between *hearing* and *listening*. You must hear to listen, but you can hear without listening.

### Hearing

You **hear** all the time—automatically. Your ears are sensory organs that receive sounds constantly and send them to your brain. You are not aware of many sounds you hear. You automatically filter out those that are of no use to you. Because so much goes on around you, you must develop this ability to filter out a lot of what you hear. You often do this subconsciously. This is necessary to protect yourself. The danger is forming a habit of blocking out sound to the point that you miss important information or do not understand it.

## Listening

**Listening** requires mental awareness in addition to the physical act of hearing. When you *listen*, you think about what you are hearing. You do more than just register the sounds. Hearing can occur without conscious thought on your part. Listening, however, actively involves your mind.

## IDENTIFYING ROADBLOCKS

A *listening roadblock* is anything that prevents you from giving your full attention to what you are hearing. The sections that follow describe some of the mental roadblocks that prevent or deter listening.

### Inattention

Most of us remember only about 25 percent of what we *hear*, which is, in part, due to *inattention*. Inattention is a major listening roadblock that we all experience from time to time.

One reason we become inattentive is that most people speak at a rate of 100 to 150 words per minute, while our brains process words much faster. That leaves us with time to think about things other than what we are listening to. Inattention can become a habit.

Other factors causing inattention can be stress or boredom. You read that you should leave your personal problems on the doorstep of the classroom. If you feel stress—preoccupied about your school work, a part-time job, your social life, family concerns—you let thoughts about these things fill up that extra brain time. When that happens, you may still be hearing but you have stopped listening.

### Distractions

Physical distractions that prevent listening often occur in a classroom. Other students, material on the walls, temperature or light level, comfortable or uncomfortable furniture, sights and sounds coming through windows—all these can distract. Recall that one reason for getting to class on time is to be able to select a seat that has few distractions for you.

### Unfamiliarity

A new field of study is full of new words and concepts that can trip you up as you listen. In such situations, you can feel that nothing you hear makes sense. Until you become familiar with the topic, you may miss quite a bit of what the lecturer says. For this reason it is important for you to keep up in your reading assignment and to review your notes after each lecture.

### Anticipation

Unfamiliarity can obstruct listening. So can familiarity if you anticipate what you will hear to the extent that you do not pay attention. You may think to yourself, "Oh, I know what this is going to be about," and tune out. A degree of anticipation is fine. Anticipation comes from being prepared. It can indicate your ability to grasp and absorb what you hear. The danger is allowing your anticipation to reach the point where you tune out and stop listening. If you tune out instructions for a test because you anticipate that this one will be just like the last, you can be in trouble.

### Preconceptions

Related to anticipation are preconceptions you may have about the topic. You may decide ahead of time that the topic is going to be boring, that the teacher is dull or poorly prepared, or in some other way prejudge what you are going to experience. If you let these preconceptions influence you, you are likely to miss a great deal that could be useful or important.

Listening roadblocks are like barriers to critical thinking: much as stereotyping and conforming make it hard to think critically, preconceptions make it hard to listen effectively.

## OVERCOMING ROADBLOCKS

In the following sections, you will read about strategies to help you overcome roadblocks to listening and to concentrate so that you can be an active listener:

### Make Associations

As you listen to the lecture, try to identify key words and main points. Write them down. Connect new information you hear to what you already know. It is easier to remember connected facts. For example, say you are in a course on electronic spreadsheets and the instructor refers to the *active cell* and the *cell pointer*. This puzzles you, but then you think of what you know about word processing. You realize that the cell pointer is like a cursor and that the active cell is where the cell pointer is.

### Create Mental Images

Suppose a science instructor says that ice has less density than water. Make that abstract statement meaningful by creating a mental image of ice cubes floating in a glass of water.

### Take Advantage of Pauses

When the instructor pauses to write on the board, for example, begin organizing your written notes. Draw diagrams or arrows connecting related points. Mark your notes with numbers or letters to indicate main and minor points. Be alert to what is happening, however. Do not become so absorbed in organizing notes that you fail to listen to what is being said. Sometimes, instructors continue talking while writing on the board.

### Ask Questions

Ask questions of yourself and of the instructor. You think you hear an accounting instructor classify equipment as inventory. You ask, "Isn't equipment an asset?" The instructor explains that this equipment will be resold. Therefore, it is inventory. If you were not questioning what you heard, you might have jotted in your notes "Equipment = inventory," which would make no sense when you saw it later.

Instructors are glad when students listen actively—and courteous disagreement is welcome. It is a good way to clear up misunderstandings or start lively class discussions.

### Combat Low-Energy Periods

If you have classes during low-energy periods, you will have to work hard to overcome listening obstacles. To be aware of when you have low-energy periods, ask yourself such questions as:

> *Am I a morning or an afternoon person?*
> *Am I less sleepy and energetic after a meal?*
> *Did I get less than the usual amount of sleep last night?*

When you have identified your low-energy periods, take these actions to combat them:

- Assume a posture that makes it appear that you are interested—be comfortable, but do not slouch and sprawl. The effect on your listening will be both psychological and physiological.

- Sit where you can hear and see instructor and chalkboard.

- Sit away from classroom windows if sun makes you sleepy.

- Stay physically alert. Move, stretch a little, wipe off your glasses, push your hair out of your eyes.

- Make eye contact with the instructor. Looking at the instructor and at charts, maps, and objects the instructor displays helps you clarify what you hear.

- If possible, sign up for courses that meet during your high-energy periods.

## Counter Preconceptions

Question your preconceptions, challenge them, test them against reality. For example:

- If you have decided that the instructor does not know the subject well, think of alternative explanations for the problem. Perhaps he or she is an expert but does not have good presentation skills.

    *Consider what you can do to make up for the poor delivery to get the most out of the instructor's knowledge.*

    *Ask questions.*

    *Look for ways to organize the material so it is clearer.*

- If you have decided the instructor does not like you, make an appointment to speak to him or her. Instructors are professionals who are doing a job. Their job is to teach, and they want to do it as best they can. Most instructors welcome an opportunity to discuss problems you might be having in their class if they know you are sincere.

- If your preconception is that the course is useless, try to find out why it is offered.

    *Speak to other students who have taken it to see if they found it worthwhile.*

---

▶ Carolyn is disappointed when she discovers that the instructor she had expected to teach the paralegal course will be away this semester. The new instructor is a paralegal himself and not an attorney as is the regular instructor. It is too late for Carolyn to drop the course, so she reluctantly goes to the first class but she decides that it will be a waste of time. She misses most of what the substitute says because she is thinking about how much more she would learn from an experienced attorney.

After class, Carolyn joins Rita and Mark for coffee. Rita and Mark talk enthusiastically about the course. Mark says, "Professor Walters' work with that large law firm sounds fascinating. Isn't it great he will organize a visit for us!"

"Yes," Rita agrees. "And he really can tell us exactly what it is like to be a paralegal. Carolyn, did you like the way he spelled out the career paths for paralegals?" Carolyn did not know. She had not been listening.

---

Carolyn prejudged the substitute instructor. She let her preconceptions get in the way of her thinking and listening. Consequently, she turned off her mind. She already "knew" the course was going to be a waste of time. Had she thought critically about this conclusion, she might have realized that an instructor who is a paralegal himself might be highly qualified to teach her worthwhile things about the profession.

## SUMMING UP

Effective listening begins even before you enter the classroom or the lecture hall. To prepare to learn from a lecture, you must use your body and your mind.

To prepare physically for listening, take these steps:

>Be rested.
>Be relaxed.
>Have ready paper, pen, and other needed tools.
>Get there on time.

If you are well rested and not preoccupied with problems, you will be ready to listen effectively to lectures. You do not want to have to ask classmates for paper or pen, which would disrupt their listening ability as well as your own.

To prepare mentally for listening take these steps:

>Clarify your purpose for listening.
>Motivate yourself to pay attention.
>Activate the knowledge you already have.
>Be aware of the lecture method.

Ask yourself questions to clarify your general and specific purposes for listening to a lecture. Try to motivate yourself by finding a connection between the lecture topic and your goals.

Listening and hearing are two different activities. Listening is active, and hearing is passive. Listening requires mental awareness added to the physical act of hearing. When you listen, you think about what you are hearing. You do more than just register the sounds.

Listening roadblocks can prevent you from listening effectively. A roadblock is anything that prevents you from giving your full attention to what is being said. Once you identify listening roadblocks, you can try to remove or diminish them. Roadblocks include:

>Inattention.
>Distractions.
>Unfamiliarity.
>Anticipation.
>Preconceptions.

There are various techniques you can use to overcome listening roadblocks. These include:

>Focusing your attention by identifying key words and
>main points as the lecture proceeds.

Associating new information with facts you already know.

Creating mental images of what you are listening to so you can make abstract statements more meaningful.

Taking advantage of pauses, while the instructor looks at notes or writes on the board, to review your notes.

Raising questions about points you do not understand.

Taking steps to cope with periods of low energy for you.

Countering your preconceptions about the topic by thinking of new ways to explain things.

## ▼ DEVELOPING YOUR SKILLS

Exercise 1

**Practice Identifying Listening Purposes**

On the lines below, write your listening purposes for:

- The next two lectures you will attend.

_____

_____

_____

- The next discussion class you will attend.

_____

_____

_____

Exercise 2

### Prepare for a Lecture

Prepare for an upcoming lecture in one of your classes. If possible, choose a lecture on a topic in which your interest is low.

- Read at least two works not assigned for that class on the topic—short essays or magazine articles—by two authors. Try to identify points of agreement and disagreement and write these on the lines below. Do the authors approach the topic in the same way? (Write your answer on the lines below.)

_____

_____

_____

_____

- Keep your reading in mind as you listen to the lecture. Does the lecturer bring up points not covered in your reading? With which author does the lecturer agree?

- After the lecture, ask yourself if your advance reading and preparation helped to increase interest in the topic.

Exercise 3

## Reviewing Class Notes

Before your next lecture, review your class notes and notes from the background reading you have done. List two facts you know that will increase your understanding of the lecture. Write these on the lines below.

After the lecture, review your lecture notes. Can you identify two more facts that you have added to your base of knowledge on this subject? Write these on the lines below.

Exercise 4

## Identifying Main and Secondary Points

After your next lecture, write the answers to the following questions on the lines below:

1. What was the main point?

   _____

   _____

   _____

   _____

2. What were some secondary points?

   _____

   _____

   _____

   _____

3. How were the secondary points related to one another?

   _____

   _____

   _____

   _____

   _____

Exercise 5

## Assess Your Listening Skills

For the next week, keep an eye—and ear—out for your listening roadblocks as you attend class and talk to others. Use those described in this chapter to help you identify your listening roadblocks. List them below and give examples.

_____

_____

_____

_____

_____

_____

_____

_____

_____

_____

_____

_____

_____

_____

_____

_____

Exercise 6

## Apply Your Listening Skills

Apply the skills you have learned in this chapter in your next few lectures. Then assess your performance. Ask yourself, "Did I use each of these techniques to help me concentrate: Always (A), Sometimes (S), or Never (N)?"

Use the chart below to check off each skill. Make copies of it for other lectures. Work to fill the (A) column with checkmarks.

| Did I | A | S | N |
|---|---|---|---|
| Arrive on time prepared to listen? | | | |
| Make associations? | | | |
| Create mental images? | | | |
| Rephrase and summarize my notes? | | | |
| Begin to organize? | | | |
| Ask questions? | | | |
| Sit "at attention?" | | | |
| Sit where I can see? | | | |
| Make eye contact? | | | |
| Avoid preconceptions? | | | |

Exercise 7

## Analyze Others' Listening Skills

If possible, attend a friend's class that you are not taking. Sit where you can see the students. Which students seem to be listening effectively and which ones do not. When you see that someone does not appear to be listening, note why you think that is happening. Check the item on the list below each time you see an example of it.

Inattention

_____

_____

Distractions

_____

_____

Unfamiliarity

_____

_____

Anticipation

_____

_____

Preconceptions

_____

_____

# 9 Taking Listening Notes

**After completing this chapter, you will be able to take effective listening notes and to use these notes to understand and remember information.**

As with reading, you remember more information when listening if you take notes. Taking notes is one way to change yourself from a passive to an active listener. Taking notes is an effective aid to learning because the more of your senses you involve, the greater your ability to remember and understand. By taking notes, you are using your eyes and your hands to aid your ears.

In this chapter, you will learn strategies for taking notes in a formal classroom situation. You can also use these strategies in many different ways outside of classrooms: on the job, at meetings, on the telephone.

As with reading, your note-taking strategies as well as the kinds of notes you take when listening will vary according to your purpose and the situation you are in.

Taking notes is only the first step in using your note taking as a study skill. After taking notes, you must clean them up and then organize and integrate them so you can retrieve the information easily. Your final step is to study your notes not only to pass tests, but also to master the material.

First in this chapter, you will learn note-taking strategies. Then, you will learn how to make these notes effective study tools.

## BE SELECTIVE

Even if you are a fast writer, it is impossible to write down every word a speaker says. Do not even try. If you try to write every word down, your concentration is on *hearing* individual words and not *listening* to what the words mean. Later, facing a large mass of notes to review and having no real sense of what the lecturer meant, you will find it hard to identify the main points.

Listen for and note only important points. There is a seeming contradiction in note taking. The act of taking notes fixes more in your memory than listening alone does. However, taking too many notes makes remembering more difficult. The reason for this is that in taking a lot of notes, you fail to focus on major points. You absorb *irrelevant* material that crowds out the *relevant*.

### Do NOT Use a Tape Recorder

You learned in Chapter 7 that using a tape recorder can be a useful way to take reading notes. You also may have seen someone recording a lecture on a tape recorder instead of taking written notes. Using a tape recorder in a lecture is NOT a good idea.

Using a tape recorder may seem like a good idea because it allows you to listen to the lecture unencumbered by note taking while recording the entire lecture for later review and study. All using a tape recorder does is delay taking notes. You eventually have to listen to the entire lecture again on tape.

Listening to a recording after the lecture, you still must separate main points from irrelevant ones. A tape recording tends to make everything seem equally important. Furthermore, although you have vocal tone for emphasis on tape, you do not have the lecturer's body language and other visual clues to help you identify main points.

Some students believe that tape recording a lecture in a difficult course will help them. They believe, for one thing, they will have the tape to listen to whenever they need to refresh their memory. You are better off, however, to take written notes during the lecture. You will learn more effectively if you avoid the recorder and rely on written notes. Taking written notes trains you to recognize important points and to focus on them. You thus do a lot of your learning in the lecture hall. Relying on a recorder can increase the time you must spend learning some material, which reduces your time to do other things.

### Identify the Main Points

You cannot always easily tell what is a main point. Sometimes, you will begin writing what you think is a main point and the instructor will shift or not develop the point. No problem. Just cross out what you have started to write. If you are not sure, make the note and cross it out later. The more you listen to an instructor, the easier it becomes to recognize main points. You need write down only important points for later review and study.

As you will read later in this chapter, there are various methods for identifying main points. In many cases, lecturers will simply say that a point is major.

### Use a Few Key Words

When you note an important point, do not write every word. Do not try to write complete sentences. Write only *key words*—those that trigger your memory. Doing this strengthens the learning punch of your note taking. Selective note taking saves you work.

Selective note taking saves you the effort of writing. It also saves you the later effort of deciphering a lot of notes and identifying main points. Using selective note taking, you do a large part of your learning and studying in the lecture hall.

If you have prepared well, you will have already encountered many key words in your reading. Listen for them and note what the lecturer says about them. Write down the word along with one or two other words the lecturer uses to define or expand on it.

Write enough so that you understand the point. For example, say you are taking an introductory class in accounting. The instructor is explaining the relationship among assets, liabilities, and owner's equity. If you write down only the three elements, you might fail to remember the relationship among them.

In this instance, the key words must include the three elements and those words that show the relationship: in this case, plus, minus, and equals. Effective key-word notes would read: assets minus liabilities equals owner's equity.

### Use an Outline Style

The outline style helps to show relationships between different points. In an outline, the position of the words and numbers or letters assigned to them indicate their relative importance and relationships. See Chapter 7 for a detailed explanation of outlining.

Even if the lecturer does not obviously use an outline format, use this form for your notes. Do not, however, become stuck trying to force everything into an outline. In some cases you will need to jot something down even if it does not fit your outline.

## USE NOTE-TAKING TACTICS

There are many simple tactics you can use during a lecture to be sure that your note taking is effective. Here are a few of them.

### Be Aware of Lecturer's Clues

Many lecturers begin by saying what the lecture is about, "Today, we will explore . . . ." They end by summing up the main points: "In conclusion, . . . ." The introduction gives you a chance to identify the main ideas, and the summary a chance to double-check your notes.

Certain words can tip you off to the overall organization of the material and to the importance of different parts:

*important factors*　　*main causes*
*to sum up*　　*by comparison*
*in contrast*　　*first . . . , second . . . , third . . .*

Include these phases in your notes. Later, if you find your notes are not clear or complete, you have a clue as to what is missing. If you did not get the second item in a list, you can ask a classmate.

### Listen for Repetition

A lecturer repeats important points to emphasize them. Make sure you write down repeated points, if not the first time, then the second.

### Watch the Chalkboard

Chances are that your lecturer uses the chalkboard as a way to emphasize points. Be sure to include in your notes anything presented on the chalkboard or with an overhead projector.

### Develop Speed-Writing Techniques

Use speed writing. Write words in shorter forms or with symbols that are quick and easy to write. In the example about the relationship among the three elements in accounting, you could use symbols:

$$\text{assets} - \text{liabilities} = \text{owner's equity.}$$

Develop your own abbreviations, but be sure you remember what they mean. Do not use the same abbreviation for different words, such as such as *com* for *communication* and for *committee.*

Jot an abbreviation's meaning in the margin. In a course on accounting, you could assume you would be hearing the phrase *owner's equity* often and decide to use the abbreviation *o.e.* to indicate it. Write in the margin the first time you use it: *o.e. = owner's equity*.

Many formalized programs of speed writing exist that you can learn, such as *Condon Notetaking*. *Condon Notetaking* teaches a combination of writing principles based on special abbreviations for common words, speednotes, and phrases that combine common phrases into a single note. Some basic speed writing techniques in *Condon Notetaking* are:

- Do not write silent letters. (For example, write *nam* for name, *tru* for true, *sum* for some, *thot* for thought.)

- Write the sounds you hear. (For example, *ruf* for *rough*, *plou* for *plough*, *stic* for *stick*.)

- Simplify your writing by eliminating such things as the dot on the *i* and *j*, the cross on the *x* and *t*.

- Do not write minor vowels. (For example, *al*, *er*, *per*, *pur*, as in *finl* for *final*, *sesnl* for *seasonal*, *egr* for *eager*.)

## Begin Organizing Your Notes

Mostly you will organize your notes during study periods. But you can begin the process during lectures. Doing so serves two purposes.

1. It helps occupy free mental time, thereby reducing the risk of inattention, and keeping you focused on the topic.
2. It helps you spot areas you are not clear about, which you may be able to clarify with a question.

Use a system of highlighting: underlining, or special symbols to help you locate important points. Stars, exclamation points, arrows, and so forth can serve for emphasis. Brackets or lines can connect ideas. Use a special color marker for points likely to appear on a test.

Mark points you do not understand or have partly missed. Mark your notes so you can find your questions quickly when you have the chance to ask them.

Do not overdo highlighting during the lecture. You will do most of your highlighting when you review your notes.

## KNOW WHEN NOT TO TAKE NOTES

There will be times during the lecture when you should not write notes. These times include the following.

### When Told Not To

Sometimes the lecturer wants everyone's full attention on a difficult subject that will have to be gone over several times. So when the lecturer says to stop everything else and just pay attention, do so. He or she will repeat the material so you can take notes.

### When the Lecturer Hands Out Material

When the lecturer hands out material covering information presented in the lecture, do not make notes of that material when it is covered. Although taking notes helps you remember, you have enough to do during the lecture getting down material not handed out. You may want to make notes directly on the handout during the lecture and later when you review your notes.

### When There Is a Clear Diversion from the Topic

The lecturer may tell an amusing anecdote or simply wander from the topic for a minute or two. She or he wants to relax. Take the opportunity to relax also. If you think that the anecdote will help you remember a point, however, do make a note of it. You could use it for a practice exercise. Do not write it word for word. Just put the key words down. Then see if you can retell the funny story to a friend.

## CLEAN UP YOUR NOTES

Every note taker will discover problem notes—unclear phrases, unnecessary sentences, words that need further definition, out-of-sequence notations. If you have trouble reading your handwriting or remembering what an abbreviation stands for, clear up such problems while the topic is fresh in your mind.

A scribbled word or abbreviation that was crystal clear to you when you wrote it down can become a meaningless scrawl a week later. That can be frustrating and, worse, it can mean that you will not understand the topic. Reviewing your notes, revising them as needed, even rewriting them, reinforces their content. As you revise and rewrite, you put your instructor's words into your own words. The material then becomes truly your own. A few other quick and easy things you can do are:

- Cross out anything that is repetitious.
- Cross out anything that is incorrect.
- Spell out abbreviations that you might not recognize later.
- Explain symbols that you might not recognize later.
- Highlight anything the instructor suggests may be on a test.
- Find and write down the definitions of any unfamiliar words.

If you took notes using only key words, now is the time to add to them to be sure you understand them. Add phrases that clarify the connections between ideas. Write the key words in complete sentences to be sure you understand them. As you are filling out and completing your key-word notes you are, of course, studying them. You are making sure you can still make sense of them later.

## ORGANIZE YOUR NOTES

When you have cleaned them up, organize your notes. Do this regularly when they are fresh in your mind. It is best to do this in the evening of the day you took them. At least organize them within a few days of taking them. This way, if something is not clear, you may remember what it should be and correct it.

Use a system that will work in the classroom and during your reading as well as later when you are working your notes. Here are some ways to organization your notes:

- **Date them.** On each set of notes put the date of the lecture or class or when you did the reading.
- **Number them.** Number the pages in each set of notes.
- **Collect them in one place.** Keep the notes for each subject in separate places. Three-ring binders are good places for notes. You can move notes around, add and remove pages easily. If you do not want to carry the binder to class every day, use a notebook with holes already punched. Later tear out the pages and put them in the binder.

Put your class and lecture notes together with reading notes on the same topic. Usually you will take both sets of notes at about the same time. Suppose, however, one week you miss a class or cannot get to the library to do a reading assignment. You will have to borrow a classmate's notes or find time to catch up on reading. In these situations, your notes on the same topic will be dated at different times.

Try to organize your notes according to how the instructor organizes the course. If the first topic in a Business Management course is on marketing, then you want to put all your notes on marketing at the beginning. When you study your notes, all the information about one topic should be together.

### Outline Your Notes

You may want to put your notes into outline form if you have not already outlined them. You do not have to rewrite them completely but simply impose on them the numbers and letters of the outline format. Refer to Chapter 7 for how to outline.

When you work your outline notes, you want to be sure that the outline is complete.

> *Does each main heading have at least two subheadings under it?*
> *Does the organization of the notes tell you that something is missing?*
> *You might have written points A and B but not C. Can you remember what point C was?*
> *Maybe there was no point C, and you forgot to cross out the letter.*
> *Perhaps you used a major head for an item that you now realize should be a subhead of something else.*

### Highlight Your Notes

You will probably use highlighter on your notes. Do not use the highlighter too soon. The tendency is to highlight too much in the beginning. Once you highlight notes, you cannot unhighlight them. As you read the first few sets of notes, you may highlight things that later you wish you had not. Things look different at the beginning, when you only have a few notes, from they way they look at the end, when you have 30 or 40 pages.

Read a batch of notes first to get a sense of the most important points, and then go back and use the highlighter.

### Create Diagrams, Drawings, and Charts

You might want to enhance your notes with diagrams, charts, or drawings of facts and information in your notes. These visual aids can help you study later on. In the process of creating the diagrams, charts, or drawings, you are reformatting information and increasing your understanding of it.

# STUDY YOUR NOTES

If you clean up and organize your notes on a regular basis, studying them will be easy and profitable. If you have two hours to study, you can be confident that you will not spend the first hour organizing.

Use the highlighted notes in this way when studying them:

1. Read the highlighted note, then look away and try to recall all the information you can that goes with that note.
2. Look back at your notes and see what you missed. Then look away and try it again.
3. Go on to another section and repeat the process.

Later go back to the beginning of your notes and see how much you remember. Note those sections you are least sure of so you can review them a third time if necessary. It is better to review your complete notes several times rather than once. If you highlight and read only once, you are less likely to recall information. Remember to use critical thinking when reviewing your notes. If something seems incomplete or wrong, check further to see why.

## Work with a Classmate

A benefit of studying with someone else is that you can compare notes, explain concepts out loud, and in other ways test your understanding. When you and a classmate compare notes, you may find that you disagree on a definition, a concept, or a fact. You then work to figure out which one is right. One of you may have missed an important point that the other can provide.

A drawback to studying with someone else is that you may just socialize and not study seriously. If you study with someone else, agree at the start on how much you want to cover and in how much time. This way you will be less tempted to get sidetracked and not finish everything you have to.

## Review for Tests

If you faithfully review your notes and texts, studying for a test will not seem so daunting. You will have developed a system of reviewing and absorbing information. When reviewing for a specific test, start with the material from the beginning of the semester or since the last test. If you feel you have a good grasp of the material, concentrate on your weak spots. Or if your professor has discussed the test in advance and you know what to expect, pay close attention to that material. You will read about taking essay and objective tests in Unit IV.

# SUMMING UP

Note taking changes you from a passive to an active listener. Note-taking skills can be useful outside the classroom, such as on the job, at meetings, or on the telephone.

Be selective when taking notes. Do not try to take everything down even if you could. Do not use a tape recorder. By taking notes, you train yourself to look for and recognize the main points during the lecture.

Identify main points, note key words and connect everything in outline form.

Some tactics you can use to make your note taking effective include:

> Being aware of the lecturer's clues.
> Listening for repetition.
> Watching the chalkboard.
> Developing speed-writing techniques.
> Organizing your notes.

You must know when not to take notes. Those times include:

> When the lecturer says not to.
> When the lecturer hands out material.
> When there is a clear diversion from the topic.

After taking your notes, you must clean them up, organize and integrate them, and, finally, study them.

No one takes such perfect notes they never need to be cleaned up. Ways of cleaning up your notes require reviewing, revising, and rewriting. Other things you can do to clean up you notes are:

> Cross out anything that is repetitious.
> Cross out anything that is incorrect.
> Spell out abbreviations that you might not recognize later.
> Explain symbols that you might not recognize later.
> Circle or star anything that the instructor suggested might be on an test.
> Find and write down the definitions of any unfamiliar words.

When working your key-word notes, put the key words into sentences to be sure you understand them.

When working your outline notes, check to see if the outline is complete.

When you have cleaned them up, organize your notes. Do this regularly when they are fresh in your mind. Use a system that will work in the classroom and during your reading as well as later when you are working your notes.

Some ways to organize your notes are:

> Date, number, collect those on the same topic in one place.
> Outline them.
> Highlight them.

If you clean up and organize your notes on a regular basis, studying them is easy.

## ▼ DEVELOPING YOUR SKILLS

### Exercise 1

**Check Your Note Taking**

With a classmate, take notes while you listen to a radio interview or watch a television documentary. Afterward, exchange notes and evaluate them for each other, using the following checklist.

**Note-Taking Checklist**

|  | YES | NO |
|---|---|---|
| Do the notes include the main points of the talk? | ☐ | ☐ |
| Do they contain the relevant details? | ☐ | ☐ |
| Do they omit irrelevant details? | ☐ | ☐ |
| Do the notes include key words? | ☐ | ☐ |
| Are they mainly in outline form? | ☐ | ☐ |
| Are the notes well organized? | ☐ | ☐ |

Exercise 2

## Practice Your Note Taking

Use the checklist below for the next week. At the end of the week, evaluate your progress. Has paying attention to these techniques and strategies emhanced your note-taking ability? Try to make them a habit to improve your note-taking skills.

## Listening Note-Taking Skills Checklist

| Technique/Strategy | Day 1 | Day 2 | Day 3 | Day 4 | Day 5 |
|---|---|---|---|---|---|
| **BE SELECTIVE** | | | | | |
| Did not write everything down | | | | | |
| Identified important points | | | | | |
| Used a few key words | | | | | |
| Used an outline style | | | | | |
| **USE NOTE-TAKING TACTICS** | | | | | |
| Was aware of lecturer's clues | | | | | |
| Listened for repetition | | | | | |
| Watched the chalkboard | | | | | |
| Developed speed-writing techniques | | | | | |
| Began organizing notes | | | | | |
| **BE ALERT WHEN NOT TO TAKE NOTES** | | | | | |
| When lecturer says not to | | | | | |
| When the lecturer hands out material | | | | | |
| When there is a clear diversion | | | | | |

Exercise 3

### Compare Lecture Notes with Classmates

After your next lecture, get together with at least one other classmate. Check your understanding of the lecture. Referring to your notes, discuss the main ideas.

Do you agree on the main ideas?

Did you both come away from the lecture with the same understanding of the subject presented?


Exercise 4

### Compare Lecture Notes with Reading Notes

Your lecture and reading notes together with their summaries, time lines, diagrams, flow charts, highlights, and symbols to emphasize main ideas or important facts can be personal in style. But your notes should represent the course work effectively. Almost anyone should be able to pick up your notes and learn something. Test this with a classmate.

After you have completed the steps described in this lesson, get together with a classmate and compare reading and listening notes for a particular topic. If necessary, acquaint each other with symbols used. Have you both

> *Picked up on the same points?*
> *Highlighted similar facts?*
> *Drawn similar conclusions?*
> *Made similar comparisons?*

Make a list of any differences you see in the two sets of notes. Consider the differences carefully to see if either is missing something important or has discovered an effective way of handling the material.


Exercise 5

### Clean Up Your Notes

Clean up your lecture notes from a recent class to be sure the outline is complete. Correct any misspelled words and write them correctly. Try to create at least one diagram, drawing or chart to illustrate an important point.

Exercise 6

## Review Earlier Notes

Look at your notes from a class that you made before learning any note-taking techniques. Do they still make sense to you? Are you taking more effective notes now? Did you use the highlight too much? Revise these earlier notes. Put them in outline form, highlight important phrases and main ideas, and boil them down into a list of key words.

Exercise 7

## Practice Identifying the Lecturer's Clues

On the lines below, make a list of clues used by the lecturer, such as phrases like "in contrast," or "main causes."

_____

_____

_____

_____

_____

# UNIT IV
# USING YOUR KNOWLEDGE

**When you have completed this unit, you will be able to use your reading, listening, and note-taking skills to improve your test performance and your workplace success.**

As a student, your main goal is to learn and acquire skills. Tests are ways of helping you evaluate whether you are achieving your goal. They are motivators because they make known the extent to which you have, or have not, mastered material.

All the study skills you acquire as a student prepare you for taking tests. The more regularly you do the routine—attend class, take notes, keep up with assignments—the better prepared you are for taking tests. More important, you will have learned and understood the material. You will have gained knowledge.

Few students, however, can afford to take major exams without investing specific time preparing for them. Taking tests does require its own set of skills. Nothing, of course, replaces preparation and study but you can develop and improve test-taking skills.

## Assess Your Test-Taking Skills

How well prepared are you for taking tests? To give yourself an idea, take this simple test. Answer the questions on the following test-taking checklist. Do not spend much time on each question, but try to answer each one honestly as to how you usually prepare and study.

**Test-Taking Checklist**

|  | YES | NO |
|---|---|---|
| Do I attend class regularly? | ☐ | ☐ |
| Do I keep up with my assignments? | ☐ | ☐ |
| Do I review my notes regularly? | ☐ | ☐ |
| Do I study every day to avoid cramming before a test? | ☐ | ☐ |
| Do I have special techniques I use to help my memory? | ☐ | ☐ |
| Do I know what my instructor expects? | ☐ | ☐ |
| Do I develop my own questions while studying? | ☐ | ☐ |
| Do I study with a classmate? | ☐ | ☐ |
| Do I read directions carefully? | ☐ | ☐ |
| Do I practice stress-reduction techniques? | ☐ | ☐ |
| Am I happy with my performance on tests? | ☐ | ☐ |

Did you answer No to any questions? In the lessons that follow, you will learn ways to turn No answers into Yes answers and poor test grades into good grades.

## KNOW TYPES OF TESTS

Most students will meet two main types of tests—essay tests and objective tests. To perform successfully on both types of test requires effective study skills. Each type requires slightly different test preparation and test-taking strategies.

**Objective tests** examine your knowledge of facts. Objective tests include true/false, matching, fill-in, and multiple-choice questions. In Chapter 10 you will learn techniques for taking objective tests and strategies for answering all four types of questions.

**Essay tests** require you to answer questions by writing your response in your own words and often in great detail. Chapter 11 will provide you with strategies for studying for and taking essay tests.

In some subjects, you will take tests that combine essay questions and objective questions. You will need to apply all the techniques and strategies you will learn in Unit IV to perform your best on these tests.

## CONTROL TEST ANXIETY

You have already studied ways to cope with stress in Chapter 5. These chapters will teach you specific tactics to use when experiencing test anxiety. Test anxiety is a particular form of stress that everyone experiences when faced with the need to perform well within a limited time.

You will learn ways to cope with this stress, such as taking the initiative, using relaxation techniques, and keeping the test in perspective. The most effective way to counter text anxiety, as you will read, is to prepare. You prepare yourself by making it a habit of using the study skills you have learned in this text.

## APPLY YOUR SKILL IN THE WORKPLACE

The last chapter in this textbook shows how you will be able to apply your skills to workplace situations. The learning that you do in school will carry over into the remainder of your life, so you should consider it a long-term investment.

# 10 Taking Objective Tests

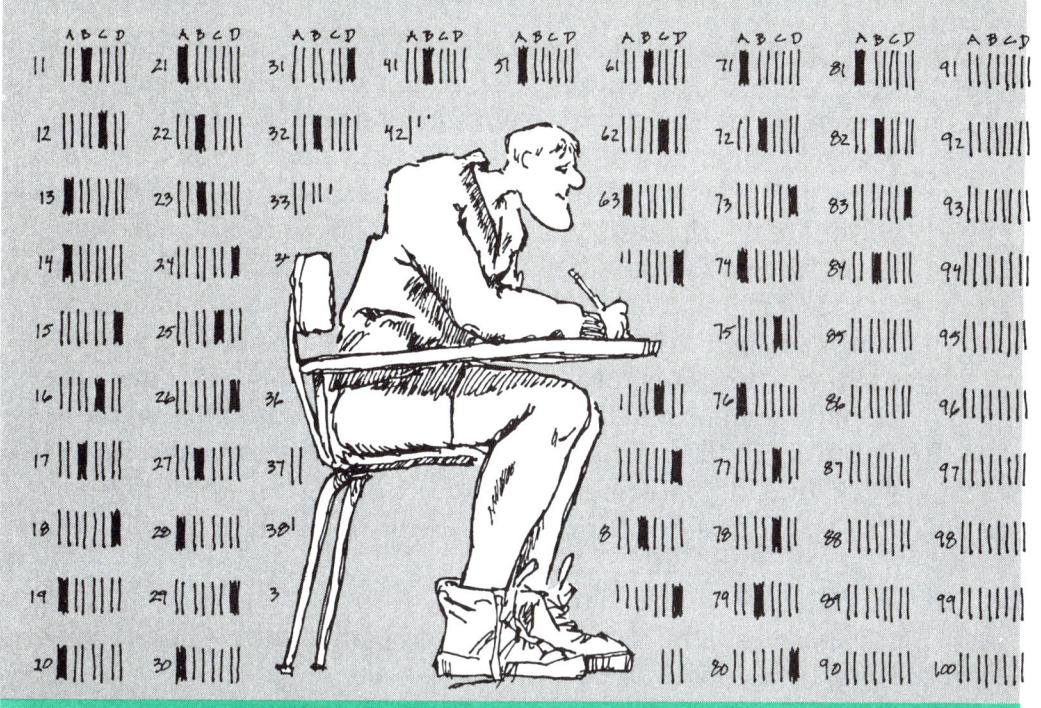

*After you have completed this chapter, you will be able to improve your test performance by applying strategies for taking objective tests.*

As you read in the introduction to this unit, objective tests include true/false, matching, fill-in, and multiple-choice questions. An **objective test** may have one of these types of questions, all of them, or any combination.

As you will see in this chapter, studying for objective tests provides ample opportunity to use critical and creative thinking. You must identify the important points, find relationships between them, and understand them before you can remember them.

## PREPARING FOR OBJECTIVE TESTS

To prepare for objective tests, use two tools: things-to-learn lists and flash cards. These tools can focus your study efforts on difficult-to-learn or need-to-know points that objective tests cover.

### Things-to-Learn Lists

Make things-to-learn lists of points you have identified for further study. These are like to-do lists, but they focus on learning. Things-to-learn lists isolate specific points that you should concentrate on. You can make a list of things to learn in a day, a few days, or a week. Create new lists as you go. You have the material in your notes. Take it out and put it into a list of things to learn. Doing this is an extension of working your notes.

Put your lists on standard-sized paper (8 1/2 by 11 inches). Leave plenty of space to add information. Set up the paper in this way:

1. Divide the paper into two columns: a narrow column (about one inch wide) and a wide one. Write the items you need to learn in the larger column. Use the narrower column to check off and mark the date when you complete (have learned) an item. Noting the date helps you keep on schedule. If you are on time or ahead of time, you get a sense of accomplishment. If you are behind, you know you will have to speed up.
2. Review your notes for points you want to work on. These may be points you are having difficulty with or must learn quickly.
3. Put no more than three things on a sheet. You are more likely to work on and complete a brief list. Long lists can discourage you.
4. Use only one side of the paper. Items on the back have a way of being overlooked.
5. Post the list where you can easily view it, such as on a refrigerator, a mirror, a desk, or a bedside table. Do not tuck it into a notebook, where it will be easy to ignore.
6. As you learn the material, write the date in the narrow column.
7. Write words of praise and encouragement to yourself in the narrow column: "Done! I did it!! Great! Good for me!!!"
8. Add other important information, such as the source of information, in the wide column.
9. Use drawings or anything else that will help you understand a point. Doodle funny drawings, for example. Do not clutter your list with irrelevant material, however. Use your creativity to further your goals, not hinder them.
10. Save the lists. When you have completed one, take it down and start another. Do not throw the completed lists away. Completed lists give you confidence. You accomplished a goal; you will accomplish the next, too. Save a record of what you have done. Put each completed list in a folder or a binder.
11. Use your lists for review. To study for an exam, take out your lists. Go over every item. You know everything on those lists. You enjoyed a sense of satisfaction from learning the material on the lists, and you created a handy tool for reviewing. Everything is right in the folder. Checking off items, seeing accomplishments grow, and having a folder full of information all make studying satisfying rather than painful.

▶ Maria is studying the history of American industries. The students have studied companies that began in this century but that no longer exist. The Studebaker Company, which had been an automobile manufacturer, is one such company. The students are learning about forces that create and destroy companies. Next Friday, the instructor will give a quiz to see what the class has learned about Studebaker.

Maria took out a piece of paper to make a things-to-learn list. She made a narrow margin on the right and, after thinking a moment, she put three items on the left:

1. Founders of the Studebaker Company.
2. Date of first Studebaker car.
3. Date of last Studebaker car.

She left space between each item. When she learned the names Clement, Henry, Jacob, John, and Peter—the five brothers who founded the Studebaker firm—she wrote them in the main column under item one and the date in the narrow column. She researched to learn that the first Studebaker was a kind of car called an electric runabout; built in 1902, it went 18 miles an hour. She put this information under item 2 with the date. She then did research to discover Studebaker made its last car in 1961, which she entered under item 3.

As soon as Maria felt she remembered these facts, she put the list in her notebook for later review and started another list. On this new sheet she put one item: Reasons for Studebaker going out of business.

## Flash Cards

You may not believe that flash cards are effective, or you may think of them as belonging in grade school. If so, you are missing an easy way to digest material you must learn. You can adapt your things-to-learn lists to use as flash cards. Be creative when making flash cards. Use your sense of humor. Use whatever helps you remember.

Make cards large enough to see easily, but small enough to carry. You want them with you so you can study them at the odd moment—on the bus, waiting for class to begin, on a quick break, waiting for an appointment. Remember reading about using found time in Chapter 4? This is a way of doing so.

You can make cards from larger pieces of paper or cardboard. Cardboard or heavier kinds of paper work best. Both 3 by 5 inch and 4 by 6 inch file cards are good.

Here are some tips for making flash cards.

- Create cards for a specific body of information.
- Use a main sentence or point for the first card.
- Write simple words (no more than three) to convey a thought on the remaining cards.
- Make sure each relates to the main thought on the first card.
- Add to each card a joke, doodle, quotation, cartoon, or anything else that will act as a memory trigger.

The exercise of preparing the cards will help you remember the points. Pulling them out and reading them whenever you have a spare moment will further imprint their message on your mind. The personal touch can help lighten the task of learning, as well as give you a pleasant association that can help you remember.

Another approach is to make an inexpensive flash card with a standard piece of paper. Divide the paper with a narrow column on one side and a wider one on the other. In the narrow column write a question, category, or word you want to define. In the wider column, write the answer. Then you can either fold the paper or otherwise cover up the answer to quiz yourself. The piece of paper is not as small as a file card, but you can fold it to fit in a pocket if necessary.

### Tape Recorder

Now is a time to use a tape recorder to your advantage. Here are two possible techniques:

- Read your notes into it and play them back to yourself while on the bus or eating a meal.
- Record questions or points from your things-to-learn lists. Later, quiz yourself, give your answers into the tape recorder and then play them back to confirm or correct them.

## STRATEGIES FOR REMEMBERING

Remembering is essential to learning. Tests encourage you to remember as well as determine how successfully you have learned specific information. Here are some easy-to-use strategies to help you remember.

- Classify data by groups.
- Number the groups.
- Connect items within groups.
- Create mnemonics.

You can use these strategies to prepare for all kinds of exams and in general studying. Since work and social life often require you to remember things—names, dates, statistics, ideas, theories, events—these strategies will be useful even after you have finished school.

As you read about these strategies you will see that you can use critical and creative thinking to remember more.

## Classify

You will rarely find isolated facts unrelated to anything else. One bit of information always connects to some other bit of information. It can be difficult to remember a specific fact in isolation. When you relate facts and see their relationship to one another, you can remember them more easily.

When you need to remember a series of facts, look for ways to group or classify them. Then you can use the groups as cues for the facts. Since there are fewer groups than there are facts, they are easier to recall. (This is like outlining: collect items under main ideas.) Consider this random list of variables affecting the ocean tides.

> Storm surge.
> Coriolis effect (rotation of the earth).
> Shape of ocean basin.
> Wind.
> Distance from sun/moon.

Quickly put the book aside for a moment and try to name the variables without looking. How did you do? Now consider this list organized or classified into two categories:

> *Predictable*
>   Distance from sun/moon.
>   Coriolis effect (rotation of the earth).
>   Shape of ocean basin.
> *Unpredictable*
>   Wind.
>   Storm surge.

By grouping items, you make them easier to remember. Instead of five unrelated facts to remember, you have only two groups of related facts. Smaller blocks of information are easier to remember than larger ones. When taking the test, you can cue yourself by thinking, "Okay, what are the *groups* of variables? What are the *predictable* variables?"

### Number

Now ask yourself *how many* items there are in each group. This will help you know if you have included everything.

You may think that remembering how many items there are in a group just adds to the things you need to remember. However, by using different levels of remembering, you reduce the strain on your short-term memory. The facts are stored in long-term memory. If you remember the number of predictable variables, you have a good chance of remembering them all. If you do not remember how many there are, you might recall one or two and no more.

### Connect

You can help yourself by making connections among the items in each category. For example, the unpredictable variables affecting tides are both related to weather. In fact, both have to do with wind.

> Two unpredictable variables
> 1. Wind.
> 2. Storm surge (caused by high wind in a storm).

Similarly, the predictable items all have to do with the earth's shape and movements. Remembering this, and that there are three items altogether, gives you another clue when you sit down to take the test.

> Three predictable variables—earth's shape and movement
> 1. Distance from sun/moon—(as earth moves closer or further away).
> 2. Coriolis effect (as the earth rotates or moves on its axis).
> 3. Shape of ocean basins.

Making connections between items is a memory aid that helps you overcome the distractions and confusion caused by test anxiety.

### Create or Use Mnemonics

Mnemonics (the first *m* is silent: "ne-MON-ics") are associations unrelated to the content of the material but that help you remember. The rhyme "In fourteen hundred ninety-two, Columbus sailed the ocean blue" is a *mnemonic* for remembering when Columbus made his famous voyage. That "two" rhymes with "blue" is pure coincidence. It has nothing to do with the events, but it helps you remember them.

When you have to memorize material, mnemonics are a big help. Many mnemonics take the form of sentences based on the first letters of important words. For instance, to remember the constituents of soil—air, humus, mineral salts, water, bacteria, and rock particles—say "*All hairy men surely will buy razors.*" The first letters of the words in that peculiar sentence are the first letters of the words to memorize. The sentence jogs your memory. It is easier to remember because its parts are connected.

You may have heard the one for the G clef musical scale. The lines of the scale are the notes E, G, B, D, and F, which makes the sentence "Every Good Boy Does Fine." You can make up your own mnemonic in this style for just about any list of terms to remember.

## TAKING OBJECTIVE TESTS

Objective tests require you to fill in blanks, to decide whether a given statement is true or false, to match information in two columns, or to select the correct answer from several choices. First you will learn general strategies to follow for taking any type of objective test. Then you will study strategies for specific types of tests.

### General Strategies

- Read all directions carefully.

- Read every question carefully before answering.

- Answer easy questions first. Do not become bogged down. If, after reading a question carefully, you cannot decide on the right answer, do not stall. Go to the next question. After answering all the easy questions, you can return to the unanswered questions.

- Look for clues in other questions. Often one question will contain clues to the answer of another question, or at least trigger associations in your mind that lead to an answer.

- Check your answers when you have finished. If there are some you are not sure of, try to leave a few minutes at the end to give them more thought. Do not change an answer unless you are certain it is wrong. It is usually best to go with your first answer.

### Fill-In Questions Strategies

- When completing fill-in questions, you usually need key words and phrases. So, if you know you will be asked such questions, be especially careful to look for key words and phrases when you study.

- Look carefully at the wording of fill-in questions. Often grammar and structure give clues to the answer required. A fill-in question for Chapter 11 on essay test terms might read as follows:

    > When you *compare* two things, you deal with both their _____ and their _____. When you *contrast* two things, you deal mainly with their _____.
    > The words "both" and "mainly" suggest that what you deal with when contrasting is one of the things you deal with when comparing. You know now that you only have to come up with two terms, not three. (The answers are "differences," "similarities," and "differences.")

- Paraphrase the statement. You may get a mental block if you keep repeating the same words over and over as you struggle to fill in the blanks. Rephrase the statement in your own words. Doing this often unlocks your memory, which simply repeating the statement does not.

### True/False Questions Strategies

- Remember that a statement is false if even one little bit of it is false.

- Be alert to exceptions to a rule. Look carefully at statements containing such words as "all," "every," "only," "no," and "none." For example, this statement is false:

    > *All trees with needles are evergreens.*

*Most* trees with needles—pines, spruce, firs—are indeed evergreens. But larch and bald cypress are two species with needles that do in fact shed them every fall. The word *all* makes that seemingly innocent statement a booby trap. If there are exceptions in the field you are studying, make sure you know them so you do not get tripped up.

### Matching Questions Strategies

Matching questions are those in which you match items in one column with those in another. For instance, you might be asked to match lists of American presidents with the years they served, authors with their works, states or countries with their capitals.

- Start with the items you know. You will then be able to apply a strategy of elimination to those that you do not know.

- Look carefully for clues.

For example, if you were being tested on American history of the early 1800s, you might be given a list of names—Hamilton, Lewis and Clark, Genet—in column A and asked to match them with descriptions in column B of what those people did. You might not recall reading about Genet. But if you read "French minister to the United States" in column B, you might figure, "Well, Genet sounds like a French name."

You might also see "Explorers of Louisiana Territory" in column B, and decide to match that with "Lewis and Clark," even if you remember nothing about them, simply because both "explorers" and "Lewis and Clark" are plural.

Try this matching test on linguistics. Match the terms in column A to their definitions in column B. You may know nothing about the subject, but if you use your head you can probably get most, or all, of the answers. Before reading further, put the number of the item in column A in the space after the column B item that it matches.

| COLUMN A | COLUMN B |
|---|---|
| 1. Noam Chomsky | Smallest meaningful units of sound in a language ___ |
| 2. morphemes | Influential figure in formal linguistics ___ |
| 3. syntax | Characteristics distinguishing one phonetic unit from another ___ |
| 4. distinctive features | The study of how sentences are structured ___ |

Here is how you would use clues to make correct matches.

"Noam Chomsky" sounds and looks like a person's name. The only phrase in column B that can really apply to a person is "influential figure in formal linguistics."

Next, there are two plural terms—"morphemes" and "distinctive features"—and two plural answers. That means that the one singular phrase left—"the study of how sentences are structured"—must go with the one term left—"syntax."

As for the remaining two, "characteristics" means almost the same as "features," and "distinctive" and "distinguishing" are nearly synonymous (having the same meaning) also, so it would be a good bet that "distinctive features" are "characteristics distinguishing one phonetic unit from another." That leaves "morphemes," which are indeed the smallest meaningful units of sound in a language.

This is a simple example, but the strategies work in more complex situations as well. There is no substitute for knowing the subject, but these techniques can enhance your performance. Simply by applying common sense, you can answer questions you never thought you knew the answers to—and learn the answers in the process!

## Multiple-Choice Questions Strategies

Close reading and common sense also pay off when you take multiple-choice tests. On these, each question has a stem—an incomplete statement or a direct question—followed by several choices, usually four or five.

- First be sure to read the directions and know what you are supposed to do. The directions may read one of these ways:

    Pick the *one* correct choice (the others are simply wrong).
    Pick the most nearly correct or "*best*" choice (some of the others may be partly right, so you need to choose carefully).
    Pick whatever number of answers are correct. For this option, you might check more than one choice.
    Pick the answer that is false.

If you cannot identify the correct answer for a multiple choice question, try these strategies.

- Try to think of an answer even if it is not one of the choices. Decide which item on the list is closest to yours. Ask yourself how they differ. How does that affect the answer? Does it have to do with the way the question is worded? Could the answer given on the test make sense under certain circumstances?

- Eliminate obviously wrong answers. Choose from those that are left. You automatically increase your chances when you do this.

- Read the question through and complete it with each of the possible answers in turn. Putting the question and the answers together this way may help you identify ones that are definitely wrong, or possibly right.

- Paraphrase each answer. Think carefully about what it means. You may discover something that you missed in your first, quick reading. Do not let the pressure of the test prevent you from thinking carefully about the answers.

When you read each question be sure you understand *what* is being asked. Try this question:

> When Columbus set sail on his famous voyage, he challenged the popular belief that
> a. the earth is round
> b. America is east of Europe
> c. the earth is flat
> d. none of the above

You might look at *a* "the earth is round"—and associate it with Columbus. If you don't read carefully you will pick the wrong answer: the question is what belief did he *challenge*? The answer is therefore *c*—"the earth is flat." This is an obvious one, but difficult questions can trip you up in this way. Read everything carefully before you answer.

With multiple-choice questions as with other kinds of questions, you can look for clues, rule out certain choices, and apply common sense. Knowing that you can use such tactics will help you be effective—not bewildered—as you prepare for and take tests.

Suppose you were taking a multiple-choice test on comparative religion after having been absent for an entire section that you never managed to make up. You see the following question and cannot for the life of you remember the meaning of the word.

> What is "Taoism"?
> a. A legendary figure in Indian mythology.
> b. An ancient Chinese philosophy and religion.
> c. A Buddhist ritual.
> d. A town in New Mexico.

You can rule out *d* immediately. Even if you know there is a town in New Mexico with a name like "Taoism" (actually it is "Taos"), in no way would you be expected to know that in a course on religion. How do you choose between the remaining three possible answers?

Look again at the word you are defining. Notice the *-ism* ending, which is so often associated with religions (Buddhism, Hinduism), philosophies (Stoicism, Existentialism), and other belief systems (communism, capitalism). The answer that reflects this is *b*. Even if you knew nothing else about the word, you would be justified in making an educated guess based only on that information. (The answer is indeed *b*.)

## SUMMING UP

Objective tests are those tests which ask fill-in, true/false, matching, or multiple-choice questions.

Helpful tools to use when studying for a test include: things-to-learn lists, flash cards, and tape recorders. Use all three to study, learn, and encourage yourself.

Strategies for remembering information are

- Classifying data into groups.
- Numbering the groups and items within groups.
- Connecting items within groups.
- Creating mnemonics.

When taking objective tests, no matter what type, use these general strategies:

- Read all directions carefully.
- Read each question carefully before answering.
- Look for clues in other questions.
- Answer easy questions first and do not get bogged down on hard ones.
- When you have finished, check your answers.

When answering fill-in questions, look for key words, understand the grammar of the question, and paraphrase the question.

When answering true/false questions, remember that a statement is false even if just one bit of it is false. Also look for exceptions.

In answering matching questions, do those items you know first, and look for grammatical clues to help with the ones you are not sure of.

In multiple-choice questions, read the directions carefully, try to think of an answer, eliminate obviously wrong answers, try out possible answers, and paraphrase each answer.

## ▼ DEVELOPING YOUR SKILLS

Exercise 1

### Practice Classifying

In the following table, classify this list of telemarketing terms into three groups: **Types of Call**, **Sales Presentation**, and **Telemarketing Methods**. Write the terms in the appropriate columns.

ending
product/service sales call
appointment call
inbound direct method
fact-finding
closing
outbound indirect method
call preparation
inbound indirect method
opening
persuading
service and order-entry call
outbound direct method
market research call
idea call

| Types of Call | Sales Presentation | Telemarketing Methods |
|---|---|---|
|  |  |  |
|  |  |  |
|  |  |  |
|  |  |  |
|  |  |  |
|  |  |  |
|  |  |  |
|  |  |  |

Exercise 2

## Identify and Connect Key Terms

Work with notes from a recent reading assignment. If you have not already done so, make a list of key terms and then put them into two or more groups. When you have done that, try to identify connections among the items in each group.

Exercise 3

## Make a Mnemonic

Write a sentence in which each word begins with the first letter of the items in the list of planets orbiting the sun. The plants are: Mercury, Venus, Earth, Mars, Jupiter, Saturn, Uranus, Neptune, and Pluto.

_____

_____

_____

_____

_____

_____

_____

Exercise 4

## Make a Things-to-Learn List

Select a passage that you have recently read for another course. Prepare for an objective test on it by making two things-to-learn lists. Put just three things on each list. Follow the instructions for creating a things-to-learn list that you read on page 208. Make your lists on separate sheets of paper.

Exercise 5

## Make Flash Cards

Prepare flash cards from the things-to-learn list you developed in Exercise 4.

Exercise 6

## Practice Taking Tests

Take the following tests. When you finish, check your answers with the key on the next page.

### Fill-In

Complete the following statements by writing the correct word or phrase on the blank lines.

1. One kind of study device consisting of 3 by 5 inch cards with a short sentence or a few words on each is called _____ _____.
2. One test-taking strategy is to do the _____ questions first.
3. When you need to remember a series of facts, look for ways to _____ them into groups.
4. You normally need to know ___ _____ and _____ for fill-in questions.

### True/False

Put a T after each true statement and an F after each false statement.

5. A mnemonic is a device for making connections among unrelated items.____
6. You need to read directions and questions carefully.____
7. For all tests, the best strategy is to answer each question in sequence before moving on.____
8. In true/false tests, a statement is true even if only a little bit of it is false.____

### Multiple Choice

Choose the best answer or answers for each question. Circle the letter of the answer you select.

Chapter 10                                      Taking Objective Tests—221

9. Which of the following is not a good strategy for taking objective tests?

   a) Read directions carefully.
   b) Read each question carefully before answering.
   c) Do not get bogged down on a question.
   d) Never go on to the next question until you have completed the previous one.

10. Select all answers that apply: Good multiple-choice test-taking strategy includes:

    a) Eliminating obviously wrong answers.
    b) Double-checking your spelling.
    c) Reading each question carefully.
    d) Using common sense.

## Key to Exercises

Fill-in. 1. flash cards; 2. easier; 3. classify; 4. key words and phrases.

True/false. 5. F; 6. T; 7. F; 8. F.

Multiple choice. 9. d; 10. a, c, d.

# 11 Taking Essay Tests

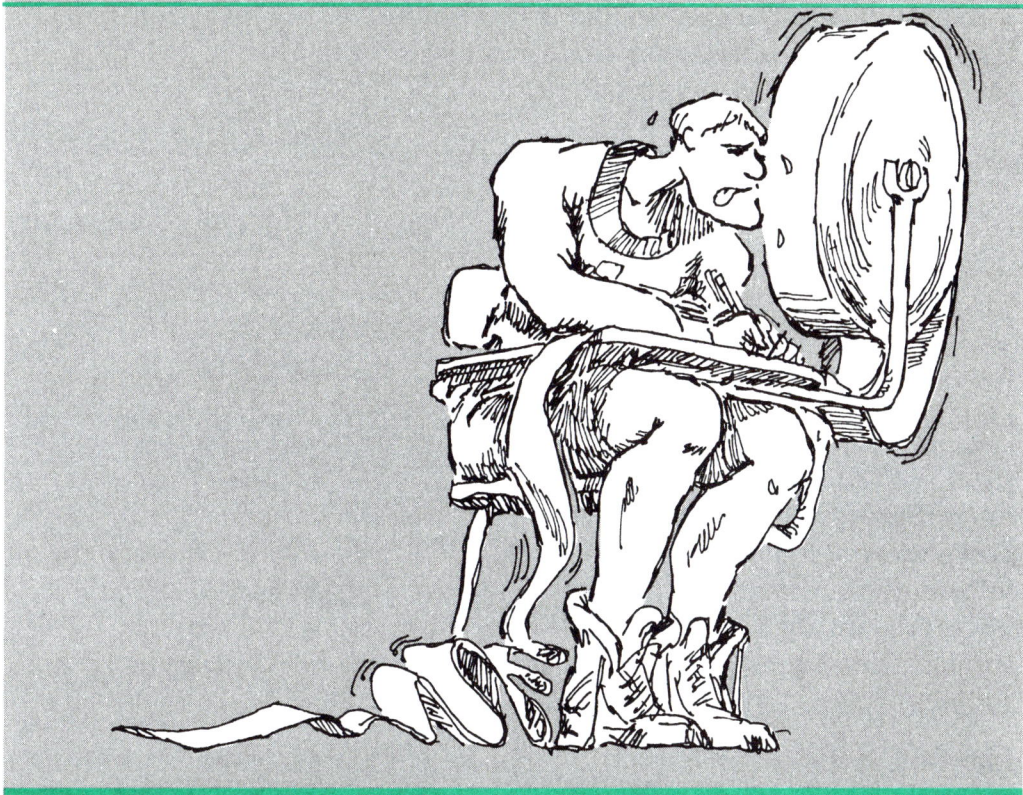

**When you have completed this chapter, you will be able to improve your test performance by applying strategies for taking essay tests.**

When studying for essay tests you will use critical thinking to interpret, analyze, and organize information before you write. Essay tests require you to write responses in your own words, which is a test of your ability to think creatively. Objective tests mostly measure your retention or memorization of facts. Essay tests are an attempt to measure your broader understanding of ideas and concepts.

## PREPARING FOR ESSAY TESTS

There are specific things you can do to increase your success on essay tests. This chapter discusses tactics for preparing to take essay tests.

### Know What Your Instructor Wants

Know what the instructor expects. Students often lose points for failing to answer the question fully or to follow instructions, even if their answers display knowledge of the subject. Avoid this pitfall. Read and follow instructions carefully. Have a sense of what the instructor expects you to learn from the course.

### Identify Major Themes

Your instructor may have a theory or an idea to convey, backed up by the facts in lectures and reading assignments. Being aware of that theory or idea is your key to understanding the course. How can you do this? In the lectures and reading:

- Watch for patterns or trends.
- Keep your ears open for words repeated throughout, even when the instructor is discussing different topics.
- Try to sum up the course with one descriptive sentence.

Ask yourself, "What is the instructor getting at?" If you do not know, make an appointment to talk with the instructor—but do so before the test.

Even if there is no one specific idea, instructors will usually have a perspective, or series of perspectives, to use as a way to organize the information. A course on bookkeeping may use perspectives of tax laws, accounting principles, and record keeping to deal with the subject. Identifying how each perspective works helps you grasp the subject.

Identifying the perspective, or even a set of facts the instructor wants to convey as the major theme of the course, will help you do well on tests. If the instructor does not identify them, review your notes and look for recurring words or ideas.

Does your course in accounting deal with legal requirements more than with mechanics? Why? In your course on data processing, are you spending a lot of time on payrolls? What does this tell you about the instructor's expectations?

### Use Study Sheets

Before a test, instructors often hand out study sheets that list the questions that might appear or give examples of the *kinds* of questions that will appear on a test. This gives you an automatic advantage when studying because now you know what material you are expected to master.

### Make Up Questions

One of the best ways to prepare for an essay test is to make up your own essay test questions. Answering the questions gives you practice, but so does thinking up the questions in the first place. It forces you to examine every facet of the subject to be sure you have covered everything.

- When thinking of questions, make sure you do not just ask factual questions (what, where, when, who, how many).

- Ask questions that make you think, expand, and make connections.

- Ask questions that require:

  | | |
  |---|---|
  | Comparisons | Reasons |
  | Evaluations | Illustrations (examples, not pictures) |
  | Descriptions | Interpretations |
  | Proofs | Conjectures |
  | Applications | What-if answers |

- Write down the answers. The answers do not require complete sentences, but they should cover all the important points.

- Keep these answers and review them. When you have answered your questions, review them to see if you missed anything. (This is a good strategy for using a study sheet also.)

## Brainstorm

Working with others is an excellent way to prepare for a test because different people usually remember different aspects of the same presentation. Brainstorming can be very effective when several people are involved.

- Brainstorm essay questions with a small group of classmates. Once you have the questions, you can answer them separately, then compare notes. Or you can discuss the answers in a group. In either case find out how your classmates would answer the questions. You will almost certainly get something from them that you might have missed yourself.

- Brainstorm the major themes of the course. Ask classmates what they think is the central idea of the course and why. Discuss the instructor's opinion on specific subjects: does the instructor disagree with the textbook, for example? Your classmates' ideas will almost certainly add to your own.

## Use Class Discussions

Class discussions are excellent ways to prepare for essay tests. They involve the same type of open-ended questions—why, explain, compare—that are so common on tests. Use class discussions to:

- Find out what the instructor expects.
- Identify what you know and need to learn.
- Test your ideas.
- Take notes on new information and others' ideas.

## Review Old Tests

Learn from your own past actions by reviewing tests you have taken. File your tests away, and before the next one:

- Review the questions and answers on the graded test.
- Make a note of successes, and read the instructor's comments. (If you did poorly on an essay test, discuss it with your instructor and find out what he or she expected in the answer.)
- Ask yourself about your test performance:

    *Did I follow the instructions in the essay question?*
    If a question asked for contrasts and comparisons, did you go over the topic point by point, or merely describe it in general terms? If the question said to present supporting data from certain sources, did you cover the sources?

    *How much did my studying help?*
    Did you study material related to the test or something different? Did the questions come from lecture material or from reading or both?

    *Did I know my material and yet find that I was still unable to put it to use?*
    You may need to seek help from the instructor if you cannot express the substance of the course. Look for general ideas to organize your thoughts.

    *Did I lose points because I spent too much time on one question and not enough on another?*
    Did you get too involved with part of a question and simply forget to include something significant? Disorganization can lose you points.

## Polish Your Notes

When reviewing your reading and class notes for a test, focus your efforts further by using these five steps:

1. Read your notes with a pen, a pencil, or a highlighter in hand. Make comments, insert new information, jot down new connections you have made since you last reviewed the notes.
2. Reduce your notes to a short memory list of key words—use mnemonics to remember them.
3. Recite the memory lists aloud. Speaking aloud brings two more of your faculties—hearing and speech—into play, increasing the effectiveness of your studying.
4. Reflect; ask questions. Look beyond the easy answers to discover connections. Relate your lists to each other.
5. Review your annotated notes, memory lists, and questions.

### Improve Your Writing Ability

Taking an essay test requires good writing and organizational skills. It is unfortunate to lose points because you cannot state your thoughts clearly in writing or because you ran out of time. You may know the material, but your instructor will not find that out if you cannot make yourself understood or are disorganized. If you are having trouble with writing:

- Seek help from a tutor. Take a course in composition, or take a course that requires you to write under time constraints.

- Use a handbook on writing, such as Strunk and White's *Elements of Style*.

- Read to improve your writing—novels, history, anything you can get your hands on. (The more you read, the better you write.)

## KNOWING YOUR TEST TERMS

Understanding words frequently used in questions helps you to do well on essay tests. A test might require you to *analyze* a point of view, to *contrast* one view with another, or to *criticize* a viewpoint. For each question, you would need much of the same basic information, but you would not write the same essay for each.

Knowing exactly the meaning of words you will frequently find in essay tests can help you find key points when you study. It can also help you organize your thoughts, decide what you need to say, and answer the right question when you take a test. Consider the following words and how you might respond to them on an essay test. Consider the role that critical and creative thinking plays in each.

**Analyze** means break into separate parts and discuss, examine, and interpret each part. To analyze America's trade with Japan, you would break the subject down into subtopics, like products sold to and bought from Japan and international trade agreements. You would write about each of those and how they relate to each other.

**Compare** means to identify the differences and similarities of two or more things.

**Contrast** means to look at two different things and show their differences. When you compare or contrast, you need to focus on particular aspects—size and shape, for instance. Do not lose track and write about the shape of one thing, the size of another.

**Criticize** means to make judgments—but not without reasons. It does not mean simply to call something "weak" or "strong." If you say a law has "weak" enforcement provisions, you need to show what makes them weak. Do not just list them and say, "These are weak." *Why* are they weak? Not enough money? Too many loopholes? To criticize, you often must analyze, compare, evaluate.

**Define** means to give the meaning. To do so, you should be specific and, usually, brief. Often, it helps to include an example. "A legume is a plant with a pod that splits into two valves, with seeds attached. Peas and beans are legumes."

**Describe** means to give a detailed, specific account. Make a picture with words. List qualities, characteristics, parts. Be as specific as you can. Do not say simply that there was a "large crowd" at the meeting; say there were almost 200 people there.

**Discuss** means to consider, debate the pros and cons of an issue, compare and contrast, describe. It does not mean to ramble. And again, it is important to be specific and to back up what you say.

**Enumerate** means to list. You may be asked to enumerate ideas, events, or reasons. Usually, if you are asked to enumerate, there are more than a couple of items to enumerate. You may have to explain why each term belongs in the list. If you are asked to enumerate the causes of bankruptcy, you should not simply write "economic policies." Explain which policies, and how they contributed to the bankruptcy.

**Evaluate** means to determine the worth of something. Did it succeed? What is its value? Is it working? When you evaluate something, you give your opinion, but you must back up that opinion. You cannot just say, "I think the anti-litter law is a success." You must cite such things as cleaner areas, the comments of sanitation officials, the amount of money paid in fines by people found breaking the law.

**Illustrate** means to give concrete examples. You can illustrate the problems facing cities, for instance, by giving the numbers of homeless people. Even when you are answering a question that does not specifically require you to illustrate, you can back up what you say by illustration with specific examples.

**Interpret** means to explain the meaning by describing and evaluating. You might, for instance, interpret a poem by describing it, citing some specific lines, then evaluating how the poem conveys a picture or an idea. You would try to show how the parts work together to give a complete, specific meaning.

**Outline** means describe main ideas, characteristics, or events. You need to be thorough, not leave out any important aspect, and not waste time trying to get the details right on some minor point. On an essay test, you usually do not need to make a formal outline, complete with roman numerals. You do need to show major points and related secondary points.

**Prove** means support with facts—usually facts presented in the text or lectures. Marshall as many relevant facts as you can, and be sure to show how they support the point you want to prove.

**State** means to show or explain precisely. If you are asked to state the reasons why the American colonies revolted against English rule, do not just write, "They were angry about taxes." Rather, explain why they thought the taxes were unfair and why this led to their revolt.

**Summarize** means to give a brief, condensed account. You should skip minor details but should try to include a conclusion, as the summary of a chapter does.

**Trace** means to show the order of events or progress of a subject. You may need to stop and think just what the beginning was. You should make brief notes before starting to write, so as not to skip things or put them in the wrong order.

## TAKING ESSAY TESTS

Being organized will save you from the "Oh no! I only have ten more minutes" blues. To be organized, use the following techniques.

### Read Directions Carefully

As with objective tests, read the directions carefully. Underline important words. Instructors often include several questions and let the student decide which ones to answer. For example, a common direction is "Answer two of the following three questions." If you did not read this direction carefully, you could end up answering all three partially instead of two thoroughly. Underline the words "<u>Answer two</u>."

## Read Questions Once Through Quickly

Read the questions once as soon as you receive the test. Then reread the questions carefully. Note whether questions have point values. (One question may be worth 20 points while three or four short questions are 10 points each.) Plan to allot more time to higher-point questions.

## Jot Down Ideas

Make notes as you read the test questions to refer to later when writing complete answers.

## Do Easiest Questions First

Answer the easiest questions first so you can work from your strengths. Clearly show the instructor what you do understand, and build your own self-confidence for tackling the more difficult questions later. Note that some instructors may assign different point values to different questions. So be aware of that when selecting which questions to answer first.

## Decide How Much Time for Each Question

Decide how much time you want to allot for each question. When that time is up, move to another question, whether you are done or not. If you have not finished, leave space and come back to it later. It is likely that you will get at least partial credit for the answer, which is better than losing all the points on an unanswered question. When you have time, go back and complete the partial answers.

## Watch Out for Modifiers

Be alert to modifiers, which can alter the meaning of the question—sometimes making it the opposite of what it seems to mean. Ones to watch out for especially are **quantifiers**—all, every, most, many, few, some, none, always, often, usually, rarely, never—and **superlatives**—best, highest, strongest, worst, least, fewest, smallest, and so on.

## Make an Outline for Each Answer

Create an outline for each answer. "What?" you might say, "take time to write an outline?" You bet. Write it on scrap paper. Your outline will prevent you from forgetting important points and from writing too much on less important ones. It will also help you plan how much time you will need to complete your answer.

### Include Outlines for Uncompleted Questions

If you run out of time, write down main ideas or sketch an outline of an answer for questions you did not get to. If you make a good-faith effort to show you know the material, the instructor may give you partial credit. Get the gist of the answer down; do not worry about polishing the writing.

### Structure Your Essay

Write a theme sentence. In your first sentence, try to state the overall theme that you will support in the essay.

Allow yourself time to write a two- or three-sentence conclusion summing up the point or points you have made.

### Check Your Writing

When you decide how much time to spend on the questions, leave about five minutes at the end to review answers and your writing. This is a very important step. Have a mental checklist of what to look for.

Check the mechanics: spelling, punctuation, sentence structure, legibility of your handwriting, and words left out (a common mistake when people hurry). Any of these errors could reduce your grade even if your material is essentially correct.

Check the content: organization, clarity, errors of fact. Make sure you have answered all the parts of the question. For example, if it said to compare and contrast, be sure you have done both.

### Work Calmly and Steadily

Work calmly and steadily. Do not panic. Keep everything in perspective. Do not let grades be the overriding measure of your self-worth. When you are calm, your thought process functions more effectively. Another benefit will be improved handwriting. (If your instructor cannot read what you have written, you need not have taken the test at all.)

## SUMMING UP

Essay tests require your critical thinking ability to interpret, analyze, and organize information and your creative thinking ability to write your answers in your own words.

There are some specific things you can do to help yourself succeed on an essay test. These tactics for preparing to take essay tests are:

> Know what your instructor wants.
> Identify major themes.
> Use study sheets.
> Make up questions.
> Brainstorm.
> Use class discussions.
> Review old tests.
> Polish notes.
> Improve your writing ability.

Also, it is important to understand terms that appear in many essay test questions. Common terms include:

| | |
|---|---|
| Analyze | Illustrate |
| Compare | Interpret |
| Criticize | Outline |
| Define | Prove |
| Describe | State |
| Discuss | Summarize |
| Enumerate | Trace |
| Evaluate | |

When the time comes to take an essay test, remember the strategies to help you. Organize your thoughts by reading test directions carefully. Quickly read all questions when you receive the test to decide how much time to spend on each. Jot down ideas and do the easiest questions first. Make an outline for your answer. Write a theme sentence and conclusion. Work calmly and steadily, and check your work.

If you run out of time, include an outline or the main ideas for unanswered questions to show that you know the material.

# ▼ DEVELOPING YOUR SKILLS

Exercise 1

## Prepare For Essay Tests

How well do you study for essay tests? In the space below check off the strategies you now use for preparing to take an essay test. Decide whether you use them always (A), sometimes (S), rarely (R), or never (N).

| In preparing to take an essay test, I: | A | S | R | N |
|---|---|---|---|---|
| Know what the instructor wants | | | | |
| Identify major themes | | | | |
| Use study sheets | | | | |
| Ask my own questions | | | | |
| Brainstorm | | | | |
| Use class discussion | | | | |
| Review old tests | | | | |
| Polish my notes | | | | |
| Know my writing ability | | | | |

Write those strategies you use sometimes, rarely, or never. Remember to use them the next time you study for an essay test.

_____

_____

_____

_____

_____

_____

# Exercise 2

## Develop Your Own Questions

Read the selection below. Develop study questions that require you to think and make connections. Write your questions on the lines below.

> Work skills are the behaviors that you use to perform and complete your work tasks. In fact, one may define a work skill as the behavior required by a work task. In other words, each work task defines a work skill. There are then as many work skills as there are work tasks. In our modern world of work, there are literally thousands of work skills. Every time a new technology is invented or an old technology modified, the possibility of several, possibly hundreds, of new work skills is introduced.
>
> For some jobs, the work skills can be learned on the job. The worker can be taught the required work skills in hours or days. For most jobs nowadays, however, workers need to be equipped with a minimum set of work skills before they can be considered for hiring. Workers learn these minimum skills in formal training courses. Some of these courses might be provided by the hiring companies themselves, but most often training courses are provided by educational institutions, both public and private.
>
> *Psychology: Human Relations and Work Adjustment*, 7e, by Rene V. Dawis, Rosemary T. Fruehling, Neild B. Oldham. McGraw-Hill, 1989, page 285.

_____

_____

_____

_____

_____

_____

_____

_____

_____

Exercise 3

## Brainstorm

With several classmates, brainstorm the answers to the questions you developed in Exercise 2.

Exercise 4

## Take an Essay Test

Take an essay test on this chapter. Answer three of the following questions.

1. State why it is important to know the differences among terms used in essay tests. Illustrate with examples.

_____

_____

_____

_____

2. Define the following: *analyze, interpret, trace*.

_____

_____

_____

_____

3. Compare and contrast the terms *outline* and *summarize*. Do you feel they mean the same thing? Why or why not?

_____

_____

_____

_____

4. Describe the purpose and content of the section on terms.

_____

_____

_____

5. Evaluate the section on terms. Does it achieve its goals? Why or why not?

_____

_____

_____

### Exercise 5

#### Write an Essay Test Question

Suppose you are going to take an essay test on this book. Pick a chapter and write an essay test question that you think might be asked on such a test. Then get together with a few classmates and compare your questions and answers. Use the space below to record your question and a summary answer. Ask a classmate to check that you have stated your thoughts in a clear and organized way.

_____

_____

_____

_____

_____

Exercise 6

Make a note on your calendar to refer to this chapter three days before your next essay test, or when you plan to start studying for it.

Exercise 7

## Review Past Essay Test

Find an essay test that you have taken recently, one that you wish you had done better on. Analyze it in terms of the skills you learned in this chapter. Try to identify what you did not do, as well as what you felt you did do, correctly. Develop a plan of action for a future essay test, emphasizing the skills you need to concentrate on. Briefly describe the plan below.

_____

_____

_____

_____

_____

_____

# 12 Succeeding in the Workplace

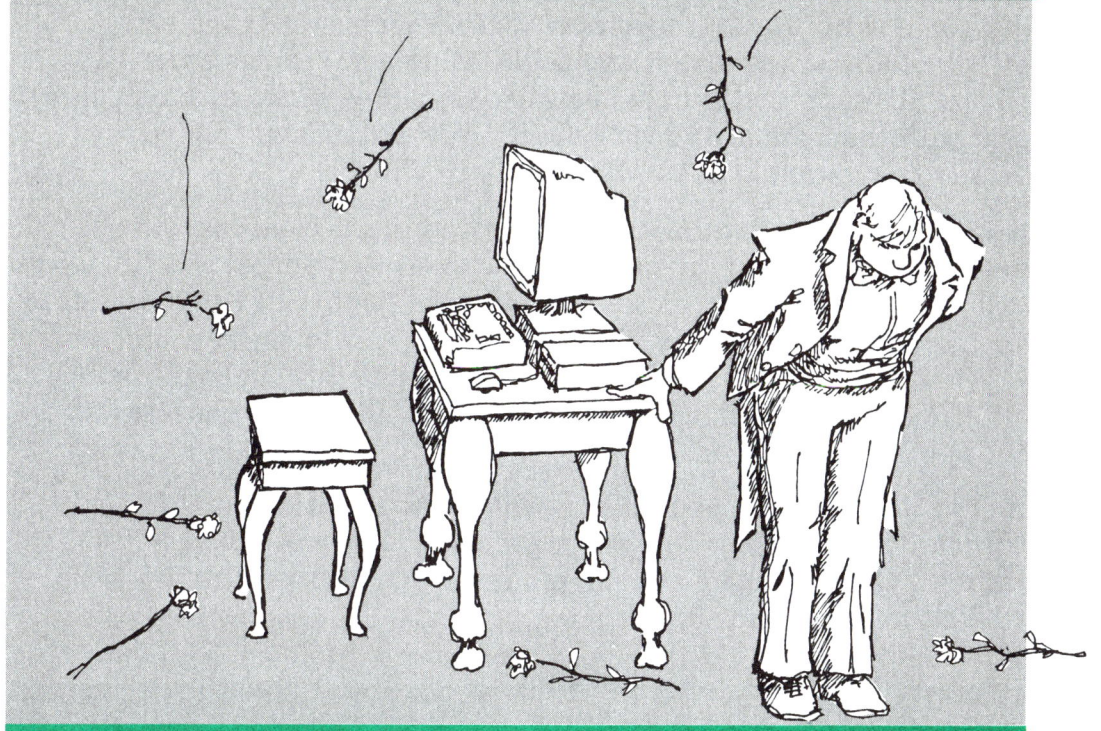

**When you have completed this chapter, you will be able to apply thinking and learning skills to workplace situations.**

This book is about learning—learning how to think and plan for yourself, learning from others through reading and listening, and finally about using what you have learned to achieve success. Learning skills are essential in school, as you know. In this last chapter you will see how the same learning skills can be applied on the job and elsewhere throughout your life.

You may think that note-taking and test-taking skills will be of no use to you once you are finished with school. Not so. You will find that these skills will serve you well in other phases of your life. Thinking, planning, learning through reading and listening, and using your knowledge effectively are all skills that will serve you well whatever you decide to do next week, next year, for the rest of your life. They will enable you to control your life and make it more the kind of life you want it to be.

Learning is a life-long project. This is particularly true in our high-tech, ever changing society.

For one simple example, consider computers. Suppose that among the courses you have taken at school is word processing. Upon graduating, you quickly get a job as an administrative assistant based on your ability to use certain word processing software. Six months later, you are good in your job and are happy with it.

Then, one Monday morning, your supervisor hands you a handful of disks and says, "Here's the newest version of our word processing software. Would you load it and begin using it as soon as possible, please? It's supposed to have some excellent new commands. I'm sure that with the manual and your ability, you will master this new version in a couple of days without any trouble."

New versions of software—for word processing, accounting, data processing, budgeting, and so forth—are released almost yearly. New technologies affect many kinds of businesses today. Those who want to keep up in their jobs must often be learning how to use new processes. If you have developed your creative and critical thinking skills along with your study skills, you will have no trouble learning how to use the new technology.

As you read the new manual, you will use your critical thinking skills to identify what is new that you must learn. You will use your creative thinking skills to relate the new elements you discover to those with which you are already familiar.

## RESOLVING PROBLEMS

Whatever job you have, you will have to do two things. First you will have to do the specific tasks, such as type letters or repair copiers, that are required to do that job. Second you will have to deal with unexpected problems that inevitably arise.

If your job is to repair copiers, you will be given the right tools to do the job. But suppose one day one of the tools breaks and you cannot perform your job. You can either simply wait for someone else to tell you what to do, or you can participate in the process of solving the problem. The more you participate in solving the problem, the more valuable you will be to your employer and the better able to help yourself. You will use critical and creative thinking to find a solution.

Another way to deal with problems is to anticipate them, be prepared for them.

### Try to Anticipate Problems

In the following example read how Miles and Toni handled a workplace problem that they shared. They were able to anticipate what might go wrong and think through a solution.

> Miles and Toni work at Fast Express, a company that delivers packages and letters overnight anywhere in the country. Each of them supervises a group of drivers in company-owned vans who deliver packages throughout the city. Miles has just read about a new office building that will open next month. He says to Toni, "I bet a lot of companies moving in will want to use Fast Express. The building is in my area, but my drivers are already so busy they can't possibly add it to their route."
>
> Toni replies, "That's too bad. You know we can't hire any more people this year."
>
> Miles and Toni decide to try to find a way to solve this problem. They know that in a few days their manager will want to talk to them about it.
>
> Toni says to Miles, "We need to do some critical and creative thinking to solve this problem quickly. I learned a technique in school that might help us. Take the word IDEA. Each letter stands for a step in creative thinking,
>
> "Illuminate your problem.
> "Develop possible solutions.
> "Ease off for a while.
> "Arrive at a solution.
>
> "You work through these steps, and I will work through the steps for critical thinking using the word SOLVE.
>
> "State the problem.
> "Organize my thoughts.
> "Learn my options.
> "Validate the implications of the options.
> "Evaluate and choose a solution."
>
> Miles is not sure it will work but agrees to try and suggests that they get together for lunch on Friday to compare solutions. He is not sure what will happen when he eases off but figures that because his week is so busy he will have no problem doing this. What he has to do is find some time early in the week to define the problem in detail and think of possible solutions.
>
> Toni decides to talk with Cory who used to be a supervisor at Fast Express. Cory might have experienced a similar problem and could help Toni validate her options.
>
> When Toni and Miles get together on Friday, they have three good possible solutions to their problem.

You can see how Toni and Miles anticipated that they would be asked to find a way to make deliveries to the new building without hiring new drivers. Here are three options they rejected and the reasons they rejected them.

Chapter 12                                    Succeeding in the Workplace—241

**Option**: *Don't deliver to the new building.*

**Rejected**: *Fast Express wants the new business.*

**Option**: *Ask the least experienced driver in Miles' group to add the building to his route.*

**Rejected**: *Unfair to driver and unwise since he is the least able to handle the additional work.*

**Option**: *Have the drivers draw straws and the loser gets the new building.*

**Rejected**: *It would not be good for morale or business to have an unwilling driver service the new building.*

Here are the three options they decided to present to their manager.

1. Toni and Miles will take turns delivering to the new building.
2. They will ask the driver in each group with the smallest route to take turns delivering to the new building.
3. They will get all the drivers together and ask which one would like the challenge of adding the new building to his or her route.

If you were their manager, what are some questions you would ask them to help you pick the best option?

## Remove Thinking Barriers

You just read about how two people tried to solve a company problem. There are times when you also have to think for yourself to solve problems that affect only you. Barriers that make thinking difficult are barriers within yourself:

- Fear of differences.
- Defensive reactions.
- Preconceived ideas.

If you learn to recognize thinking barriers within yourself, you will make any task easier, including job hunting.

Here are two examples of people who were first blocked by thinking barriers and then learned to remove them.

▶ Connie would like to work at the Acton Company where her friend Liz works. But Liz has told her that the head of personnel is a real jerk and does not hire recent graduates. She says the only reason she got her job was because her older brother works there.

Connie decides not to apply. Then the job counsellor at school says to her, "Now Connie, you're the one who is being a jerk. How do you know you won't be offered a job. The head of personnel at Acton called me just the other day to say he had three openings for recent graduates. The only way you know you won't be offered a job is if you don't apply."

Connie decided that she should not let her preconception of the personnel manager hold her back. She will wait to form an opinion of him until after she has had an interview with him.

▶ Barry has had one interview for the position of sports reporter for the local newspaper. He is excited about getting the job, which is just what he wants. The interview went well, and he thinks he only has to wait for the offer to be made. To his surprise, he finds the following message on his answering machine from the paper's editor-in-chief,

"We are very impressed with you, Barry, and plan to make a decision soon on the position of sports reporter. There are two other candidates for the job, but I want to tell you that you are my first choice. To be fair to all three candidates, however, we are asking each of you to submit some samples of your writing. If you could drop them off tomorrow we will read them immediately. Thank you and I hope to have favorable news for you no later than Friday."

Barry is angry about the request and decides he does not want the job after all. He watches the basketball game with his friend Wayne that evening and tells him about the call. Wayne says that he had three interviews and waited a month before he was offered his job. He says, "They're just trying to be fair to everyone and make the right choice. Your writing is great so just take in some samples. I'm sure you'll get the job. Include that piece on the tennis match last summer. They'll be really impressed!"

Barry is lucky to have a friend like Wayne who does not let his defensive reaction prevent him from getting the job he wants.

## PLANNING FOR SUCCESS

In Chapter 3, you learned how to develop a vision of your future and to set short-term, mid-term, and long-term goals to achieve that vision. People set goals for themselves. As employees they also set goals for themselves, their departments, and the entire company. The company president may set a goal to open up a new branch store next year. The manufacturing manager may set a goal to reduce plant costs. The product manager may set a personal goal of taking a course on presentation skills that will make her more effective in her job. Because she will then be able to sell more of the company's products, she will be eligible for a bigger commission. As you can see, job-related goals help the individual who sets them and the company.

## Set Work Goals

It is important to set goals for the work you want and also to accept that your goals will change from time to time. It is not always easy to know what you want to do, but the process of setting goals helps you clarify what you want to do. See how it worked for Ray and Anna.

▶ Ray has worked for five years for an automobile dealer in the service department. He likes the dealer but knows there is no opportunity to advance. He and his wife Anna plan to have a family and Ray thinks that now would be a good time to make some long-term plans for a secure job. He decides to open up his own business of servicing cars and sets the following goals.

**Short-term** (by the end of next month): go to the bank to find out whether he can get a loan to get started.
**Mid-term** (by the end of the year): take a course on how to start your own business.
**Long-term** (by the end of next year): open up the business.

One day the dealer says to him, "I know you are thinking of starting your own business, but have you considered buying a franchise instead." He tells Ray that there might be less risk in franchising than in starting his own business. Ray knows that franchising has to do with buying a license to sell the products or services of another a company. He knows that McDonald's and Midas Muffler both sell franchises, and in fact the dealer has a franchise to sell cars. He decides to change his first short-term goal to learning more about franchising.

Ray eventually decides to buy a franchise rather than start his own business. It takes him three years to do it, but he is making a profit by the end of the following year. The automobile dealer has closed his showroom and retired to Florida. If Ray had not planned ahead, he would have ended up being out of work when his first child was born.

## Set Personal Goals

For many people, a job is a large part but by no means everything in life. It is important to set goals that are not job related as well.

> Carol has a 6-year-old daughter, and she wants to start saving money for her daughter's college education. If her daughter starts college when she is 18, Carol has 12 years to build up her savings. Carol works for a large insurance company that offers several savings plans. Carol knows that if she buys shares of the company's stock, she has a chance to earn more money than if she buys government savings bonds. She also knows she has a greater chance of losing more from investing in stocks. She sets her goals like this.
>
> **Short-term goal**: determine how much money she will need for her daughter's college education.
> **Short-term goal**: look at reports of earnings over the past five years for the company stock and for savings bonds.
> **Short-term goals**: arrange to have part of her paycheck invested in two accounts, one for stocks and one for bonds.
> **Mid-term goal**: at the end of each year review how much money her investments have earned and shift money from one account to the other if it seems a good idea.
> **Long-term goal**: send her daughter to college.

Ray and Carol both find that by setting long-term goals they can deal with stress more easily. When the daily work load gets heavy or someone in the family is sick, it helps to remember that they are working toward a long-term goal that they will be proud to reach.

## READING AND LISTENING FOR RESULTS

In Unit III you read about effective reading, listening, and note taking. If you acquire these skills in college, you will have many opportunities to use them later on. Reading and writing, listening and speaking are all part of the communication process, and communication is essential for business and society to function smoothly. Because you cannot always carry around with you someone else's knowledge, whether written or spoken, you have to be able to record it yourself.

### Reading and Note Taking at Work

In work situations, you will probably not take reading notes and put them in a notebook dated and numbered the way you do in school. Nevertheless, you will often find you are taking notes. Common work situations that require taking notes include the following:

- Your boss hands you a report and says, "Please read this and let's discuss it tomorrow." You read it and make notes to refer to tomorrow in your discussion. Without taking notes, you will find it harder to remember what you want to say.

- You receive a complaint letter from a customer and want to show it to your manager, the head of customer relations. First, you highlight the main points of the letter, and then you check the files and make a few notes in the margin of the letter to explain what went wrong.

- You read an interesting article in a trade magazine about some aspect of your business. You make notes summarizing the article, put them in a memo, and send the memo and article to your coworkers.

- You plan to sign up for health insurance offered by your company. You read the booklet describing the plan but do not understand everything in it. You make notes of your questions so that when you call the benefits manager, you get all your questions answered at once and do not have to call back.

As the examples above illustrate, the purpose of taking reading notes in work situations is often not to show what you know but to deal with a problem more efficiently.

You can decide how to handle the complaint letter more quickly if you have all the facts at hand when you talk to your manager. You will not waste your time or the benefits manager's time if you have a written list of questions about what you do not understand when you make your call.

### Listening and Note Taking at Work

Sometimes people think they will look foolish if they take notes when someone talks to them at work, but this is a mistaken idea. If someone has something important to say to you, especially if it involves details, you will be wise to take notes.

One of the most frequent cases of note taking in an office is taking a phone message. You note whom the call is from, whom it is for, the caller's phone number, and a message, if there is one. Much aggravation is caused among office workers because of inaccurately recorded phone messages.

Look at the example below and count the number of times that someone has to listen and understand what someone else has to say. How many times should someone be taking notes?

> Aileen is a sales representative. Today she makes a sales call to a customer to present the company's newest product. The customer explains that he will not buy the product now and gives a reason. The customer then places an order for a quantity of another product and asks for it to be delivered by a certain date.
>
> Aileen returns to her office and goes to see her boss, the sales manager. He has just gotten off the phone with another sales representative who has just gotten a large order. He hears what Aileen says but does not understand a word of it because he is not listening. Instead, he is thinking about how to ship the large order that the other sales representative has just told him about.

In the example above, there were at least three times when someone listened to someone else: Aileen listened to the customer, the customer listened to Aileen, and the sales manager listened to the other sales represpresentative.

If Aileen is an experienced sales person, she may not need to write down the customer's reason for not buying the new product as long as she listens well and understands what he says. But even an experienced sales person should write down the details of an order.

The example also illustrates a common problem in business. Aileen talks to her boss, but he does not listen. A related skill to listening is knowing how to get someone's attention so that he or she will listen to you. The best Aileen can do in this situation is go back to her boss later when he is not distracted or put her information in a memo and send it to him.

## USING KNOWLEDGE TO PERFORM WELL

There are many times on the job and in your personal and social life when you have to use your knowledge to perform well. At work you may have to explain the office procedures to a new employee. The better you can explain the procedures, the sooner the new employee will be sharing the work load.

In your personal and social life, you will explain things to children, to friends, and associates. People take satisfaction from knowing they understand something and can share that knowledge with others, even when it is no more complicated than telling a friend about a great book.

Depending on the kind of work you do, you may have more formal occasions for using your knowledge to perform your job well.

> Rudy is a product manager for a computer company. At the next sales meeting, he will present the newest computer to the sales representatives. This means he has to learn everything he can about the new computer and organize the information in a clear and understandable way. He will explain everything he can about the computer to the sales reps and answer questions they have about it.

Rudy will prepare to give his sales presentation by drawing on skills he used in school to study for tests. He will first make sure he understands all the main points about the new computer and have all his facts correct. Next he will make flash cards to help trigger his memory of what he wants to say. He will ask himself questions by putting himself in the position of a sales representative. Any questions he cannot answer he will write down and find the answer to before the presentation.

There are a number of technical details, so he will create a mnemonic to help him remember them. He also will want to compare the new computer to the competition and use illustrations of ways the computer can be used. At the end of the presentation, he will summarize what he has said being sure to restate the most important points.

Rudy will be using skills that he acquired in school to prepare for taking objective and essay tests. By setting aside enough time to prepare, he knows he can reduce the stress he feels about giving the presentation. Just to be on the safe side, he will go over the entire presentation with a colleague ahead of time to get the colleague's reaction and to find out whether he has left anything out.

## SUMMING UP

The same learning skills that you learn in school can be applied on the job and elsewhere throughout life. These skills include note taking and test taking, as well as thinking, planning, and using your knowledge effectively.

You will use critical and creative thinking to find solutions to workplace problems. The more you participate in solving a problem, the more valuable you will be to your employer and the better able to help yourself.

Another important aspect of solving workplace problems is anticipating. If you can anticipate what might go wrong, you are more able think of a solution or, better still, prevent a problem in the first place.

Barriers that make thinking difficult are barriers within yourself: the fear of differences, defensive reactions, and preconceived ideas.

People set goals for themselves. As employees they also set goals for themselves, their departments, and the entire company. It is important to set goals for the kind of work you want to do and also to accept that your goals will change from time to time. It is not always easy to know what you want to do but, surprisingly the process of trying to set goals helps you clarify what you want to do.

For many people, a job is a large part but by no means everything in life. It is important to set goals that are not job related as well.

In work situations you will probably not take reading notes and put them in a notebook dated and numbered the way you do in school. Nevertheless you will often find you are taking notes.

The purpose of taking reading notes in work situations is often not to show what you know but to deal with a problem more efficiently. You can decide how to handle a situation more quickly if you have all the facts at hand.

Sometimes people think they will look foolish if they take notes when someone talks to them at work, but this is a mistaken idea. If someone has something important to say to you, especially if it involves details, you will be wise to take notes.

A common problem in business occurs when one person talks to someone who does not listen. A related skill to listening is knowing how to get someone's attention so that that person will listen to you.

There are many times on the job and in your personal and social life when you have to use your knowledge to perform well. Depending on the kind of work you do, you may have more formal occasions for doing this in your job. A good example of this would be giving a sales presentation where you could draw on the skills you learned for studying for exams.

# ▼ DEVELOPING YOUR SKILLS

Exercise 1

## Use Your Skills at a Business Meeting

Attend a business meeting and practice using your listening and note-taking skills.

Possible choices include:

> A local chamber of commerce meeting.
> A stockholders meeting for a local business.
> A faculty meeting or meeting of a school committee.
> A meeting of a local government agency or department.

Do some research ahead of time so you have some idea of what will happen at the meeting. Do this by getting an agenda for the meeting, talking to the person running the meeting, or talking to some one who has attended similar meetings.

Select a topic to be discussed at the meeting and take notes on it. Then interview at least one person who spoke on the topic.

Write a report on what you learned.

Exercise 2

## Research an Organization

Research a local company or organization (social, cultural, political, or athletic). Find out such things as when it was organized or founded; what it makes or what service it provides; how it is structured; who the officers are; and whatever else you can.

Next find out what the the short-term and long-terms goals of the company or organization are.

Write a report on what you learned.

*PERFORMANCE MASTERY*

# Using Your Skills

## PROJECT ONE

### Conduct a Job Search

Apply the skills you have learned in this course to conduct a job search. Use the steps below as a guideline.

1. Use critical and creative thinking to research and write a concise definition of the job you would like to have. Use resources such as the *Occupational Outlook Handbook* and the *Dictionary of Occupational Titles* to generate ideas of possible jobs.
2. Develop a plan to review and evaluate the possibilities you have identified so as to establish the pros and cons of each. Start by brainstorming to list the information you need to get, for example

   - The kind of company or organization offering this position.
   - The kind of education and skills required.
   - The type of entry-level jobs in the field.
   - Where such jobs are available.

3. Make your selection and describe it and your reasons for selecting it to a person whose opinion you value.

4. Make a list of short- and mid-term goals that will lead to your obtaining this job.
5. Conduct further research by interviewing someone who knows something about this job and by reading at least one article about it. Take listening and reading notes of your research.

Now take either one of the following actions:

**Alternate A.** Write a report that states what the job is, why you want it, and what you learned about it from your research. Conclude with a summary of how you plan to get this job.

**Alternate B**. After you have researched the job you may decide that it is not for you after all. If this happens, write a report that states what you found out about it from your research and two reasons why you do not want this job. Conclude with a statement that includes:

- What kind of job you think you might like instead.
- Why you would like it.
- How you plan to find out more about it.

# PROJECT TWO

## Set a Long-Term Goal Not Job-Related

For most people, their job is only part of their life. They want to achieve other goals as well that give them enjoyment and that enrich their life emotionally, spiritually, or intellectually.

Select a goal of this type for yourself. Make it a long-term goal, one that you will not fully achieve in less than five years and that could take twenty years or the rest of your life. Look at the examples below:

- Develop a skill, such as playing the saxophone well enough to perform in an amateur group.
- Build a house or a car.
- Read the complete works of Shakespeare.
- Climb the highest mountain in each state in the United States.
- Live for six months in the country of your ancestors.
- Become a leader in a social, political, religious, educational, athletic, or environmental organization.

This is a good project for creative thinking. Often people do not allow themselves to think much about goals not related to earning a living. To identify this important goal you want to:

- Brainstorm to think of as many possibilities as you can.
- Relax, ease off, and return to thinking about it.
- Avoid being critical of yourself or too quick to rule out possibilities.
- Do not let others talk you out of it if you really want it.

Remember you can take as much time as you need to achieve it. The important thing is to identify it so you can start working on it. Once you have identified this long-term goal, do the following.

1. Write it down.
2. Write down two short-term and two medium-term goals that lead to achieving your long-term goal.
3. This is not supposed to be job related, but ask yourself if this goal can be related in any way to your job goal. How might having this goal help you do your job?

# Index

## A

Activity
  goal-related, 64, 80
  high, low priority, 88
  non-goal-related, 64, 80
  realistic, 86
Adler, Mortimer J., 46
Attitude, 30
  positive, 51–53

## B

Bias, self-serving, 36–37
Biological forces, 54
Books, elements of, 128–129
Brainstorm, 11, 56–57, 225

## C

Career, 55–58
  decision chart, 64
  vision, 59
Change, resisting, 35
Class discussion, 153, 225
Communication process, 245
Conflict, 100
Conforming, 35
Consequences, 19–20, 33
  immediate, 19
  long-term, 19
  pros and cons, 20
  short-term, 19
Criticism, 36

## D

Daydreaming, 12
Deadline, 82, 89, 98
Decision, 14, 17, 30, 32, 62
  informed, 64
  snap, 38
Decision-Making Matrix, 63
Defensive reaction, 35
*Dictionary of Occupational Titles (DOT)*, 56
Drugs, 104

## E

Ego, 36–37
Elements of Style, 227
Energy period, 81, 88, 175
Environmental forces, 54
Exercise, 108

## F

Fact, 13–16
Facts, classify, 211–212
Fanatic, 31
Fault, finding, 36
Feelings, negative, 31
Fiction, 13
Flash cards, 207, 209–210
  main point, 210
  on-the-job use of, 248

## G

Generalization, 35
Goals
  career, 64
  conflicting, 62
  job related, 244
  long-range, 63
  long-term, 47, 59–62, 243
  mid-term, 59–62, 243

257

personal, 244
prioritize, 62–64, 65
realistic, 66, 103
review, 61
setting, 38
short-term, 47, 59–61, 63–64, 243
as a student, 204
unrealistic, 103
vision-based, 59, 75
work, 244
in writing, 62
Goethe, 88
Guilt, 31

## H

Habits, 78–80, 81, 89,
  bad, 78
  four good study habits, 88–90
  good, 78
Hearing, 120, 188
  physical act, 173
  vs. listening, 172
Hypocrite, 31

## I

IDEA, steps to creative thinking, 8, 241
Influences
  biological, 54
  environmental, 54
  friends, neighborhood, 30
  parents, family members, 30
  socioeconomic background, 30
Interview, 55

## J

Job, 56, 58
  entry-level, 32
  solving problems on, 240–242
  use of knowledge on, 247
  using study skills on, 248

## K

Key word, 152, 174, 227
Knowledge, use of, 247

## L

Learning, life-long project, 239
Learning skills, 239
Lecture, 174, 224
  listening to, 171
  main topic of, 170
  method of presentation, 172
  purpose, 170
Lecture notes, *see* Note taking (listening)
Life, as a journey, 49, 58
Lincoln, Abraham, 53
Listening, 3, 169, 188, 239, 245
  activate your knowledge, 172
  active, 174, 187
  hearing, 172
  mental awareness, 173
  motivate yourself, 171
  not passive, 172
  obstacles to, 121
  phone message, 246
  preparing mentally, 170–172
  preparing physically, 169–170
  purpose for, 170
  roadblocks, 173
  vs. hearing, 172
  at work, 246–247
  *see* Note taking (listening)
Listening roadblocks
  anticipation, 174
  inattention, 173
  overcoming, 174–176
  physical distractions, 173
  preconceptions, 174, 176
  unfamiliarity, 173
Listening skills, 118
Listening techniques, 120
Lowell, James Russell, 30

# M

Main point, 174, 248
Memorizing, 8
Memory, 37
  long-term, 212
  short-term, 212
Memory aid
  mnemonics, 212–213, 227
Mental image, 175
Mnemonics, 213
  use of on the job, 248
Motivation, 47

# N

Note taking, 245
  strategies for
  supplemental reading, 150
  textbooks, 150
  at work, 245–246
Note taking (listening)
  clean up, 192–193
  compare with classmate, 195
  diagrams, charts,
    drawings, 194
  highlight, 191, 194–195
  key word, 189, 193
  main point, 188–190
  organize, 193–194
  organizing, 191, 193
  outline, 189, 194
  selective, 189
  speed writing, 190–191
  study of, 195
  tactics, 190
  tape recorder, 188
  when not to take notes, 192
Note taking (reading), 130, 133
  chart, 156–159
  diagram, 156–159
  drawing, 156–157, 159
  five groups, 151
  key word, 153
  main point, 151, 153–154
  organizing, 161
  outline, 154
  outline (key word), 154–156
  outline (sentence), 154
  picture, 156
  questions in the
    margin, 159–160
  secondary points, 154
  strategies, 150
  studying, 161
  summary, 151–153
  supplemental material, 150
  tape recorder, 160
  textbooks, 149
  write questions, 159–160
Note-taking skills, 239
Note-taking techniques, 112, 121
Note-taking tools, 170
Notes, 174, 227
  classroom, 193
  lecture, 175, 187
  listening, 175, 187
  reading, 149

# O

*Occupational Outlook*
  *Handbook,* 56
Opinion, 13–16, 32
Option, 18, 56
Organizational skill, 227
Outline, 154, 156, 230–231
  arabic numerals, 155
  lecture notes, 190
  main point, 154
  major point, 155
  roman numerals, 155
  secondary point, 154, 155
  subcategory, 155

# P

Planning, 81, 239
Possibilities, pros and cons, 17
Posture, 175

Priority, 64
Problem, 20, 38
  define, 17, 19
  solve, 19
  summarize, 16
Problem solving, 240
Propaganda, 13

## R

Reading, 3, 46, 55, 227
  aloud, 135
  central to learning, 123
  clarify purpose, 123–125, 131
  creatively, 136–137
  for directions, 118–119
  focus attention, 130–133
  to gain knowledge, 119–120
  general purpose, 123–124
  know elements of books, 128
  to learn, 118
  make up questions, 134
  monitor yourself, 133–135
  motivate yourself, 125–126
  motivation, 131
  outline notes, 130
  overhaul, 135–137
  passively, 149
  for pleasure, 118
  prepare yourself, 123
  preview, 127–128, 132, 134–135
  purposes for, 118, 124
  reread, 135–136
  selective, 119
  skimming, 129–130, 132, 134–135
  speed, 135–136
  strategies, techniques, 123
  summarizing, 135
  use knowledge you have, 126
  at work, 245–246
  *see* Note taking (reading)
Reading obstacles
  distractions, 130
  inattention, 130
  overcoming, 132
  procrastination, 130, 132
  uninteresting, 131
Reading skills, 118
Reading techniques, 130
  highlighting, 132
  make connections, 133
  mental images, 132
  monitor yourself, 133
  summarize, 134
  think ahead, 135
Recreation, 84
Reference book, 90
Remembering
  mnemonics, 211
  strategies for, 210–213
Research, 15

## S

Schedule, 75, 80–81
  daily, 80, 85–87
  general time-use, 80–82, 84–86
  long-term, 80, 82–84
  overloaded, 99
  test dates, 82
  weekly, 80, 84–85
  write it down, 80
Self-image, 52
  positive, 53
  vision, affect on, 51
Sense of time scale, 77
Solution, evaluate, 20
SOLVE, steps in critical thinking, 16, 241
Speed writing
  *Condon Notetaking*, 191
Stereotype, 34–35
Stress, 48, 173, 248
  avoid, 104
  change, 101
  change yourself, 107
  concentration, 110
  confront, 104

constant, 100
control of, 103, 107–110
defining, 98
degree of, 102
diet, 109
good, positive, 100–101, 103
harmful, 103
invited, 101
long-term, 98–100
managing, 97
meditation, 109
moderate, 101
as motivator, 110
optimal level, 100–101
ordinary, 100
perception of, 102
physical exercise, 108
producers, 97
public speaking, 104–105
relaxation, 109
response, 107–108
seek help, 110
short-term, 98–100
test, 107, 110–112
uninvited, 101
Stress management, 48
Strunk and White,
*Elements of Style*, 227
Study
find suitable place, 89
keep up with
assignments, 89
necessary tools, 89–90
set specific time, 89
tools, 89–90
Study habit, 112
Study sheet, 224
Success, planning for, 243

# T

Talent, 30, 54, 56
Tape recorder, 188, 210
Task, 81
big, 88
complex, 101
difficult, 126
high-priority, difficult, 84, 87
routine, 60, 84, 86
Test, 8, 12, 89, 98, 191, 210, 224
mastery of, 120
as motivator, 204
review for, 195
Test (essay), 205, 223, 248
instruction for, 223
legibility of, 231
preparing for, 223–227
punctuation, 231
review old tests, 226
sentence structure, 231
spelling, 231
taking, 229–231
terms, 227–229
Test (objective), 205, 223, 248
fill-in, 205, 207, 214
general strategies, 213
matching, 205, 207, 214–216
multiple-choice, 205, 207, 216–217
preparing for, 207–213
taking, 213–217
true/false, 205, 207, 214
Test anxiety, 206, 212
Test stress, 110–112
Test-taking checklist, 205
Test-taking skills, 110, 204, 239
Things-to-learn list, 207–209
Thinking, 239
barriers, 33, 37, 242
creative, 2–4, 5–13, 16, 33, 37, 56, 136–137, 149, 152, 207, 223, 240
creative (IDEA), 8–11, 16
creative, techniques for, 11
critical, 2–4, 5, 13–20, 32–33, 37, 57, 103, 149, 153, 177, 207, 223, 240
critical (SOLVE), 16, 20
discipline, 29

Index—261

experiences mold, 29
imagining, 3
independently, 35
as an individual, 4, 29, 34, 36, 37
influences, 30
overcome barriers to, 37
problem-solving, 3
random, 3
remembering, 3
for yourself, 32
Thinking barriers, 33–34
conforming, 35
defensive reaction, 34–35
fear of difference, 34
groups, social, 34
stereotyping, 34
Thinking skill, 2, 4
Thought pattern, 35
automatic, 36
Thoughts, organize, 17
Time, 78
found, 88, 209
major resource, 75
Time management, 75, 88, 103
manage yourself, 77
as study skill, 48
To-do list, 58, 64, 80, 84–85, 88
prioritize, 65
review, 66
written, 65, 87
Tutor, 227

# V

Values, 15, 30, 54, 56–57
acquiring, clarifying, 30–31
compromise, 31
experience, 30
functional, 32
parental influence, 31
peer influence, 31
reevaluate, 31
Vision, 57–60, 62, 103, 243
importance of, 49
influences on, 51
know yourself, 29, 53
as motivator, 47, 50
negative, 50–51
positive, 50–51, 55
realistic, 55
refine, 57
as self-fulfilling prophecy, 50
steps toward, 52
values affect on, 51

# W

Workplace, study skills in, 206 239–248
Write, 19, 84, 86, 112
Writing, 12, 57, 75, 227

262—Studying Smart